Praise for *The Smart Way to Your Ph.D.*

"*The Smart Way to Your Ph.D.* is a wonderful new resource. There's great down-to-earth advice here for every stage in a graduate school career. Easy to skim, re-read and understand, it is enlightening and informative for faculty as well as their students."

–Erich Ippen, *Professor of Electrical Engineering and Computer Science,* Massachusetts Institute of Technology

"*The Smart Way to a Your Ph.D* is a thoughtful and through guide for graduate students already in a Ph.D. program or those contemplating joining one. Dr. Farkas effectively deals with a range of topics (such as time management, writing and defending one's thesis, and finding a job), and bases her suggestions on interviews with former and current graduate students. The book is packed with friendly, accessible, and practical tips and suggestions. I am happy to endorse the work and recommend it to doctoral students and even their mentors."

–Brinda Charry, *Assistant Professor, Department of English,* Keene State College

"During graduate school, students can get 'stuck' or feel demoralized about how their work is going, or about their relationship with their advisor. *The Smart Way to Your Ph.D.* provides easy-to-use information to help graduate students identify how and why they're stuck and offers strategies to help them move forward."

–Robin S. Rosenberg, Ph.D., *Clinical Psychologist*

"After reading all the stories, I was surprised by how many of the situations seemed familiar to me and how much of the advice rang true, despite differences in fields, institutions, and degree programs. I would recommend this book for all prospective, current, and recent graduate students. Adding this book to every graduate school library and office of student affairs would go a long way toward giving the students the resources they need to progress and succeed in graduate school and beyond."

–Heather Mernitz, *Assistant Professor of Physical Science,* Alverno College

THE SMART WAY TO YOUR Ph.D.
200 Secrets from 100 Graduates

Copyright ©2009 by Dora Farkas

Published by Your Ph.D. Consulting

All rights reserved. Printed in the United States of America. No part of this book may be reproduced or transmitted without written permission from the author, except for the inclusion of quotations in a review. For more information please visit www.yourphd.com.

First edition

Designed by Chung Chiang
Cover and inside illustrations by Gábor Reisz

Includes bibliographical references and index.

ISBN: 0-9821092-0-2
ISBN-13: 978-0-9821092-0-5
Library of Congress Control Number: 2008910633

The Smart Way to Your Ph.D.

200 Secrets from 100 Graduates

Dora Farkas, Ph.D.

Published by
YOUR PH.D. CONSULTING
Arlington Massachusetts

FIGURES AND TABLES

ACKNOWLEDGEMENTS

This book compiles the contributions of over 100 people. First and foremost, I would like to thank the 100 Ph.D.s who volunteered to be interviewed. They generously contributed their time and offered many valuable suggestions to make this book useful and accessible to current and future doctoral students.

I am also grateful to the following faculty members, deans, and counselors for contributing to and reviewing parts of this book: Brinda Charry, Professor of English at Keene State College; Sarah Delaney, Assistant Professor of Chemistry at Brown University; John Essigmann, Professor of Biological Engineering at MIT; Robert Frost, Assistant Professor of Education at Oregon State University; Brian Hampton, Assistant Professor of Geological Sciences at Michigan State University; John Nonnamaker, Associate Director at the MIT Careers Office; Katherine O'Dair, Associate Dean for Graduate Student Life at Boston College; Karl Reid, Associate Dean and Director of the Office of Minority Education at MIT; Robin Rosenberg, Clinical Psychologist; Steven Tannenbaum, Professor of Biological Engineering at MIT; Joel Voldman, Associate Professor of Electrical Engineering and Computer Science at MIT; Jessica White, Assistant Professor of Education at Oregon State University; Ann Yelmokas McDermott, Associate Professor at Cal Poly State University; and Mary Ziegler, Information Technology Consultant at MIT.

A special "thank you" goes out to my two brothers-in-law, William Jiang, Chief Librarian at the Patient and Family Library of the New York State Psychiatric Institute, and Chung Chiang. Thank you, Will, for revising the section on library research and for all your creative suggestions. My readers are very fortunate to benefit from your experience! Chung, thank you for helping me design my cover and for answering questions about graphics design. Also, thank you for doing an outstanding job with the typesetting!

I would also like to acknowledge Karen Ivy and Scribendi Services for editing my manuscript, and Gabor Reisz for designing the illustrations on the cover and the inside of the book.

I am also deeply grateful to my family in Hungary. I would not be where I am today, were it not for the support of my parents, János and Zsuzsanna Farkas. They taught me to love math and science from a very early age, but also emphasized the importance of writing and communication skills (which is probably why this book came about). Their enthusiasm and encouragement have motivated me to pursue a Ph.D. in the first place, and then to write a resource guide for future students. I am especially thankful to my father, who suggested the title of this book, as well as the domain name of its website, www.yourphd. com. I would also like to thank my brother, Ádám, for being so excited about my research and for making me feel like a very special sister.

Finally, I would like to thank my husband, Leaf, for his unconditional love and support. His sense of humor, patience and creativity have always lifted my spirits up and motivated me to keep writing. Thank you, Leaf, for always believing in me and for helping me make this book a reality.

Disclaimer

This book is not a substitute for academic or medical advice. All decisions regarding your doctoral dissertation should be discussed with your thesis supervisor. Consult with your physician if you experience any symptoms of anxiety, depression or repetitive strain injury. Furthermore, any changes to your diet or lifestyle should be made under the supervision of a health professional. The author and Your Ph.D. Consulting are not liable or responsible for any loss or damage allegedly caused by the information in this book. We have made every effort to ensure that the information in this book was correct and updated at the time of publication, and assume no personal responsibility for any inaccuracies, omissions or typographical errors.

Imagine it is a warm, sunny day in late spring. You are standing in a long line with your peers, all of you dressed in caps and gowns, when suddenly, you hear the music: It is time to go. Your pace is slow, and you walk tall, in unison with the drums. Your friends, colleagues and professors nod with respect to you, and you know that your family is smiling proudly. Stretching your neck allows you to see piles of diplomas on the stage, and a faint smile sweeps over your face at the thought of your recent accomplishment: You finished your Ph.D. thesis. It is now on the shelf of your university's library, bound in shiny black leather with golden lettering on the front. Recalling your challenges from the last few months, you still sigh at the relief you felt when you realized that the journey was over, and that you did it. You earned the highest degree offered by an academic institution. You have earned your Ph.D.

Did this scenario bring you a momentary state of bliss? If you are thinking about going to graduate school—or if you are already there—you are probably wondering how some students complete their Ph.D.s in a short time, while others struggle for many years. Your field of study, financial situation and access to mentoring certainly will influence how long it will take you to earn a Ph.D., but they are not the only factors. During the time I was a graduate student at MIT, I noticed that even within the same research groups, there were significant differences in terms of the length of time necessary to complete doctoral dissertations. It quickly became clear that the graduate school experience is not influenced solely by funding, field of study or guidance from a thesis advisor. What other factors can influence how long it will take you to finish your Ph.D.? One of my surprising observations was that the students who graduated relatively quickly did not necessarily work the most during graduate school. In fact, they usually worked reasonable hours and enjoyed hobbies on the weekends. They knew how to work *smarter*, not just *harder*.

What does it mean to "work smarter"? Are these "smart" doctoral students the same ones who had perfect grades in college? The answer to this question came to me during graduate school, when I was a resident tutor in an undergraduate dormitory. One of my responsibilities was to advise students who were having personal or academic problems. I held group sessions to help them organize their time, study efficiently and learn test-taking skills. Having been an undergraduate just a few years before, I empathized with their difficulties: studying volumes of books for exams, solving challenging problem sets, writing lengthy essays and fighting sleep deprivation from the overwhelming workload.

Although college life is busy, most undergraduates know what they need to do to graduate. Graduate school, however, will present you with an entirely different set of challenges. Your job is to propose and complete an original research proposal and to defend your work in front of a committee. Unlike in college, where you might have felt overburdened by deadlines, in graduate school you need to be your own boss and decide what to do and when to do it. Therefore, I came to the conclusion that an undergraduate education usually does not instill all of the skills needed to earn a Ph.D.

During the time I worked on my own dissertation, I realized that one of the pitfalls of the graduate school system was that students often had to face challenges without the benefit of an organized support system. In college, there were between 20 and 100 students in most classes, and sometimes as many 400. When the homework sets were impossible, we commiserated together; when the tests difficult, we all received poor grades. As one of my professors said, "There is protection in numbers." Such protection is not available in graduate school, however. Your project is yours alone; you can make it or break it. If you fail, you fail alone. Fortunately, it does not have to be this way. What if you could learn from former doctoral students about the skills necessary to succeed in graduate school?

In order to write this book, I interviewed 100 individuals who had earned Ph.D.s, to find out what they considered the most important elements of success in graduate school. I asked them questions such as:

- What was your biggest challenge, and how did you cope with it?
- Was graduate school what you expected? If not, what were the biggest surprises?
- How did you deal with your advisor being unsupportive (in cases where they had indicated a difficult professor)?
- How did you motivate yourself to work on your thesis?
- What strategies did you use to become more efficient in your research?
- How did you choose your career path?
- What is the number one piece of advice you would give to prospective graduate students?

(See the appendix for the complete list of questions.)

I was amazed by how eagerly former graduate students contributed to this book. Some of them had finished in three years, while others had struggled for many more; all of them, however, had learned important lessons about what it takes to earn a Ph.D. and become an independent researcher. In fact, I collected over 200 pieces of advice and sorted them into appropriate chapters. These "secrets" of success are shown in bold throughout the book (next to the diploma icon shown on page xxii), and also collected under the headings "From the Ph.D. Secret Archives."

I interviewed Ph.D.s (or equivalents thereof)* from 46 universities across the country, in nearly 40 fields. (See the appendix for the list of majors and schools.) In order to protect the identities of the interviewees, I use fictional names throughout the book. There were 70 interviewees from the sciences, engineering and mathematics, and 30 Ph.D.s from the humanities, social sciences and arts. These numbers reflect the approximate ratio of Ph.D.s awarded in these fields: two-thirds from the sciences, engineering and mathematics, and one-third from the humanities, social sciences and arts. Given that some of the challenges are specific to men or women, I balanced my pool by including 51 men and 49 women.

How did I find all these Ph.D.s? I started with just a handful of friends, and after each interview, I asked whether they could recommend anyone else who would like to be interviewed. The answer was

---

*Note that not all fields award a Ph.D. as the terminal degree. For example, education majors earn an Ed.D. and fine arts majors are awarded an M.F.A.

usually "yes," and I thus gathered my interviews primarily by word of mouth. I was also curious about resources for minorities, married students and international students. To learn more about their challenges, I interviewed Ph.D.s from these subpopulations and included their advice throughout the book and in the appendix. To make this book more complete, I also asked professors about their expectations from graduate students, and how their perspective on the Ph.D. process had changed since they became advisors. Finally, I consulted with deans, counselors and librarians regarding resources and career advice for doctoral students.

After collecting information from these interviews, I concluded that there were fundamental differences, but also many similarities across the various fields of study. Students in the humanities, social sciences and arts struggled to find funding—a luxury that many doctoral candidates in the sciences, engineering and mathematics take for granted. On the other hand, students in the sciences, engineering and mathematics were frustrated by irreproducible experiments or malfunctioning modeling software, whereas humanities, social sciences and arts majors did most of their research in libraries, museums, studios, and offices, without worrying about instruments breaking down. Interestingly, however, most Ph.D.s believed that the major challenges in graduate school were not academic. As outstanding students in college, they were not intimated by difficult research projects. Most Ph.D.s found that the major challenges of graduate school were learning how to become independent, finding ways to motivate themselves, communicating with difficult advisors, dealing with stress, and finding a suitable career path. Their stories and coping strategies are summarized in the chapters that follow.

I also sought insights from guidebooks written for doctoral students. I found advice on how to choose a department and advisor, how to find financial support, how to write a thesis and how to find a job. Most of these books, however, did not have advice on how to be more productive in graduate school. I did come across many productivity-enhancing guides written by business professionals, and I wondered whether the advice in these books would be helpful for doctoral students. After reading these books and discussing the techniques with former students, I realized that many of the strategies developed for the corporate world were also applicable in graduate school. Therefore, in the following chapters, I will frequently refer to books written by management consultants and executive coaches, and highlight their strategies for learning how to motivate yourself, overcome worry, communicate effectively and organize your time, space and thoughts.

How should you use this book? The book is comprised of seven stand-alone chapters, which will guide you through the entire graduate school experience, from the pre-application phase to the job-searching stage. Reading the entire book and trying to master all these strategies at the same time would be very difficult, if not impossible. Many of the skills discussed might also appear nitty-gritty or even irrelevant until you reach a particular stage in your studies. Thus, it is best to skim through the entire book first and then read the relevant chapters and appendices as needed. Also, check the extensive reference section in the appendix periodically, as it will help you find funding, online research tools, ergonomic typing aids, and job-searching resources. If you are in the early stages of your graduate student career, look though the later chapters on thesis-writing and job-searching as well, so you can plan ahead for these challenges. If you read through the entire book, you will notice some repetition of "secrets" across the chapters, especially those regarding self-motivation and organization; this is no accident. There are some common threads of wisdom that are applicable throughout graduate school. In other words, the organizational skills you need during the first few years—to pass your qualifiers and write your thesis proposal—will also be relevant towards the end, when you need to do an in-depth literature search and write a dissertation. With practice, you can incorporate these strategies into your daily routine until they become second nature.

What was the number one piece of advice from former graduate students? Briefly, before you enter graduate school, really make sure you want a Ph.D. Do not commit to this long journey because your friends are going, or because you do not know what else to do. Furthermore, in order to have a fulfilling experience, you need to consider the financial aspects and logistics of going to graduate school. Thus, the first chapter of this book is about laying your foundations. I will share with you how to find funding, how to choose an advisor, and what types of questions to ask during your campus visit.

In the second chapter, I will discuss the typical challenges faced by students on the road to becoming independent researchers. How do you develop a productive daily routine? How do you stay focused throughout the day? How do you keep yourself motivated after experiencing inevitable setbacks? I have also compiled the top 10 secrets from former students, to help you design an original and realistic research project for your dissertation.

The third chapter will be particularly useful when you want to be more efficient, without having to work longer hours. As many Ph.D.s have observed, productivity comes in bursts, and you can harness this energy if you learn how to pay attention to your work habits. You will learn how to identify high-priority tasks, how to budget your time efficiently, how to organize your space and how to manage your to-do list.

I divided the fourth chapter into three sections, all devoted to discussing how to take care of your mind and body. In the first section, I will show you how to deal with anxiety and minimize stress in your life. You will learn the top 12 ways to beat worry, and even make it work to your advantage. One of my observations during graduate school was that students who consumed healthy diets were also more focused and productive. In the second section, I will discuss what constitutes balanced nutrition: what foods are best for staying sharp throughout the day, and how you can incorporate a healthy and affordable diet into your busy lifestyle.

The third section of chapter four is about a common but rarely discussed epidemic: repetitive strain injury (RSI). RSI in your hands and arms can prevent you from working on a computer, and it is thought to be caused by excessive typing, pipetting, playing instruments, or participating in certain sports. Given that I had never heard of this condition before graduate school, I was surprised that 28 of the 100 Ph.D.s I interviewed (more than one in four) had suffered from RSI while working on their dissertations. Some experienced relatively mild symptoms (e.g., fatigue and aching in arms), while others had to eliminate all activities involving their hands for weeks or even months. Recovery from RSI can be time-consuming and expensive, because it involves long periods of rest and physical therapy. During my recovery from RSI, I realized that had I known more about this condition earlier, I could have easily prevented it. I considered this issue so relevant to graduate students—as they heavily use computers—that I dedicated the third part of chapter four to this topic.

Good communication skills are an essential part of scientific research. Unless you are able to communicate your results effectively, your accomplishments will go unnoticed. Whether you want to communicate with your advisor, group members or a collaborator, you need to deliver your message clearly. In chapter five, I will discuss the principles of effective verbal communication, as well as the common mistakes you will need to avoid in graduate school. Once you learn these skills, you will no longer dread "the talk" with your advisor (i.e., when you will graduate), and you can also be sure that he or she will listen to what you have to say.

Many students are also apprehensive of another type of communication: writing. If you have little experience writing long manuscripts, pulling together a doctoral dissertation can seem daunting. Yet, you need a written thesis to graduate. In chapter six, I will show you how to develop an efficient writing process, use writing to explore your ideas and stay motivated day after day. Many Ph.D.s commented that graduate school was also an excellent opportunity to improve their presentation skills, which were essential for their career advancement. In the second part of chapter six, I will share with you their secrets for becoming better public speakers.

What happens after you defend your thesis? Do you know what you want to do after graduation? Do you know where to begin looking for a job? With the increasing number of people earning Ph.D.s, it is a challenge to find a suitable position. Many Ph.D.s also question their career paths; they are no longer sure that they want to become faculty members, or even stay in their fields of research. What are some other career options for Ph.D.s? In chapter seven, I will discuss both academic and alternative careers, and strategies and resources for exploring both paths.

To summarize, this book will show you how to:
- Prepare for graduate school
- Write your thesis proposal
- Keep yourself motivated (no matter what!)
- Increase your productivity

- Decrease stress and anxiety
- Incorporate a healthy diet into your busy lifestyle
- Prevent and treat repetitive strain injury
- Communicate with your advisor, thesis committee, and coworkers
- Write your thesis efficiently
- Become a better public speaker
- Land your dream job

Are you ready? Let's get started!

 "Secrets" of success are shown in bold throughout the book next to the diploma icon.

CHAPTER 1:
LAYING THE FOUNDATIONS FOR GRADUATE SCHOOL

"Create a definite plan for carrying out your desire and begin at once, whether you are ready or not, to put this plan into action."
Napoleon Hill (1883–1970)
Author of *The Laws of Success*

When you enter graduate school, you are making a huge investment in yourself. You will sacrifice a lot of time, and many paychecks, in the interest of earning another degree. Think for a moment about how much more money you could earn, if you entered the workforce directly after you completed your bachelor's or master's degree. As one of my college professors emphasized, you should do a Ph.D. only if your "inner fire" is burning with a desire to do research. Before embarking on this journey, ask yourself two crucial questions: 1) why do you want to earn a Ph.D.? and 2) how you will prepare for life in graduate school?

It is essential to clarify your plans before you start graduate school, and sometimes even before you apply. The more concrete and detailed your goals are, the more positive your graduate school experience will be. In fact, one of the major regrets of previous Ph.D. students was that nobody told them about the challenges of graduate school and how to plan for them. In this first chapter, you will begin to lay the foundations for your graduate school experience by examining the following questions:

- Why do you want to go to graduate school?
- What are your criteria for choosing a school, department and advisor?
- Do you have an adequate academic background for your coursework and thesis?
- Do you have a financial plan?
- Do you have a support group to turn to in times of need?

- How do you plan to relax and maintain your health?
- If you are an international student, have you thought about the cultural adjustments?

Should you pursue a Ph.D.?

Each year, approximately 40,000 students earn doctoral degrees in the United States, which is approximately twice the number of Ph.D.s earned each year in the 1960s (see www.nsf.gov/statistics/srvydoctorates/). Of those 40,000 Ph.D.s, approximately two-thirds earn degrees in science, engineering or mathematics, and one-third in the social sciences, humanities or arts. This ratio was approximately the same in my interview pool: I spoke with 70 Ph.D.s who earned degrees in science, engineering or mathematics, and 30 Ph.D.s who majored in the social sciences, humanities or arts.

When I asked my interviewees why they decided to do a Ph.D., the most common answers were: "I wanted to become a professor," "I really like research" or "I wanted to teach at the college level." Other answers were more surprising: "I was not ready to work in the real world yet" or "I did not know what else to do with a bachelor's degree in biology."

Students who wanted to become professors, do research or teach at the college level were on the right track. Almost all teaching and research positions in academia require a Ph.D. What about those looking for employment outside academia? Are the degree requirements so clear in other careers as well? Mack, a chemist in a pharmaceutical company, observed that researchers with master's or even bachelor's degrees frequently achieved positions as high as Ph.D.s after they had been at the company for several years. At his previous company, however, they only promoted Ph.D.s to senior- and management-level positions.

Given this lack of clarity regarding degree requirements, how do you know whether a Ph.D. is what you need? Talk to others who have been in your position a few years before. Begin networking within professional organizations in your field, as well as with members of your alumni association. Also, ask about job opportunities in your school's career office, to determine which positions require a doctoral degree.

 Begin networking within professional organizations and your alumni association, to understand how a Ph.D. will influence

job opportunities. Will it help you access the right jobs? Or will it close down some opportunities that you are interested in?

Students who go to graduate school because they are not familiar with their career options are almost *asking* for trouble. The key to success in graduate school is to have well-defined career goals. Students without a concrete plan struggle; they do not know what they want to do after graduation, so naturally they will not know which projects will give them the necessary skills. Nick, a physicist-turned-patent agent, commented that graduate students usually think more about their careers after graduation than before they enter a doctoral program. "If you want to have a positive experience in graduate school, think carefully about the career paths that interest you. I have a job that I love, but it is not one that requires a Ph.D."

I also asked former students whether graduate school was more or less difficult than they had expected. Most Ph.D.s found graduate school to be more challenging than they had predicted. Students with experiences matching their expectations were those who had had concrete plans regarding their 1) lifestyle during graduate school, and 2) career plans. Sam, a physicist who completed his doctoral thesis in three and a half years, attributes his success to detailed planning. During his first semester, Sam and his advisor mapped out a plan for graduating in four years, including the specific skills Sam wanted to acquire along the way. He remained flexible and modified his plans as necessary, but he completed all the important milestones in three and a half years. As he recalled the challenges he had to overcome in completing his research project, he commented that "graduate school is hard, so only do it if your career goals require a Ph.D."

 Be in charge of your future and clarify what you want to get out of your Ph.D., in terms of your education and career advancement.

What options do you have if you are not sure you want to pursue a Ph.D.? Some people work for a few years before they apply to graduate school, to have more time to weigh their career options. They work as technicians, consultants, research assistants and teachers, which also gives them the opportunity to earn some money before returning to school. Alison, a biochemist, went back to graduate school after five years in industry. She finished her degree in three and a half years, a record time for her department. Alison attributes her quick progress to her five years of "pressure-free" research training in the pharmaceutical industry. "I was also more mature than my classmates, which helped me to stay focused on my goals," she said. On the other hand, it can be difficult to return to school after having been a professional for a few years. Tim, a chemical engineer, joked that the toughest part about going back to graduate school after being accustomed to a well-paid industry position was getting used to living on a graduate student stipend. "My wife and I had to move to a smaller place and learn how to cook instead of eating out so much."

 If you are unsure about whether a Ph.D. is for you, get a job after your bachelor's or master's degree, and then explore your career options.

If you are still in college, talk to graduate students in your field. Approach teaching assistants and resident tutors, and ask them about their lifestyles and career goals. Also think about how you would handle the challenges of graduate school. Can you visualize yourself living on a small stipend for many years? Are you comfortable with the uncertainty of not knowing when you will finish? Are you excited by research? What kind of a career do you imagine for yourself? Do not be shy about asking questions, because most graduate students will be happy to share their experiences.

Parts of the application package

After you have decided that you do want to earn a Ph.D., it is time to evaluate the various graduate programs. First, talk to your professors and ask which schools are considered to have the best graduate programs in your field. Second, research each of those schools to learn more about their curricula and areas of research. (In the appendix, I have listed some resources that will help you choose graduate programs to match your criteria *vis-à-vis* fields of study and desired geographical area. I have also listed the website for the *US World and News Report*, which ranks graduate schools each year.)

Apply to multiple graduate schools, but remember that each application will cost both time and money, so choose only as many schools as your budget and time will allow. Most graduate school applications will require the following four components:

- Your official transcript (usually forwarded by your student services office)
- Letters of recommendation (often forwarded separately by those who write them)
- GRE test scores
- Personal statement or graduate admissions essay.

How can you maximize your chances of getting into the graduate school of your choice? In the final year of your undergraduate studies, there is probably not much you can do to change the contents of your transcript. Shortcomings in this area can be addressed in your personal statement or admissions essay (see below); many universities will respect that grades are affected by personal adversities, for example, but you can "package" or "spin" those adversities as valuable learning experiences. (In any case, remember that your student services office will probably require some advance notice to send a transcript, so do not wait until the last minute to order it.)

Ask professors who supervised a previous research project, either during the summer or as part of your curriculum, to write your recommendation letters. Look for mentors who will describe you as the diligent, enthusiastic student you are. Give your professors sufficient notice (about one month) to write your recommendations, and do not hesitate to remind them, if you have not heard back from them as the deadline nears.

Most students consider GRE tests to be a nuisance, but you can significantly boost your application package if you know how to prepare for them. Depending on the programs you are applying to, you might need to take both general and subject GRE tests, so check the requirements for each application. The best way to approach GREs is to do practice tests. Your library or local book store will have study guides that you can use for practice. If your scores are not satisfactory, think about taking a review course. Review courses will not only motivate you to study, but they will also help you learn strategies for tackling the test. Since there is a lot of material to study, it is generally recommended that you begin preparing for the test three to six months in advance.

 Take the GRE test early, in case you need to improve your score, or to get it out of the way before you are overwhelmed by application deadlines.

Your personal statement is the part of your application package that will distinguish you from the other applicants. In order to write this essay, you will need to ask yourself the types of questions mentioned earlier in this chapter:

- Why do I want to go to graduate school?
- What are my career goals?
- How will I fit into each program?

Also ask yourself more personal questions, such as:

- Who motivated me to pursue a higher degree?
- Were there any life-altering events that led me in this direction?
- Which extracurricular projects are the most important to me? (If you had a leadership role or won awards for any hobbies or sports, that would certainly strengthen your application.)

Your essay will also give you the opportunity to explain any gaps in your academic record or shortcomings in your transcript.

- Did you need to take off time during college for personal or financial reasons?
- Are there shortcomings in your transcript that need explaining? Were you able to make up for these gaps later on? For example, did you receive a poor grade in an introductory class, followed by an excellent grade in an advanced class?

In your personal statement, mention any other distinctions that will strengthen your application, such as:

- Academic and non-academic awards and honors
- Internships
- Jobs
- Any other hobbies or experiences that you consider important in your personal development

Given that you have limited space for your essay (often with strict word-count limits), you might not have the chance to address all of these issues. Ask your professors and counselors to revise your essay, and to give you feedback about what to include. See the appendix for GRE study guides and graduate essay reference books.

How to choose the right school

The best way to prepare for graduate school is to gather information about each program you are applying to. Look at the resources in Appendix B, including graduate school rankings on the website of *US News and World Report*. Also, think about the following questions:

- Will the school support you financially during your Ph.D. program?
- Is it important for you to be close to your family, or do you want to move to a new area?
- Is the school located in an area where you can pursue your hobbies, such as visiting museums or skiing?
- What is the weather like? (This is actually a very important consideration for many people.)
- What is the average time taken to complete a Ph.D.?
- What kind of career counseling does the school have?
- Will you need to rent an apartment or are there graduate student dormitories?

Second, talk to current students or graduates from your prospective department. Most departments will give you a chance to network during the campus interview. Take advantage of this opportunity and ask more specific questions, such as:

- What are the biggest challenges in graduate school?
- What kind of background do you need for graduate-level classes?

- Is it realistic to expect yourself to do research while taking classes?
- What are the qualifying exams like?
- Are there regular social events, or do you need to be proactive to meet other people?
- Will you have the opportunity to be a teaching assistant?
- Do students get opportunities to go to conferences?
- Are there regular thesis committee meetings?
- How do students find their first jobs?

Most likely, you will get a variety of answers to these questions, depending on whom you ask—even within the same department. Make sure, however, that the general culture of the department fits your expectations regarding coursework, the nature of the research, social life and the types of jobs that students get after graduation.

Research each school before you visit the campus, so you can ask the students and faculty specific questions about their program.

Some students shy away from programs that require them to be teaching assistants. They either do not like speaking in front of groups or feel that teaching would draw time away from their research responsibilities. Casey, a mathematician, felt just the opposite. She thought that being a teaching assistant was one of the most valuable parts of her graduate education, because it gave her the opportunity to contribute to the department. If you are concerned about teaching assistantships, inquire about your department's requirements and talk to current students, if possible, about their experiences.

Some students avoid programs that require them to be teaching assistants. While teaching assistantships are time-consuming, most Ph.D.s felt that it helped them improve their public-speaking skills and prepare themselves for faculty positions.

In summary, it is crucial to plan your doctoral studies in advance, and in as much detail as possible. Unlike a job that you can quit, you need to "tough out" graduate school if you want to walk away with a diploma. You can preclude a lot of frustration if you know what to prepare for. Maybe it is impossible to find the absolutely perfect graduate school. (Many of us do end up in Boston, where the temperatures reach 0°F (or −18°C) in the winter.). However, if you know what the right questions are, and where to find the answers, you will be maximally prepared for a positive Ph.D. experience.

Most surprises in graduate school fall into one of the following categories:
* *Research: not going as fast, or not as interesting as expected*
* *Advisor: not helping enough, or micromanaging a project*
* *Lifestyle: working late, not having enough money, feeling lonely, or not having the opportunity to pursue hobbies*

Planning your finances

If you are like most students in America, you have probably put yourself and your parents in debt by the time you graduated from college. Now, you want to go to graduate school, which can also be expensive. Many universities will cover your tuition and provide you with a stipend for the duration of your Ph.D. program. You might need financial aid, however, if your tuition is not covered completely by your program, or if your stipend is not sufficient in covering your expenses. The most common types of financial aid for Ph.D. students are: 1) fellowships and 2) student loans.

Evaluate your financial situation before you enter graduate school, to determine how much money you will need to borrow, and what sources of income will be available to you.

Most fellowships are provided by government organizations, and will usually provide you with a few years of funding. In addition, winning a fellowship will look prestigious on your résumé and enhance your marketability after graduation. In addition, if you win a fellowship, you will have more options when you choose a professor and project, because you bring your own funding. Make sure, however, that you choose a project that your advisor is invested in. Marla, a biologist with a fellowship, chose a project that her advisor was not interested in. As a consequence, she did not get sufficient guidance from him. She considered her fellowship a "double-edged sword," because it liberated her advisor from having to pay attention to her research. Jacob, another student with a fellowship, received sufficient—or possibly too much—attention from his advisor, because he worked on a very crucial project in the lab. Fellowships are advantageous if you have significant research experience and know what you want to work on. Jeffrey, an electrical engineer, joined a group after having won a fellowship, and he constructed his own project with little guidance from his advisor. He enjoyed his independence and did not miss his advisor's input regarding his research.

Professors will usually encourage you to apply for fellowships, because they will save them money and will make your résumé more impressive. Fellowships are available in almost all fields of study, including humanities, science, engineering, environmental sciences, agriculture, arts and education. See appendix A for more information on field-specific fellowships.

 Fellowships will give you more freedom to pursue research projects that are interesting for you. Choose a topic in which you and your advisor have expertise, so that you will have sufficient guidance during your studies.

The government and private organizations also provide low-interest loans for educational purposes. The most common loans are 1) Stafford loans, 2) graduate PLUS loans and 3) private/alternative loans. In order to qualify for loans in America, you must be an American citizen with a good credit history and be enrolled in an eligible university. Graduate Stafford loans are either subsidized or unsubsidized, depending on the student's needs. Subsidized loans are provided on a need basis to low-income students. Subsidized loans do not accrue interest until after the student has graduated. Unsubsidized loans are awarded to all eligible students, but they begin accruing interest from the time the loan is taken out. Graduate PLUS loans are federally backed loans, depend on the student's credit rating rather than their financial needs, and can be used to cover a significant portion of the cost of education. Private alternative loans are also low-interest and students can defer repayment while in school, unemployed or serving in the military. Graduate student loan consolidation is a good way to save money when repaying loans, particularly if the repayment begins while the student is still in school. Turn to the appendix for online information about applying for different types of financial aid.

It is essential to construct a detailed financial plan before you enter a doctoral program. What is the minimum amount of money you need every month to survive? If your stipend is not sufficient, what other sources of income do you have? Are there options for part-time jobs? During your planning, consider the following expenses:

- Health insurance
- Food (campus dining can be very expensive)
- Clothing
- Car insurance/gas
- Rent and utilities,
- Airfare to visit home
- Childcare (if applicable)

If you decide to apply for loans, think about your financial situation after your Ph.D. How much debt will you have accrued by the time you graduate (including your undergraduate loans), and how much do you expect to earn after you graduate? If your department does not cover tuition, your debt could be in the tens of thousands of dollars. Leona, an art history major, decided to go to the school that gave her the best financial package. "I knew that as an assistant professor in art history, I would not be able to repay graduate loans. I had to take out about $5,000 to cover my expenses during my last semester, but my loans would have been much higher at the other universities, which did not even provide tuition."

 Take out only as much debt as you can comfortably repay after graduation.

It can be tough to make ends meet in graduate school, but it is not too early to start thinking about a savings or retirement plan. The earlier you start investing your money, the more time it will have to earn interest. Try saving $50, $100, or more every month and put it into a savings, investment or retirement plan. If you wait until you have a "real job," you will find that your expenses will also increase (particularly if you buy a house and a car and have children), so your disposable income might not be much higher. Max, a postdoctoral fellow, started his Roth IRA in graduate school, and he had a surprising amount of money in his retirement account, even before he got his first job offer.

 Start a savings or investment plan in graduate school. The earlier you start your plan, the more time it will have to earn interest.

Choosing the right advisor and research group

Your choice of advisor is one of the most important decisions in graduate school. During my interviews, I observed that there was almost a 100% correlation between a student's happiness in graduate school and their satisfaction with their advisor. Furthermore, one of the most common suggestions from Ph.D.s to prospective graduate students was "Choose your advisor wisely." Some Ph.D.s also noted that other students in the group got along better or worse with their advisors. In other words, there is no professor who is perfect for everyone. You need to investigate who is the best "fit" for *you*.

How do you begin your search for your thesis advisor? One of my college professors told me to choose an advisor who 1) did interesting research and 2) was easy to get along with. To satisfy the first of these requirements think about what areas of research interest you the most. Look up all of the professors in the departments where you are applying. Remember that you will be working on your doctoral dissertation for several years, so choose a topic that is truly exciting for you. Apply to departments where you can visualize yourself working for more to one professor, because you might not get your first choice of advisor.

If you cannot choose your advisor in advance, choose a program which has multiple professors in your area(s) of interest.

Some departments will allow you, or possibly even expect you, to do rotations before choosing an advisor. Rotations are an excellent opportunity to explore the day-to-day duties of graduate students, and to become familiar with the personalities of the professors. Once you have narrowed down your general research area, consider the following questions:

- Am I looking for a hands-on or a hands-off advisor?
- What is the atmosphere of the research group?
- Is your advisor understanding of personal situations?

The advisor's involvement in student research was one of the most important considerations that former graduate students were thankful they had made, or wish they had made. A hands-on advisor will meet with you frequently to discuss your progress. Students with little research experience, or ones who appreciated continuous supervision, usually benefited from this type of mentoring. "My advisor was always on top of my research, so it was easy to be motivated. He was also a great person to turn to for advice, because he was so involved in our research," said Linda, a biologist.

 If possible, do rotations to find which advisor and research group are the best matches for you.

Some students recognized only a few years into their program that they needed more intense mentoring than they were receiving. Fred, a biochemist, commented that his Ph.D. stretched out longer than he expected because he was not able to manage his project due to his lack of experience. "My advisor gave me a lot of independence, and an entire year passed without any progress. After I talked with him, we designed a project that I had more experience with, so I could finish it within a reasonable amount of time."

Hands-off advisors can be a good fit for students who have research experience and want to be independent. "I already had a lot of experience in this field as a result of my master's thesis, and it was great to have an advisor who gave me all the tools, and let me explore many different ideas without checking up on me frequently," said Greg, an electrical engineer. Karl, a physicist, noticed that his advisor was hands-on with new students, but gave his senior students more independence. By his final year, he was able to finish his thesis without much guidance from his advisor. Ask senior students from the department about the advisor's style and determine whether you have the appropriate academic background and personality for that group.

The interactions that you have with your lab members will also have a significant impact on your productivity. "My advisor did not help me with my thesis, but I received so much support from senior students and postdoctoral fellows that I did not really need his guidance," recalled Helen, a biologist. Paul, a biomedical engineer, said that the strength of his research group came from the diversity of expertise of the lab members. "Our research was very interdisciplinary, and having people with a variety of different backgrounds really helped me design experiments." Paul also noted that having good relationships with his lab members helped him cope with stress and be more productive in the lab. "My group went on excursions and ski trips very frequently, and sometimes my advisor came along, too. I had a really good relationship with everybody in my group, and I think it was because I had the opportunity to get to know them well outside of work."

 Do not isolate yourself from your community, especially your research group. Participate in your department's social activities, to build your support network.

Some students have personal issues that need special attention. International students, for example, usually take longer vacations, although less frequently than other students. If you need to travel overseas once or twice a year, will your advisor be supportive? If you have a long-distance relationship with your spouse, will your advisor allow you to take long weekends to visit him or her? Will your advisor allow you to work from a different city, if you are just doing computer work? While you are "shopping around" for advisors, ask how different professors would react to a special situation you might have.

Find an advisor who will be supportive of your education as well as your personal life.

Also consider how supportive your advisor will be of alternate career plans. Sandy, a biophysicist who decided to study public policy after graduation, emphasized the importance of diversifying your academic background by taking classes outside of your curriculum. Sandy's advisor was supportive, but unfortunately, not all advisors encourage extra coursework. "My advisor was very unsupportive of me taking a French class, even though I wanted to work in France after graduation. I could barely convince him to sign my registration form," said Lee, a biochemist.

Diversify your background by taking courses outside of your department and finding out about alternative careers.

Preparing for coursework and qualifying exams

A frequent response to questions about the biggest challenge in graduate school was: "finishing the coursework and taking my qualifying exams." The coursework can be particularly challenging if you are changing fields or you come from a school that had a different curriculum. If you feel unprepared for your graduate classes, can you take a higher-level undergraduate class to fill in the gaps? Do not feel embarrassed to take a course with undergraduates (even freshmen), if it will help you with your studies. "My department expected us to take their undergraduate biochemistry course, even though I already took one in college. Some of it was review, but I am glad that I got a refresher in DNA chemistry, because that ended up being very important for my research," recalled Kay, a molecular biologist. While some students found their graduate courses easier than their undergraduate ones, almost all Ph.D.s I interviewed found their qualifiers (sometimes called "comprehensives" or "preliminaries") challenging.

If the coursework is too difficult, consider taking some higher-level undergraduate classes to learn the basics.

What exactly does a qualifying exam entail? Schools vary in how they "qualify" students for their Ph.D. program, and you can find out the details of these exams in your first year or even during the application process. You might need to take one or more written exams, and possibly also an oral exam. In some schools, students are expected to write a research proposal, either for their thesis or an unrelated topic. Critiques of these research proposals are frequently crafted to indirectly test a student's knowledge of his or her coursework. Most Ph.D.s confessed that they probably "over-worried" about their exams. The exams (or the critique of the research proposals) were challenging (sometimes more difficult than expected), but the preparation was less stressful when the students realized that the purpose of qualifying exams was to test whether they understood the major ideas discussed in class, rather than the nitty-gritty details of the coursework.

How long did it take students to prepare for qualifying exams? In the case of written exams, students spent two weeks to a month reading over their notes and taking practice exams. Preparing research proposals was significantly more time-consuming—typically one to three months. The greatest resource for studying was the community: Students formed small groups to review class notes or critique research proposals. In addition to helping them prepare for exams, these groups served as support networks for the balance of their graduate program.

Discuss with your advisor his or her expectations regarding research while you are taking courses and studying for qualifying exams. Can you take some time off to focus on your studies? Many advisors will let you take a break from your research while studying for exams. Take advantage of this opportunity and concentrate on your coursework. Lia tried to be a "superwoman" during her first year in graduate school, by working full-time in her laboratory while taking courses. By the end of the first semester, however, she was burned out from working 12-hour days on a regular basis. She felt fatigued and unmotivated to continue working. When she realized that her burnout was a result of her heavy workload, she focused on her coursework until the qualifiers were over. Afterwards, she found that she was able to concentrate better on her research, once she did not need to worry about the exams.

Why do some students want to quit graduate school?

Perhaps you are already in the middle of your program and you are wondering whether it is worthwhile to finish your Ph.D. Given the significant investment you have already made, the idea of *not* finishing graduate school should be considered carefully. Dennis, a chemical engineer, considered quitting after three years. "I told my friends that I did not want to finish, because I was tired of being frustrated all the time. One of them laughed and said that almost every graduate student thinks about quitting at least once. It's just part of the process. I kept that advice in mind until I finished, about three years later."

 If you are not satisfied with your choice of school, department or advisor, consider switching groups. Change is scary, but consider how the change will improve your quality of life and the course of your career.

Why do some students consider leaving graduate school? If you planned well, you probably secured yourself an excellent graduate program, sufficient funding, and a reliable support network. Despite your best efforts to plan, however, there might be surprises. Research is unpredictable, and so is funding. You might have to be a teaching assistant, for example, more frequently than you expected, which could lengthen your program by an extra semester or year.

Larry, a biologist, was in his fifth year when he left graduate school. His project was not progressing, and he knew that his advisor would not let him graduate for at least another two years. Larry had always been drawn to law, and he researched his options for going to law school. He found a law firm to pay for his law degree, if he agreed to a few years of internship. Larry quit graduate school, but he did not leave empty-handed; he had published several papers (which give him more credibility as a patent lawyer) and his department granted him a master's degree. The lesson from Larry's story is that if you quit, you need to have a plan. Larry had secured a financial plan, as well as a vision for his future career as a patent lawyer.

Some students consider quitting when their funding, or that of their advisors, runs out. If your advisor leaves, you might need to switch groups, departments or even schools. Sharon, a neuroscientist, found out that her advisor decided to move to another university thousands of miles away. While many of her group members were unhappy with this change, Sharon considered it an opportunity to familiarize herself with a new town and research environment. At the time, Sharon was not married, but she acknowledged that students with families had to make difficult choices. Some of them switched advisors, and those who were close to finishing actually moved to the same city as the professor. If your advisor leaves your university, inquire whether you could finish your research in another professor's group or work long-distance.

Bridget, an art history major, struggled continuously with money during graduate school. Some of her classmates quit their programs because they could no longer support themselves, but Bridget found a part-time job in a museum. "It was difficult to work and study at the same time, so I worked on my thesis, on and off. My thesis took eight years, but much of that time was spent in the museum learning about art." Bridget's commitment to her job turned out to be an asset. She received multiple job offers in academia, and she attributes that success to her work experience.

 If you struggle with funding, look for a part-time job that will contribute to your learning experience.

Another option besides quitting is to take a leave of absence. (Your advisor might not be happy about this, but it is *your* life and career at stake.) James, a computer science student, took a leave of absence to start up his own company. His company was successful, but he decided to pursue an academic career path, rather than stay in the corporate environment. After a two-year absence, James returned to school, once he found the right person to replace him in the company. Universities have rules about how long your leave of absence can be, so consider such restrictions before you make your decision.

A common reason that students want to quit is that they feel that they are not smart enough to be in graduate school. The feeling of not being "smart enough" has been termed by Dr. Valerie Young, a life coach with a Ph.D., as the "impostor syndrome." (see www. Impostorsyndrome.com). The "impostor syndrome" refers to the feeling that you are not good enough, and that other people might soon discover that you are not as intelligent as they thought you were.

Graduate students, for example, might feel that they are not talented enough to finish a Ph.D., and that a mistake must have been made when they were accepted into graduate school. If you ever experience these feelings, remember that a Ph.D. is *meant* to challenge you. Mike, an aerospace engineer, pointed out that it was during the most stressful times that he was able to acquire the skills needed to become an independent researcher. If you are intimidated by obstacles along the way, bear this in mind: Each year, over 40,000 students earn a Ph.D., and more than 1,300,000 people have earned a Ph.D. since 1920—all in the United States alone. *If they can do it, why not you?*

 Most graduate students consider quitting at least once, because they think they are not smart enough to earn a Ph.D. If you have these feelings, realize that unforeseen challenges are a normal part of the Ph.D. process.

Considerations for special student populations

Married Students

Henry, an engineering major, found out soon after he started graduate school that his wife, Ally, was expecting a baby. Their initial excitement dampened when they realized that having a child during graduate school would put significant financial strain on their family. Ally was self-employed, and her income was not enough to allow them to afford a babysitter. "After our son was born, Ally could only work when I had time to watch the baby. As I got closer to finishing my thesis I had less time, and Ally had to put her career plans aside. The worst part was that we didn't know when I would finish, and our financial situation was uncertain," Henry recalled.

Having children during graduate school is a challenge for most students. Lisette and her husband were both graduate students when their first child was born, and they had to pay for daycare in order to finish their degrees. "My parents gave us a loan to pay for child care, because we would not have been able to finish school. I was embarrassed to ask them for money, because it was almost as much as paying for a college degree. Now that my husband and I have jobs, we are gradually paying my parents back," she said. Some students were also fortunate to have grandparents watch their children on weekends, so they could have a break or, more frequently, have additional time to work on their dissertations. "My parents watched my son for an entire week so that my husband and I could go on vacation. It was right before the final rush to wrap up my thesis, so I really needed a break," said Claudine, a biochemist.

Married graduate students without children also faced dilemmas. Tony, a physicist, and his wife had to relocate when he started graduate school. They moved to an area where there were not many career opportunities for his wife, and it took her a few months to find a job. Once they settled down, however, Tony enjoyed the married graduate student lifestyle. "I worked from nine to five just like my wife, so that we could spend time together in the evenings. Having a wife forced me to have a regular schedule, and made me more productive at work. I also enjoyed coming home and knowing that I could complain to somebody about my day at work."

If you are married, there are several questions you need to ask yourself (and your spouse) before you decide to pursue a Ph.D. Will you be able to support your spouse and children financially? Will a doctoral dissertation take too much time away from your family? How does your spouse feel about living on a small stipend for several years? If you need to relocate, will your spouse be able to find a job? Remember that your spouse's and children's emotional support is essential to your success in graduate school, so discuss your options with them before you make a decision.

 If you are married, consider your family's quality of life before you decide to go to graduate school.

International Students

Anna, a biophysicist, observed that one of the disadvantages of being an international student was that she was not able to make informed decisions like her domestic classmates. " I did not have a chance to look at the campus, meet the professors, or talk to the students. I think it is very important to find out as much as you can about each university before you make a decision. Fortunately, telephone interviews and the Internet helped me find a school and choose an advisor." Anna was able to settle in relatively easily, because the university had a community group of students from her country. "I don't know what I would have done without my friends. They were there to support me when I had difficulties or just needed a break. I also met my husband through this student group."

In addition to cultural adjustments, international graduate students also need to think about travel visas, especially when they need to find employment. "It was not that difficult to get a student visa, but I was not allowed any grace period without a job after graduation," said Eunice a biologist. "I found a postdoc quickly, but my advisor lost his funding a few months after I started. I e-mailed a bunch of professors, hoping to find another position, because otherwise I would have needed to go back to my country. I was very lucky to find another position in the same city, so I did not even need to move." Eunice found her new postdoctoral position through a professional contact. As an international student, you will find that it is even *more* important to network, because you might have a limited grace period between positions.

If you are an international married student, you have additional questions to think about. Will your spouse need to learn English? Will he or she be able to find a job? Does your university provide a community for spouses of graduate students? "It took a little time for my wife to get her work permit, so we were just living off my salary. Fortunately, my school offered me a stipend that was slightly higher than normal, because I was married," said George, a humanities major. Once she received a work permit, George's wife, Maria, worked in a coffee shop while looking for a job as a webpage designer. Unfortunately, employers did not find value in Maria's overseas college diploma, so she decided to earn a master's degree in order to find employment. Maria enjoyed going back to school, but she and George struggled financially for years. "We had to save money for Maria's education, so we barely made ends meet. One year my department was not able to offer me a stipend, and I had to work part-time in addition to working on my thesis. That was the most difficult time for us." In retrospect, George thought that their financial situation could have been less stressful, had they contacted an international students' group at George's university and explored the resources available.

If you are an international student applying to graduate schools in the United States, see http://educationusa.state.gov/ for resources.

If you are an international student, find a community group that will help you adjust to cultural changes and find professional contacts.

Minority Students

Francis, an engineering major, worked in his industry for 15 years before deciding to go back to school to earn a doctorate in education. As an African-American, he was interested in the factors that encouraged or discouraged minority students from pursuing higher degrees; in fact, it interested him so, that it became the subject of his dissertation. "During my research I realized that many minority students felt that higher degrees were unattainable for them. They did not have many role models, and viewed graduate school as a hostile environment for minorities." Francis now works at a research university and part of his job is to counsel minority students about opportunities in higher education.

According to Francis, summer research programs can play an important role in encouraging minority students to apply to Ph.D. programs. Through these programs, students have the opportunity to learn about research and meet faculty from other universities. Furthermore, there are also many fellowship programs available exclusively to minorities, to help them cover the cost of their education. See the appendix for a list of summer research programs and fellowships specifically for minority students.

FROM THE PH.D. SECRET ARCHIVES:

Refuting common myths about graduate school

What are your preconceptions about graduate school? What do you think the expectations are? Do you think that your study habits from college will serve you well (and sufficiently) during a doctoral program? It turns out that in order to succeed in graduate school, you might need to "unlearn" many of the lessons from the undergraduate years. Here are some common myths that former graduate students believe can make your life unnecessarily difficult:

Myth #1: My thesis must be groundbreaking. In 1923, a young French physicist named Louis-Victor de Broglie earned a Ph.D. at Sorbonne University in Paris for demonstrating that all matter had a wave-like nature—a phenomenon which became known as wave-particle duality. Six years later, de Broglie won the Nobel Prize in Physics for this work when was only 37 years old. We all enter graduate school thinking that we need to do something astonishing to earn our degree, yet de Broglie's accomplishment of earning a Nobel Prize for his Ph.D. thesis is the exception rather than the rule. In fact, the real goal of a Ph.D. is not to make cutting-edge discoveries (although that does happen sometimes), but rather to learn how to do research. If you expect yourself to do pioneering work in graduate school, you will probably make your life harder than it needs to be. A distinguished professor at MIT put it succinctly: "My students usually think that they have to do more than they actually need to." He did not expect groundbreaking work from his students (although he was one of the world's leading experts in his field), but he did expect carefully thought-out theses that demonstrated to him that his students were able to carry out independent research.

Myth #2: My work has to be perfect. Perfectionism is a vestigial attitude from college. We are used to striving for perfect SAT scores, perfect GRE scores, and a perfect GPA. Research works a little differently. Yes, you should be meticulous, but is there such a thing as a perfect thesis? Experiments are not perfectly reproducible. In fact, one generally expects a 10–20% percent-error between data sets. Perfectionism can also take its toll during the writing of a thesis. Constant re-writing of text that does not really need it can cause "tunnel vision" and lack of balance in your life. How do you know you have written a "good enough" thesis? Consult with your advisor and read other theses from your department to see what constitutes a doctoral dissertation. You might be surprised at how much you have already accomplished.

Myth #3: If I want to become an independent researcher, I need to do everything by myself. In college you might have been expected to solve problems completely on your own. Research, however, is rarely a solitary endeavor. If you read through the acknowledgements in doctoral dissertations, you will see how many people contribute to the completion of a single project. How do you convince people to help you? How do you make your voice heard in a group meeting? How do you seek out collaborators and persuade them to work with you? If you do not yet have experience with working in teams, graduate school might provide that opportunity for you. The important thing for now is to realize that it can be challenging to do everything by yourself, but you *do not have to.* If you find it challenging to work or communicate with others, skip ahead to chapter five, which discusses how to master your people skills.

Myth #4: I need to abuse my body to get my work done. In college and possibly at a job prior to graduate school, we were used to short deadlines. We had to study for exams announced just a few days in advance, or complete a progress report handed to us the day before the deadline. We stayed up late (or all night) to complete our work. Perhaps the all-nighter paid off and we passed our exam or won approval for our progress report. Most likely, however, our body needed to recover after such a workload before it was ready for the next challenge. Back, then we were "sprinting"— we had to complete many small projects fast. In graduate school, in comparison, we are running a marathon. When you ask first-time marathon runners what their goal time is they usually reply: "I just want to finish." Similar to the tortoise that beat the hare in a race, we need to pace ourselves, if we want to cross the finish line. Consider the following statistics: The world record for running a marathon (42.195 km) is about 2 hours and 4.5 minutes, and the record for a 100 m sprint is 9.7 seconds. If marathon winners were to keep their pace for a 100-m race, they would finish in 17.7 seconds— a posting that would not even qualify them for the race. Nevertheless, this pace is sufficient to earn a gold metal in a marathon. When you drive yourself more than you are capable of—or more than you need to—you jeopardize your work and also your health. If a sprinter tried to keep his pace for a marathon, how long do you think he would last? (http://www.marathonguide.com/history/records/index.cfm and http://en.wikipedia.org/wiki/100_metres has more details on these very illustrative statistics.)

Jack, a senior graduate student, was editing a book comprising over 30 chapters from many contributors, all while also writing his own dissertation. It was early December and he wanted to complete most of the editing by the end of the year. He stayed up every night until 3 a.m. (and rose at 7 a.m.), ignoring the early signs of a cold. He soon came down with such serious pneumonia that he had to be hospitalized. His recovery was slow and his wife had to take unpaid leave from work to care for him. His illness resulted in a significant setback for his work, as well as financial hardship for his household. When we push ourselves to do more than we are capable of, we run the risk of developing an illness—or on a more subtle level, a burnout. When we are burned out, we feel depressed and unable to motivate ourselves. In chapters two and three, I will show you how to develop a healthy working schedule, and to maximize productivity while avoiding a burnout. In the meantime, give your body the rest and exercise it needs, to balance out your "brain work." Even Socrates himself was a gymnastics student. Need we say more?

Myth #5: If I want to complete my dissertation, I have to work all the time and give up my hobbies and friends. If you feel overwhelmed by your work, it is worth asking yourself: How much of my stress is real and how much of it is self-imposed? There is nothing wrong with working on weekends (in fact, sometimes we do have to miss a movie night with friends, in order to meet an important deadline), but when you work long hours make sure that your time is spent wisely. Nora, a mathematician, spent most of her free time training for dance concerts. Even during the busiest times of the semester, she would speak passionately about her performances. At the same time, she was also applying for an internship at NASA. "How do you have time for dancing?" I asked her. "Oh," she replied, "if I couldn't dance, I would die." I did not understand her reply at the time. When I found out, however, that she had stellar grades and was accepted into the NASA summer program, it prompted me to start swimming three times a week (a hobby which I had put aside previously). Eventually, exercising evolved into daily routine, and it is a habit that would be very hard for me to break now. After swimming, I always feel so refreshed, that I now understand why they call pastimes "recreation. After exercising I truly feel like I "re-created" my energy. It is important to set aside a regular time for recreation. At the very least, if you enjoy your hobbies, they will probably give you an energy boost, and you will have more motivation to work on your project.

Myth #6: My advisor will tell me exactly what I need to do to complete my thesis. There is a wide range of personalities when it comes to advisors. Some professors will try to micromanage your project, while others will meet with you infrequently. No matter how hands-on your professor is, however, it is unlikely that he or she will tell you exactly what you need to do to graduate. In fact, you would not want an advisor who outlines all the details of your thesis, because then there would be nothing left for you to learn. Some students are disappointed in their advisors when they realize that they get less help than they initially expected. On the other hand, the need for guidance decreases as students mature. Kim, a biologist, confessed that she wished her advisor gave her more freedom during her last year. Keep in mind that regardless of your advisor's style, *you* are ultimately responsible for the completion of your Ph.D. thesis. In chapter five, I will cover the essential skills for communicating with your advisor, in case you feel that you need to get more or less guidance from him or her.

Myth #7: I can just wait until my studies are finished to start writing my thesis. There are a number of reasons why starting to write your thesis early can speed up your progress. Remember that in order to graduate, you need a *written* thesis. That is your end product, your ticket to the outside world; you cannot turn in ideas that are still in your head. Regardless of what kind of device you engineered or how exciting your results are, you cannot graduate until you submit a written thesis. Which part of the thesis do you write first? I would suggest writing your table of contents. Most theses are built around addressing a single question or hypothesis, and when you write a table of contents, you can see whether your work actually answers the question you proposed. Many graduate students have a tendency to "miss the forest for the trees": They get so caught up in the day-to-day details of their work that they forget the "big picture." While writing your table of contents (or a detailed outline), you will be reminded of your overall goal, and you will also be motivated to work more on your project. Most likely you will need to modify the outline as your research progresses, but keeping the big picture in mind will help you to stay focused. If you can imagine trying to build a house without drafting blueprints first, you can understand the importance of developing an outline before doing anything else.

Another good reason for starting to write your thesis early is to evaluate your research as you go. Does what you have done so far make sense? How much have you accomplished and how much remains to be done? If you publish papers or present at conferences, many of these questions will be answered, and can help you construct your final dissertation. In chapter six, I will discuss strategies to help with the thesis-writing to make it quicker and more enjoyable. (That's right, writing *can* be enjoyable—that's why I wrote this book!).

If you think that it is too early to begin writing your dissertation, write as much about your research as you can. Publish research papers, send progress reports to your thesis committee, submit conference abstracts, or put together presentations for your department. The more written material that you have and the more you have analyzed your research, the better prepared you will be to write your thesis when the time does come.

Myth #8: If I do not have good data a few years into my Ph.D., I might as well quit. I have been going to thesis defenses since I was an undergraduate, and I quickly learned that productivity in graduate school was not linear. The first time I went to a thesis defense was after my sophomore year, when I worked in a chemistry lab during the summer. The thesis defense candidate graduated after six years of study and research, and noted that she had collected most of her data in the last six months. It took her five and a half years to figure what she wanted to do and how to do it, and six months to collect the data. Those five and a half years were not wasted, because during those years she completed her coursework, passed her qualifiers, surveyed the literature, learned experimental techniques, and chose a relevant topic for her thesis. After the defense, a senior scientist remarked that sometimes it takes five years to define the right question. Maybe the topic is so new that it is not clear in which area one can make a significant contribution, or maybe the scope of the project is so ambitious that it cannot be completed within a reasonable amount of time. For multiple reasons, it can take a few years until the right question crystallizes, at which time you will feel ready to collect data.

Occasionally, interpreting the data is the real challenge. During my third year in graduate school, I went to a defense that I thought was one of the best I had ever attended. The topic was interesting, the data was analyzed meticulously, and the student was eloquent as she presented her work. After the defense, I walked up the stairs with a professor who had been on her thesis committee. I told him that I was not sure my thesis could ever be as interesting as hers. He looked at me with surprise and said, "You should have seen what she had six months ago. Her experiments were mostly completed, but the data was confusing and we were not sure how to interpret it. She did a nice job, though, of reanalyzing the data and complementing it with new findings from other groups." I kept this comment in mind while I was writing my thesis, and I did not let "confusing data" intimidate me anymore. In fact, I found that some of my most exciting results came from experiments where my data was different from what I expected.

How to lay the foundations for graduate school

Step 1 (before and during the application process): Decide whether earning a Ph.D. is the right choice for you.

- Will a Ph.D. help you achieve your career goals?
- What is your financial situation? Will your job after graduate school pay for the debt you incur?
- Will you be able to manage your family responsibilities, as a graduate student?
- If you are an international student, do you know how to obtain the necessary travel visas for you and your family? Are you aware of all the adjustments you will need to make? Is there a community from your native country near the university?
- If a Ph.D. is the right choice for you, but this is not the right time, can you postpone it for a few years?

Step 2: Begin the application process. (See the appendix for resources.)

- Find out more about the schools, departments and individual professors you want to work with.
- Complete the application forms for each school.
- Write a great admissions essay.
- Ace your GRE examination(s).

Step 3: Make a detailed financial plan for each program.

- How much will graduate school cost you? Does your program cover tuition and/or pay you a stipend?
- Will your school pay for medical insurance?
- If you need extra income, where can you apply for fellowships? (This is a step that you could also do before you have been

accepted to graduate school. Some professors will automatically accept you, if you bring your own funding.)
- Is it realistic to expect that you can work a part-time job while working on your thesis?

Step 4 (after you have been accepted): During the interview process, assess the advantages and disadvantages of each program.
- Is the department a good fit for you, in terms of curriculum and research?
- Are you satisfied with the social life in your prospective department?
- Consider the location of the school: Is proximity to your family a priority?
- Does the school or town offer opportunities to pursue your favorite sports and hobbies?

Step 5: Choose an advisor that will be a good fit for you.
- Evaluate how much guidance you will need, and whether you prefer a hands-on or hands-off advisor.
- Is the research exciting?
- Does your advisor have sufficient funding for you? Will you be required to pay your own tuition or be a teaching assistant?
- Do you prefer to work for a tenured or untenured professor? Will the professor come up for tenure in the middle of your thesis? If your professor does not get tenure, will you be able to handle the changes that may occur, as a result?

Step 6 (after you have started graduate school): Build a support network.
- Get to know your classmates.
- Socialize with your research group members.
- Attend seminars and department events where you can meet other professors, graduate students and postdoctoral fellows.
- Join professional organizations and network at conferences.

Step 7: Establish a life outside of work.
- Set aside a few hours every week, as well as some time for relaxation every day.
- Pursue sports that are fun and re-energizing for you.

- Join hobby and special interest groups where you can meet new people.

What is next? Once you pass your qualifying exams, or possibly even before, you will need to start planning a thesis project. Do you know what your research area will be? Are you aware of all the electronic resources available, to help you with your research? Should you work on something that is very innovative, or would you rather stay with a more conservative project? Once you have the freedom to do research, how can you keep yourself motivated to work? The next chapter will guide you through these questions, so that you can construct an exciting research project with realistic goals.

Changing advisors: *Stella's and Maya's stories*

More than one Ph.D. pointed out the importance of changing advisors, if you see no future for your thesis in your current group. Some students have the courage to take action, while others hesitate, perhaps too long. Stella was working on her Ph.D. for four years when she realized that the project she had been assigned to would never generate interesting results. Her advisor insisted on continuing the current project, even though the results were irreproducible. Frustrated with the lack of progress, Stella approached another professor in the department and asked him whether he would consider taking her as a student. She had already known this professor to be a dedicated mentor to his students, and was sure she could succeed in his group. Fortunately, he agreed to hire her, and she graduated four years later, after completing a productive and fulfilling research project. Stella believes that changing her research group was the best decision she had made in graduate school. "My first advisor and I never got along, even before we realized that the project did not work. I think that she did not have much respect for me, which was the reason that she did not pay proper attention to how my work was going."

Maya, too, was dissatisfied with her advisor. He was not interested in mentoring her, and she had to work on her own throughout the entire dissertation process. She considered working for a senior professor in her department, but thought that he probably did not want to hire more students because he was close to retirement age. After one of Maya's friends finished her qualifying exams, she announced that she found a great advisor: the one that Maya had wanted to work for! "I wish I had at least asked him whether he would consider taking another student," Maya said. " I just assumed that he wanted to retire soon and was not interested in mentoring anybody else. I did finish my Ph.D., but it could have been a more satisfying experience with another professor."

Finding funding: *Cheryl's, Portia's and Billy's stories*

Finding funding for a Ph.D. in the humanities, social sciences or arts is frequently a challenge. Students usually need to work part-time in order to support themselves—and often their tuition is not covered, either. How are they able to finish their degrees? Cheryl, a literature major, recalls finding funding a continuous challenge. "Every year, I had a different solution for making ends meet. My tuition had to be covered by research and teaching assistantships, because my department did not always have funding. I suppose the advantage was that I got a lot of experience teaching, which is what I do now. In order to support myself, I also had to take a second job, usually as an administrative assistant or tutor. It was very tough to find the time to work on my dissertation, and I had to learn to manage my time very wisely. It is important to think about your financial situation very carefully, before you begin your Ph.D. program. Secure yourself as much funding as you can from fellowships. Some of my friends also took loans, but you have to make sure that you do not take more than you can repay after graduation."

Portia, an education major, took a job after her master's degree, in order to gain more experience before returning to school. After she decided to pursue a Ph.D., she was awarded an assistantship from the university, in which she would help edit one of their journals. With her tuition covered, she could focus on her studies; she finished her Ph.D. in three years—a record time. "My husband and I were very economical with our money by cooking most nights rather than eating out. Fortunately, I did not need to get a job in addition to being an editor, so I had free time to pursue hobbies such as rock-climbing, hiking and biking."

Fellowships can significantly enhance progress on a Ph.D. thesis, by allowing the students to focus on their work rather than having to balance a part-time job and their research. As an international student, Billy knew that she would not be able to finish her Ph.D. without proper funding. "Finishing my Ph.D. in English was difficult enough, even with a fellowship," she recalled. "I applied to many schools, but I considered only those that offered a financial package. My friends who did not win fellowships took significantly longer and struggled more, because they also had to support themselves while working on their dissertations."

CHAPTER 2:
BECOMING AN INDEPENDENT RESEARCHER

"Whatever you think you can do or believe can do, begin it.
Action has magic, grace and power in it."
Johann Wolfgang von Goethe, German writer, (1749–1832)

After I passed my qualifiers, one of my friends laughed and said, "The easy part is over!" At first, I did not understand what she meant. After all, I had been taking courses for a year and a half, and I spent my entire winter vacation lugging around heavy books to study during any free minute I had. Could a thesis be more difficult than that? The answer was both "yes" and "no." Preparing for my doctoral exams was overwhelming, because there was an infinite amount of material to study. Yet, I knew what I needed to do, and the more I studied, the more prepared I felt.

During the completion of my thesis project, however, I was constantly plagued by questions: Am I going in the right direction? How much more do I need to do? Will my committee approve of my project? It is essential to continuously reassess progress on your thesis, but how can you be sure that you are going in the *right direction*? In this chapter, you will learn the following essential skills for becoming an independent researcher:

- Developing a productive daily schedule
- Designing an original and realistic research project
- Keeping yourself motivated

Challenge #1: Adapting to the graduate student lifestyle
Developing a sustainable daily schedule
Sandra, a computer science student, was so excited to be part of a famous research group that she spent all of her free time studying and doing research. She worked 12–14-hour days, and by the end of her first semester, she was exhausted. "I think it is very important

to pace yourself," she said, "because you will burn out quickly, if you focus on trying to please everybody. It can be very tempting to be an 'eager beaver,' in order to impress your supervisor and colleagues, but you really need to take care of *yourself* if you want to finish your dissertation." As she tried to balance coursework, research and community activities, Sandra faced the same challenge as most other graduate students: In an environment where there are few real deadlines, how do you determine what your ideal daily schedule should be?

 Avoid the "eager beaver syndrome," because you will soon become exhausted and unmotivated.

While researching the answer to this question, I realized that most graduate students have the flexibility to set up a schedule that meets *their* personal and academic needs. I once visited a biochemistry lab around 9 a.m. and was surprised to see only one student in the lab. "No one slacks off here," the professor explained. "Most people will be here by 10 a.m., some after noon, but everyone gets their work done." He was right. Some students came in after 12 p.m. but they stayed until the early hours of the morning. Others, with families for example, were in by 7 a.m., but left by 5 p.m. Everyone had to develop their own work schedule—a flexibility that might make students uncomfortable, after the rigidity of undergraduate coursework.

Not all supervisors give their students freedom to set their own hours. Leslie, a biology student, found graduate school to be more structured than college. "In college, I had the luxury of sleeping until my classes began, which was usually around 11 a.m. In graduate school, I had a real boss, and I had to answer to him on a regular basis. I did not have a chance to slack off." Most students, however, developed their own schedules. Patrick, a chemist, was always the first to be in his lab, because his infant son woke him up around 5 a.m. He reasoned that he might as well go to work at the break of dawn when all of the instruments were free, and then leave early to relieve his wife of the evening chores. Sally, a biochemistry student, usually arrived with her morning coffee at 11 a.m., but stayed until 8 or 9 p.m.. Her schedule was shifted towards the evenings, because she was active in graduate student groups that met late at night.

What is the best schedule for *you*? Are you a morning person or an evening person? Do you like to begin your work before everybody else gets in, or do you like to finish it after everybody else has left?

 To determine your daily schedule, ask yourself the following questions:
- *Does your supervisor expect you to be at work during certain hours?*
- *During what time of day are you most productive?*
- *Do you have any commitments to your family or community that determine your schedule?*

Once you have set a schedule, try to maintain it. It is tempting to sleep late on some days, but you will be most productive when you keep a regular work and sleep schedule. There will be days when you will feel tired or unmotivated, even after you have rested enough. It is normal for your energy and motivation to go up and down in cycles. On your "tired" days, be more forgiving of yourself, and make as much progress as you have the energy for. If you feel excessively tired, check with your doctor to make sure you are not sick.

 In order to maximize your productivity, maintain a regular schedule. Be forgiving of yourself on days when you feel tired, but return to your regular schedule as soon as you can.

How to stay focused throughout the day

Let us assume that you have set up a regular schedule, such as 9 a.m. to 6 p.m. How do you stay focused throughout the day? If you have ever tried to read or study for nine hours straight, you know that it is impossible to concentrate for such a long period of time. Nevertheless, there are occasions (e.g., when studying for qualifying exams or writing a paper) when it will be necessary to put in many hours of work to meet a deadline. The key to maintaining your productivity throughout the day is to take regular breaks. How frequently should you take a break? How long should your breaks be? What should you do during your breaks?

Jim, an electrical engineer, told me about the following strategy for structuring his days. When he was doing experiments, it was easy to set up an agenda, because his experiments dictated his schedule. The challenging days were those when he had large blocks of time for reading or writing. His trick for staying sharp all day was to alternate 45 minutes of working with 15 minutes of rest, and he enforced this schedule with a stopwatch. If he came across a difficult problem, he forced himself to keep thinking about it until his timer rang. Jim said that one of the most important skills for overcoming challenges was to have the patience to keep working when he got stuck; it was tempting to take a break when he got confused, but he realized that the problems would still be there, unresolved, when he returned. By staying for just a few extra minutes after encountering a challenge, he motivated himself to define exactly what had to be done to resolve each problem.

 In order to stay focused for a long period of time, try alternating 45 minutes of work with 15-minute breaks.

On the other hand, Jim took his 15-minute break after 45 minutes of work, even if he was in the middle of something. He would finish writing the sentence or equation he began, but he said that the 15-minute breaks were essential for his mind and his body, and so he adhered to them strictly. During his breaks, he stretched his limbs, analyzed his work, organized his desk and decided what he should work on during the next 45-minute work period. While other students procrastinated on such "house-keeping" activities, Jim claimed that cleaning up gave his mind a rest so he would be sharp for the next 45-minute session. With this strategy of forcing himself to work through difficult problems while also sticking to a predetermined break schedule, he was able to get so much work done during the day that he graduated in less than four years—all while pursuing sports and maintaining an active social life and regular sleep schedule.

 Use your breaks to stretch your limbs, organize your desk and get a drink of water.

Be careful about taking breaks that could "eat up" your entire afternoon. Sarah, a biologist, found it challenging to plan her daily schedule so that she could get her work done and still have a few breaks to allow her to relax. She usually took breaks by going out to coffee with friends, but found that these excursions often took at least an hour. As a consequence, she had to make up for the lost time by staying late at work. Another "time trap" was using the computer during her breaks. Initially, Sarah took breaks to check e-mail or surf the web, but these activities did not "refresh" her, and they usually took more than 15 minutes. "I tried to stay away from the computer when I took a break, but it was very hard, because I felt compelled to check my e-mail very frequently." Instead of staying at her desk during her breaks, Sarah decided to get a drink of water or chat with friends. If she had to stay at work late to finish experiments, she also took a few longer breaks during the day to get snacks or take a walk around campus.

 Take a few long breaks during the day and use them for exercising, walking or getting a snack. Students found that breaks at the computer (e.g., checking e-mail or web-surfing) were time-consuming and not refreshing.

Balancing work and play

In response to the question, "How did you relieve stress during graduate school?" almost all the Ph.D.s emphasized the importance of socializing with a supportive community group and pursuing a hobby or sport on a regular basis. A hobby can be as simple as regular walking or cooking at home. Corinne, an art history major, spent many of her evenings preparing exotic meals. "I loved cooking, because it gave me instant gratification. With my research, it took months or even years to see measurable progress."

Other students pursued sports and hobbies they had picked up during college or high school. Kris, a chemist, played jazz music with a band on Friday nights. Playing music reenergized him, and his jazz band also became his support group. Lucas, an electrical engineer, made it a rule to relax on Friday nights and all of Saturday. He used this free time to go to the movies with friends and explore hobby groups on campus. He did go back to work on Sundays, and found that he was more motivated to get organized for the rest of the week. Mandy, a computer scientist, liked to stay at work late, but was disappointed that her university gym was closed by the time she was ready to exercise. Thus, she found pockets of time during the day when she was usually not productive (particularly the mid-afternoon), and she used those hours to exercise. Afterwards, she returned to her office, and stayed as long as necessary, knowing that she had already completed her workout for the day.

 Set aside a regular time every week to socialize with your support group, or to pursue hobbies or sports.

Challenge #2: Developing your research plans

Marc, an electrical engineer, described graduate school as being thrown into the Atlantic Ocean with a paddleboat. If you are lucky you might get vague directions from your advisor, but more frequently, you will find yourself as the captain of your own boat. How do you get to the other side? Before you begin the journey of your doctoral dissertation, ask yourself the following three questions:

1. *Where* is the other side?
2. What resources do I need, to get there?
3. Where is the roadmap that will give me the directions?

It is very rare for students to have answers to all three questions when they begin graduate school. In fact, the catch-22 of graduate school is that you are there to become an expert, but how do you come up with a plan for your thesis if you do not have any expertise to begin with? How do you even know what constitutes a suitable thesis proposal?

A good proposal is one that is *robust*. It is not easily swayed by Murphy's Law (i.e., anything that can go wrong will, and usually at the worst time). Your thesis proposal is the blueprint for your doctoral dissertation (and your life, for the next few years), so plan a project that can be completed with the available resources in a reasonable amount of time. Invest sufficient time into this proposal, because the more you polish it, the better you will understand the background, methods and research questions.

How do you construct a good thesis proposal?

1. Choose a research area that you are passionate about.

When you begin your research, your advisor might give you a choice of dissertation topics. What criteria should you use to make this decision? In this section, I offer several tips on how to construct your thesis proposal, but the most important advice that former graduate students have given is that your thesis topic should cover an area that you are truly passionate about. Regardless of your field, you will have good days and bad days. On good days, you will be enthusiastic and motivated to work. On bad days, you might question whether your research makes any sense, and you might even doubt your ability to graduate. If you choose a meaningful topic, the setbacks in your research will not bring you down. You will still be working in an important field, and you will still be learning the skills and expertise necessary for your career.

2. Choose a topic that can be completed with the available resources in a reasonable amount of time.

What are the resources that you will need for your thesis? First, you will need funding. If you are on a fellowship, you might have limited time to complete your thesis. Justin, an engineer, received three years of funding from a fellowship, and his advisor agreed to fund him for one additional year. On his first day at work, Justin asked his advisor: "What project can be completed in four years?" As his thesis progressed, he periodically met with his advisor to talk about how to finish his thesis by the time his funding ran out. Justin was able to graduate in four years, by working on projects that were realistic for his timeframe.

Another important resource is expertise. Ivan, a chemist, chose an exciting topic for his thesis. The problem was that neither he nor his advisor had sufficient expertise for the project. One year after he began his project, Ivan had made little progress. "We actually changed my thesis topic to something that was closer to my advisor's field of research. After that, my project progressed more quickly because he was able to give me more guidance."

3. Look for projects that are educational and incorporate market-able skills.

Think about your progression through graduate school as a pyramid (see FIGURE 2-1). As the figure shows, you become more and more specialized with each passing year, with fewer and fewer people being experts in your field. An adage among many advisors in graduate school is: "You learn more and more about less and less, until finally you know everything about nothing." By the time you graduate, you will be part of a small community of people who specialize in your particular area. On the other hand, you will probably need a diverse skill set after graduation, so it is important to avoid the common mistake of narrowing your pyramid too quickly. It is not necessary to learn all the subspecialties, but do familiarize yourself with the background literature and technical skills in your field.

Some students make the mistake of focusing only on finishing graduate school quickly, rather than taking advantage of learning opportunities. Ted, a physicist, finished in less than four years; in retrospect, he wishes that he had stayed in graduate school longer. Now a research scientist, Ted realizes that he could have benefited from exploring different projects in his group. "I was so focused on finishing quickly, that I did not take the opportunity to learn about the different aspects of my field."

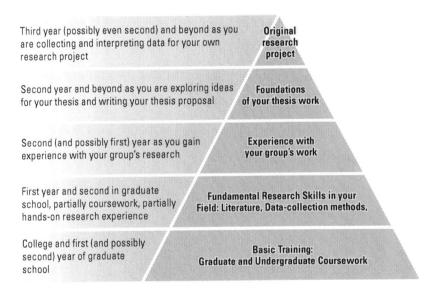

Figure 2-1: Development of doctoral dissertations

It is also important to think about your marketability. Colin, a chemical engineer, chose a thesis topic that had few practical applications. "My thesis project was so obscure, I was unemployable after graduate school. I actually had to do a postdoctoral fellowship to rescue my résumé and learn some practical skills."

How do you diversify your education while focusing on your thesis? Jamie, a chemistry student and liquid chromatography expert, decided to pick up some cell culture expertise during his final year. His buddy Terry—a cell culture expert—decided to learn liquid chromatography. Oddly enough, Jamie was hired into an industrial cell culture laboratory, and Terry was invited to multiple job interviews because of his liquid chromatography expertise. As these examples show, it is frequently possible to design a small project towards the end of your thesis to help you to learn new skills that will bolster your post-graduation employability.

4. Visualize your finished publication(s).

Sean, a physicist, had an advisor who outlined each paper, even before the research had started. He wrote down what questions he wanted to answer, and what each graph and table should show. This method was so helpful for Sean, that he still designs his research papers in advance. "In the end, the papers did not turn out exactly as my advisor prescribed, but it was a good way to get his students motivated and focused."

As you plan your papers, write down the answers to the following questions:

- What is your central hypothesis or research goal?
- What is the motivation for this study?
- What have other groups contributed to this research?
- What methods do you need to learn, to complete this project?
- What are the possible outcomes or results of this study?
- What will your tables and graphs, if any, show?
- How does this work contribute to your field of research?

Visualizing your publications will motivate you to work, because most graduate students feel a sense of pride when they hold their very first published paper in their hands. Most likely, the answers to these questions will change with time and you will probably have several setbacks. Fortunately, most students become more efficient as they progress through graduate school. Your cumulative experience will pay off during your final year, when you are racing to finish your research and your dissertation simultaneously. In the meantime, work on defining your questions and methods meticulously, so that you will have a realistic plan to work with.

5. Set well-defined goals for your thesis.

At the beginning of this section, I listed the three most important questions that you need to ask, in order to write a good thesis proposal. The most important question is the first one: "Where is the other side?" In other words, what do you hope to accomplish? After six years of graduate school, Sophia scheduled a job interview, because she assumed that she would graduate the following semester. When she asked her advisor about a date for her defense, she was dismayed to hear that she could not graduate until she completed yet another project, which was estimated to last six months. Not only did Sophia have to cancel her job interview, she also lost the motivation to finish her thesis. The six-month project actually took an entire year. In retrospect, Sophia admitted that she did not communicate with her advisor as frequently as she should have. "I just assumed that once I published a few papers, he would let me graduate, but clearly he wanted me to finish a project that was very important to him." It is therefore essential that you and your advisor agree on what needs to be completed while you write your thesis proposal, and also throughout your graduate program.

6. Determine how you will accomplish your goals.

While planning your dissertation, visualize each step of your research:

- How will you get started?
- What resources will you need?
- What steps do you need to take, and in what order?
- How will you know when you have achieved your goals (i.e., made it to the other side)?

Your research will probably not go exactly as you planned it, but if you want to answer these questions in a written thesis proposal, you will have to review the literature and discuss your ideas with your advisor. It is not embarrassing to ask basic questions such as: Why did we decide to do this study? Why did we take this approach? How will we execute this project?

What do we need to do first? What is the appropriate research protocol? Keep communication open with your supervisor, but do not become too dependent on him or her. After a thorough literature search, you will come up with your own ideas, but always discuss them with your advisor before you invest too much effort. You do not want to waste time on a project that will not be considered valuable!

7. Select a project that balances novelty with established research.

Given that you want to finish your thesis within a reasonable amount of time, should you research a novel or "hot" area, or go with a "safer," better-understood topic? One way to answer this question is to visualize your-self at every stage of your thesis. How will you make it happen? Can you gather the resources and complete the work by your proposed graduation date? Most likely, your project will take longer than you anticipated, so allow some flexibility to account for contingencies. In fact, one former student estimated that everything took two to four times longer than he had expected. (He did finish his Ph.D. in four years, so his overall planning skills must have been quite good.)

If you have little expertise, begin your work by exploring questions in well-understood areas. For example, you could learn the basics of your field by extending the research projects of previous students, or trying to reproduce their data. Starting your research in an area where the meth-odology has been established will teach you the research skills needed in your field. Once you learn the basics, you can expand your research by exploring novel areas, and building your own unique niche.

8. Establish a network of professors in your committee who will drive your research and give you constructive feedback.

Selecting a good thesis committee is another essential component of a successful doctoral dissertation. A good committee can motivate you, focus your research and possibly help moderate any disagreements with your advisor. The frequency of committee meetings will depend on your department. Some students met with their committees only once in graduate school, whereas others presented their research every six months. Whichever is the case for you, choose faculty members who are approachable and have expertise in your field. Also, do not be shy about meeting with individual members, if you need advice. One advantage of meeting with professors regularly is that they will be continuously updated on your research, and so there will be no surprises at your committee meeting. In addition, keep your advisor on top of your communications with other faculty members, so that he or she will also be aware of the status of your project.

9. Have several backup plans for your thesis proposal, in case you reach a dead end.

Research is unpredictable and you would not want your doctoral dissertation to hinge on good luck. It is quite frustrating to have to cross your fingers continuously for your studies to go well. When your results do not come back to you the way you expected them, you might even lose the motivation to continue working. How can you avoid such a disappointment?

Gerald, a chemical engineer, always had three or four alternatives for every research plan. "I never worried about my experiments not working out, because I always had several alternative directions, in case I ran into a dead end." In fact, most of Gerald's experiments did not turn out the way he wanted them to. In addition to the backup plans he had built into his original proposal, he continuously generated alternatives to his written plan. Using this approach, Gerald avoided disappointment and frustration. "I did not waste much time during my Ph.D., because I always had a plan of what to do next. That is probably why I finished more quickly than my classmates." (He finished in four years, in contrast to the five years typical for his department.)

10. Do a thorough literature search before you choose your topic.

Many schools require a written thesis proposal, which forces students to review the literature thoroughly. A thorough literature search will give you the necessary background to answer the following questions:

- ◆ Do you have all the necessary resources and expertise?
- ◆ Is your timeframe realistic for this project?
- ◆ What practical applications does your topic have?

Online resources will provide you with a wealth of information, to help you build the foundation for your thesis. In the next section, I have listed a few electronic databases for the most common fields of study. I also list many free-access databases in the appendix (categorized by field of study), but you should check with your library for subscription-based services.

Using online research tools

With so many articles being published every day, it is a challenge to keep track of advances in research. In this section, I discuss some free-access and subscription-based databases that can help you remain informed. When you browse databases, also check whether they offer alert services (such as RSS feeds, discussed later in this chapter) that will notify you electronically when articles with your selected keywords are published.

 Sign up for electronic alert services from relevant databases.

Free-access databases

The appendix lists many free-access databases, which you can search from any computer. One example of a free-access web-based search engine is Google Scholar (GS), available at scholar.google.com. It indexes articles across an array of disciplines. Released in 2004, GS includes most peer-reviewed online journals from the world's largest scientific publishers. Google also has other free services that could be useful for your research, such as Google Patent, Google Government, Google Directory and Google News. Google Patent is a search engine that indexes seven million patents from the United States. Google Government allows you to simultaneously search websites from local and federal governments, as well as government agencies and the news. Google Directory is a search engine organized by categories such as arts, business, health, and society. You can search for keywords within the main categories, or click on the subcategories and bring up several related websites, including other search engines and databases.

MEDLINE (pubmed.gov) is compiled by the US National Library of Medicine (NLM); it includes abstracts in medicine, nursing, pharmacy, dentistry, veterinary medicine and health care. This database has over 17 million records covering approximately 5,000 publications, from 1950 to the present. While the abstracts are free-access, you usually need a license to view the full-text articles. Some of the articles that are linked to MEDLINE, however, are of no cost. If your computer does not have access to university-based subscriptions, you can search through Pubmed Central (pubmedcentral.gov), which is a database of free-access articles. You can make your searches more efficient by setting up a MEDLINE account for free, which allows you to set up alert services and customize your searches. For example, you can restrict the set of journals you want searched, thereby reducing the number of entries in your alerts. Another way to specify your searches in MEDLINE is to take advantage of the MeSH database (available under PubMed services). The MeSH database indexes journal articles in the life sciences, according to a hierarchy of categories. By selecting which categories you want to include in your search, you can significantly reduce the number of abstracts you need to browse. MEDLINE also provides access to other free databases, including those that index chemical structures and protein and gene sequences. While the subscription-based databases described in the following sections are very powerful, the free databases mentioned here and in the appendix also have access to a significant number of journals.

For more examples of free-access databases categorized by field, see the appendix.

Subscription-based databases
Multidisciplinary databases
- *Academic Search Premier* is the world's largest scholarly, multidisciplinary database; it contains full-text articles for nearly 4,700 publications and abstracts for nearly 8,200 journals. This collection indexes information from most areas of academic study, including science, engineering, humanities, arts and social sciences.
- *MasterFILE Premier* provides full-text articles from more than 2,100 general periodicals in a broad range of disciplines, including general reference, business, education, health, general science, multi-cultural issues and much more. In addition to full-text articles, this database provides indexing and abstracts for more than 2,800 publications.
- *WorldCat*, the world's largest bibliographic database, catalogs the collections of approximately 10,000 libraries from more than 90 countries. It contains over 90 million records corresponding to 1.2 billion physical and digital entries in 360 languages. WorldCat can be browsed from libraries that subscribe to services provided by the Online Computer Library Center (OCLC). In order to navigate this catalog, many institutions subscribe to FirstSearch, an online search engine that provides access to dozens of bibliographic databases, including more than 85 million records from WorldCat.

- *Historical Newspapers* is a service that allows users to browse *The Times* and *The New York Times* via four archives: (1) *Palmer's Index to* The Times (covers 1790 to 1905), (2) *The Official Index to The Times* (covers 1906 to 1980), (3) *The Historical Index to The New York Times* (from 1851 to September 1922), and (4) *Palmer's Full Text Online, 1785–1870,* which contains the full articles referenced in *Palmer's Index to The Times.* Many libraries also subscribe to *The Times* and *The New York Times* and provide access to the complete archives, as well as more recent articles.
- *Web of Science* includes five major databases: (1) Science Citation Index (SCI), (2) Social Sciences Citation Index (SSCI), (3) Arts & Humanities Citation Index (A&HCI), (4) Index Chemicus and (5) Current Chemical Reactions. These five databases cover about 8,700 of the leading journals in science, technology, social sciences, arts and humanities.
- *JSTOR* is an archive of articles from about 500 peer-reviewed scholarly journals in 42 disciplines, including math, science, ecology, business, political science, linguistics and music. Depending on the publisher, articles become available one to five years after publication.

Scientific databases
- *The Web of Science* provides access to the Science Citation Index (1900–present), Index Chemicus (1993–present) and Current Chemical Reactions (1986–present). The Science Citation Index allows users to search for articles that cite earlier publications. Index Chemicus and Current Chemical Reactions can be used to research information on chemical compound, structure and reaction data.
- *EMBASE* covers the biomedical and pharmacological sciences; it contains over 11 million records from over 5,000 biomedical journals, from 1974 to the present.
- *Ovid Technologies, Inc.* (frequently referred to simply as *Ovid*) provides access to online bibliographic databases, journals and other products, chiefly in the health sciences.
- *Scopus* is one of the newest abstract and citation databases for science and medical research, with 15,000 peer-reviewed journals from more than 4,000 publishers. It has access to 33 million abstracts, 386 million scientific webpages and 22 million patent records from five patent offices.

- The *INSPEC* database indexes literature in physics, electrical and electronic engineering and computer science, and includes over 3,400 technical and 10 million bibliographic abstracts.
- *Chemical Abstracts Services* provides two databases, *CAplus* and *Registry*. *CAplus* indexes bibliographic information and abstracts from chemical journals worldwide, chemistry-related articles from all scientific journals, and patents. *Registry* has information about 33 million organic and inorganic substances, and also 59 million DNA sequences.

Mathematics
- *Mathematical Reviews,* published by the American Mathematical Society, contains synopses of articles in mathematics, statistics and theoretical computer science. In 1980, *Mathematical Reviews* was integrated into *MathSciNet,* a subscription-based database with access to over 55 years of *Mathematical Reviews* and *Current Mathematical Publications,* from 1940 to the present.
- *Zentralblatt MATH (ZMATH)* is an abstracting service that provides reviews of articles and other publications in mathematics. The *ZMATH* database contains over 2.6 million entries from about 3,500 journals, from 1868 to the present.

Humanities and social sciences
While articles in the sciences are usually centralized in a few databases (e.g., PubMed in the health sciences), information in the humanities, social sciences and arts is scattered across many different sites. This section discusses a few wide-spectrum databases, but you may need to look through the more subject-specific services provided by your university.

- As mentioned, *Web of Science* provides access to five databases, including the SSCI and the A&HCI. The SSCI provides access to over 1,700 journals covering more than 50 disciplines, and the A&HCI covers over 1,000 journals.
- *Humanities Abstracts* covers over 500 English-language periodicals in the areas of archaeology, classical studies, art, performing arts, philosophy, history, music, linguistics, literature and religion, going back to 1994.

- *The Humanities & Social Sciences Index Retrospective 1907–1984* contains nearly 1,200 periodicals with records as far back as 1907. It has more than 1,300,000 articles from North America and Europe, including over 240,000 book reviews.
- *The 19th Century Masterfile* provides access to eight million citations from 60 indexes that cover 19th-century literature. This database includes *Poole's Index to Periodical Literature* (1802–1906), the *Index to Periodicals* (1890–1902), *The New York Times* (1863–1905), *New York Daily Tribune* (1875–1906), *Palmer's Index to The Times* (London; 1880–1890), and the *Library Journal Cumulative Index* (1876–1897).
- *America: History and Life* covers the history of the United States and Canada from prehistory to the present. This database contains over 530,000 entries from 1,700 journals, going back as far as 1954. In addition to articles, *America: History and Life* includes 6,000 citations of book and media reviews from over 100 key journals covering US and Canadian history.
- *Historical Abstracts* has access to 2,100 journals published in 90 countries. This database covers all world history from 1450 to the present, excluding the United States and Canada.
- The *International Bibliography of the Social Sciences (IBSS)* is a subscription-based online bibliography for social science, compiled by the London School of Economics and Political Science. *IBSS* focuses mainly on four social science areas—anthropology, economics, politics and sociology—but also includes other interdisciplinary subjects, such as the environment and gender studies. *IBSS* includes 2.5 million references from articles, books, and approximately 2,800 journals; many full-text articles are available through the subscription.
- The *PsycARTICLES* database covers general psychology and specialized, basic, applied, clinical and theoretical research. The database contains more than 40,000 articles from 53 journals, as published by the American Psychological Association (APA) and other organizations.

Business, journalism, and law
- *ABI/INFORM,* one of the largest business databases, covers business, economics, management, foreign affairs and marketing. *ABI/INFORM Complete* features 4,055 journals (including nearly 3,000 full-text titles), full-text access to *The Wall Street Journal* (going back to 1984) and also 18,000 full-text doctoral and master's theses.

- *LexisNexis* is one of the world's largest collections of public records, particularly of legal and business information. *LexisNexis* is divided into two sites that require separate subscriptions: www.lexis.com is intended for legal research, while www.nexis.com is intended for journalism research. The Lexis database contains all the current statutes and laws of the United States, as well as public records (e.g., current mailing addresses for almost every living person in the United States, property deeds, mortgages, voter registrations, motor vehicle registrations, marriage and divorce records, professional licenses and liens). Nexis has news stories from most of the major English-language periodicals, back to 1986 and some going back as far as the mid-1970s. Universities usually subscribe to *LexisNexis Academic,* which is a less expensive version of the database.
- *Westlaw,* one of the primary online research services for lawyers and legal professionals in the United States, includes more than 23,000 databases of case law, state and federal statutes, administrative codes, newspaper and magazine articles, public records, law journals, law reviews, treatises, legal forms and other information resources. In addition, *Westlaw* features KeyCite, a citation-checking service that allows customers to determine whether cases or statutes are still considered good law. It does cost money to access legal information, but Westlaw allows anyone with a credit card to retrieve citations. Westlaw is one of the chief competitors of *LexisNexis*, as both databases are very pervasive in legal research.

Databases providing news and newsfeeds
- *Dialog,* the largest provider of online information databases and global news sources, has access to 800 million unique records comprising over 12 terabytes of information. A compendium of 900 databases, *Dialog* provides access to 150,000 scientific and technical journals, 11,000 news and industry publications, and patent data from 60 countries, as well as pharmaceutical drug pipelines.
- *Factiva* indexes information for the business and education communities. *Factiva* products include access to more than 10,000 sources (such as newspapers, journals, magazines, news, and radio transcripts) from 152 countries in 22 languages, including more than 120

BECOMING AN INDEPENDENT RESEARCHER

continuously updated newswires. Both *Dialog* and *Factiva* are powerful databases with alert services, but both are too expensive for many academic institutions.

• *Google News* is a good resource when *Dialog* and *Factiva* are too expensive, as it provides access to 4,500 news sources in English and—best of all—it is free.

Most students do not have time to browse all the relevant databases, but you can request to be notified when articles with your keywords appear in the news. Perhaps somebody just discovered a new application of your research that can help you redefine your career plans. News websites usually publish their information in a format called Real Simple Syndication (RSS). RSS is based on XML, and is an emerging standard in web technology. You can sign up for an RSS Reader, such as Google Reader, for free. Afterwards, you will no longer need to visit multiple websites to get your news, because they will all be centralized and channeled to your RSS Reader. Some websites do not have RSS feeds, but you can still gather information from them by using a special service called "Page2rss" (available at http://www.page2rss.com/). For a summary of information on RSS readers, see the appendix.

 Centralize your newsfeeds through an RSS reader.

Conferences

Also, take advantage of another very valuable resource: networking. Conferences and professional meetings can inspire a new direction in your research and career. Subscribe to the journals or newsletters published by your professional organization (there is usually a discount rate for students and postdoctoral fellows), so that you can keep up with the latest research and job ads. To search for conferences and trade shows in your field, visit www.allconferences.com, www.eventseye.com and www.conferenceguru.com.

 Keep track of conferences and trade shows, to find out about research developments and career opportunities.

Challenge #3: Staying motivated

Why do students lose motivation in graduate school?

What is it about graduate school that leads many students to become disillusioned and unmotivated? Why is it that some students become disgruntled or bitter, while others remain positive and enthusiastic? Are the enthusiastic students the "lucky ones" whose projects just happened to work well? The answer, surprisingly, is *no*. In fact, it is the other way around. They are not necessarily happy and enthusiastic because their projects are going well, but rather their projects are going well *because* they are able to remain positive and focused, despite their hurdles.

I used to chat with students after their thesis defenses, in order to understand how they overcame the challenges of their dissertations. Not long ago, I spoke with Ty, who completed his Ph.D. in three and a half years, and I asked him how he managed to complete his thesis so smoothly. He looked at me with surprise and said "My thesis did not go smoothly at all. I was frustrated all the time with my experiments. But I just kept doing research until something worked out." All students, no matter how long or short or how experimental or theoretical their theses, have setbacks. Their strategy: just pick yourself up and keep working.

At this moment you are probably thinking, "Gee, that sounds easy, but how do I stay motivated? What if my project does not work out and I have to stay in graduate school longer than expected? What if I need to leave before finishing?"

If I could name one trait that sets productive students apart from unmotivated ones, it would be this: feeling like they are in *control* of their thesis and their future. If you feel like your thesis is going nowhere, or going somewhere but you are not sure where, of course you feel frustrated. Students in control of their theses also know where *they* are going. They are committed to becoming professors, want to start their own company, or know what kind of industry they will join. Or, they do not know where they want to work, but they know they love research. In order to create a feeling of control over your project and your future, you need to continuously re-evaluate your progress and ensure that your actions are helping you reach your goals.

 In order to keep yourself motivated, remind yourself of the "big picture" of your thesis, as well as your career goals.

BECOMING AN INDEPENDENT RESEARCHER

What if you have already lost sight of your original thesis goals and career plans? When you begin graduate school, you are dropped into a big ocean with your little paddleboat and told to get to the other side. It is not surprising that after many shipwrecks you might become frustrated, sometimes chronically so. Graduate students love to commiserate about non-productive lifestyles and aloof advisors (these are almost standing jokes in graduate school), and it is very relieving to share stories over a Friday night beer. It is very important, however, to distinguish funny stories from what we *believe*. How can you be motivated in an environment where you feel miserable?

Feeling unmotivated and being unproductive actually form a vicious circle: The more you believe you are unproductive, the more unmotivated you will feel, and the more unmotivated you are, the less productive you will be. Before you know it, you will be on a downward spiral with no idea on what went wrong or where your time went! Why not turn this around? If you learn to motivate yourself, you can turn this spiral right-side up again. Even the tiniest accomplishment will increase your self-confidence, your motivation and your energy levels. Soon, you will have completed one part of your project (perhaps a small one, but progress is progress) and then another one, and soon you will be truly coming a step closer, each day, to completing your thesis.

 Be a self-starter and take initiative to get your thesis work done. Do not wait for others to motivate you.

How do you start? First, you will need to examine the reason for feeling unmotivated. Is it a lack of interest in the project? Is your project not challenging enough? Or is the project too complicated? It may sound odd to say so, but you might be unmotivated if you (possibly subconsciously) find the project too difficult, in which case your mind is so overwhelmed that it shuts off. At the end of this chapter I offer a story about Rob, who became motivated again after he communicated honestly with his advisor. Have you approached your advisor to try to find a project that is suitable for you? If it is impossible to find an exciting project in your group, would you consider changing your advisor?

Lack of motivation can result from frustration with your specific project, which does not necessarily indicate loss of interest in your field of research.

A second reason why some students lack motivation is that they feel isolated. They cannot connect with other students, and they lack an appropriate support group. Gillian, a history major, started a weekly seminar series in her department. All students and faculty were invited to attend and discuss certain topics related to research in the department. "Organizing this seminar series really helped to boost the morale of the department. It also helped me become more motivated about my research. I would encourage all students to participate in or organize their own community-building activities," Gillian said.

Participating in community activities can boost your morale. If you do not find one that you like, organize your own events.

Finally, address the non-academic areas in your life that might be subconsciously distracting you from your thesis. Are there any worries in your personal life that require attention? Think about whom you can talk to about your worries. Do not be shy about approaching people, even if you think they are difficult to communicate with. (See chapter five for tips on better communication.) A word of caution: It is important to see a doctor if you frequently experience fatigue or lack of energy. Remember that the earlier you recognize your symptoms, the faster you can receive treatment.

If you cannot concentrate on your work, attend to the non-academic areas in your life that might be distracting you from your thesis.

A three-step plan to overcome procrastination

What exactly is procrastination? How does it differ from a lack of motivation? Procrastination is the habit of regularly putting things off. It is the "I'll get to it tomorrow" excuse, when you know you could do it today. Lack of motivation is one reason for procrastination, but it is not the only one. For example, if you did not get paid to work, of course you would procrastinate doing your job, or quit altogether. The tricky thing about procrastination is that it can occur, even when there is an incentive. Did you ever put off an important project until right before a deadline, because you did not feel like working on it?

The tools for learning how to overcome procrastination are the same, whether you are a graduate student, a professor, a secretary, a CEO or a homemaker. Once you learn a few simple rules, you will be able to motivate yourself to work, regardless of how your research is going or how you feel on any given day.

STEP 1. Ask yourself: Am I procrastinating?
I once asked Simon, a chemical engineer, whether he ever procrastinated working on his dissertation. He laughed and responded: "Of course I procrastinated, I was a graduate student!"

Procrastination attacks most graduate students (and people) at one point or another. In fact, I like to think of it as a common cold: Unless you take proper precautions to avoid it, you will probably catch it. However, procrastination is not necessarily a bad habit. As I will explain in the next few sections, procrastination is a signal from your body: There is something about your project that needs to be changed. It is actually a relief to realize that there is nothing wrong with you; you are just procrastinating, and probably for a good reason. On the other hand, procrastination can become a problem if you do it habitually, and you do not take the time to realize why you are doing it.

 Never beat yourself up for procrastinating. Be patient, and take one small step at a time to get your work done.

During graduate school, I had to prepare a seminar about my research for a local company. It was difficult to motivate myself to work on my presentation, because whenever I started to practice my talk, I would begin daydreaming. After several attempts, I finally realized that I was procrastinating because my presentation was dull. How could anyone else be interested in this presentation, if even *I* found it boring? I then started to brainstorm about the most exciting aspects of my research, particularly those that were relevant to my audience. Once I realized why I procrastinated, I took notes on new ideas and redesigned my seminar. I constructed detailed charts and graphs and summarized how our research was relevant for the company. As a result, the presentation was a success!

 Procrastination might be a signal from your body that something about a particular project needs to change.

How do you know that you are procrastinating? You might have a strong sense of guilt about a task you have been putting off, or you might even distract yourself with other activities that will keep you busy (e.g., web-surfing, e-mailing, an excessive social life). My friend Luke was always helping others; he claimed that he never had time for his own project, but it seemed like every time he finally got a chance to start writing his own thesis, he suddenly realized that he had to help someone use an instrument or go out for coffee with a friend. Procrastination can also disguise itself as a hobby. John, an engineering student, started graduate school without any prior dance experience, yet within a few years he became an excellent salsa dancer. He competed at events and taught classes, yet he never found time to do his thesis. He was still in school a year after all his classmates had graduated, with no idea of when he would finish his dissertation. (In this book, I emphasize the need for recreation, but it is important to recognize when your extracurricular activities are interfering with your thesis.)

 Recognize any busywork (e.g., e-mailing, web-surfing) or social activities that consistently take time away from your thesis.

STEP 2. Get organized for unpleasant tasks.
Think about a task that you have been putting off for a while, such as cleaning your closet, organizing your filing cabinet or writing a letter to a friend. What is holding you back? Most people mistakenly believe that you need to be motivated first, before you can do something, but it is actually the other way around. If you begin *doing* something, you will fuel your motivation. The most dreaded part of doing most tasks is *starting* them. Once you begin the task (even if you complete only a very tiny part of it), you will be motivated to finish it. Most of the time, you will find that the

BECOMING AN INDEPENDENT RESEARCHER

project was not as unpleasant or as drawn-out as you had previously anticipated.

 Results will motivate you to work more. Try to get something to work, even if it is just a tiny piece of the overall project.

One reason that you might put off a task is that you are not properly organized. I used to procrastinate filing important papers, because I never set aside time to organize my filing cabinet. I always thought that organizing my cabinet would take hours and I never seemed to have enough time. It turned out that organizing my cabinet was a time investment with a very high return. It took less than an hour, and it saved me a lot of time when I looked for papers later on. I no longer procrastinated when my advisor asked to see references, because I knew exactly were to find them. I also realized that once I began organizing, it was no longer a dreadful task. It became interesting to look through my files, recycle old papers, and set up new files for my current research.

Occasionally, you might need to make a small investment, time- or money-wise, to get organized. Perhaps you need your own pair of scissors, a tape dispenser, or a stapler so that you do not have to run into the main office every half an hour. You can also turn dreaded tasks into pleasurable activities, if you combine them with something fun. For example, I began listening to my MP3 player while filling out tax forms, paying bills and cleaning the house. I was surprised at how much I looked forward to filing taxes, once I had the luxury of listening to my favorite tunes.

 Combine unpleasant tasks with a fun activity, such as listening to music or working with a friend.

Another reason that we might procrastinate is that the task seems so overwhelming, we do not even know where to start to make a dent. If you are faced with a large pile of books to review, or a complicated data set to analyze, you might stare at your work and ask yourself: Where do I start?

The strategy for handling any task, no matter how complicated, is the same: Visualize the end result, and define exactly what needs to be done. Take out a pen and paper and write down everything that you need to do to consider your project completed. If you need to analyze a complicated data set, for example, your task might have multiple parts. You might need to organize your data in chronological order, plot it in charts and perform necessary statistical analyses. As you proceed through your to-do list, you might find that your task is more complicated than you originally thought. Perhaps the data was handed to you in such a disorganized file, that you will need to spend hours or maybe even days putting it in a logical order. Regardless of how complicated or simple the task is, visualizing and writing down your goals will move you into *results-oriented thinking.* You will no longer dread the task, because you will be focused on *what* you need to do and *how* to do it. This example reinforces that one of the most powerful strategies to overcome procrastination is to *assess the task in as much detail as possible, before you begin to execute it.*

 If a task seems too complicated, focus on the individual parts and visualize the desired results.

Of course, if you believe that this project will take an unreasonable amount of time, talk to your supervisor. If your advisor is not involved in your research, he or she might not have realized how complicated the project is. During your discussion, present your to-do list and explain why you think this task will take too long. It is much better to talk with your advisor before you start a complicated project, than after you have invested significant time into a project that leads nowhere.

If you discover that you are procrastinating, ask yourself if there is a particularly dreaded task that is holding up your progress. Neal, a chemist, procrastinated an experiment when he ran out of chemicals, because he hated waiting in line in the supply room. Sue, a biologist, delayed calling tech support because they kept her on hold for a long time. Is there anything that you can do to make the dreaded tasks more pleasant? In these scenarios, for example, Neal could have gone to the supply room in the morning when there was no line, and Sue could have waited for tech support using a headset or speakerphone, so that she could do her work while on hold.

If you find yourself procrastinating, spend a few minutes getting organized. A clean workspace will inspire you to do more work.

STEP 3. Change your self-talk.

Another factor that affects your motivation is your self-talk. Graduate students might feel like they are at the mercy of their advisors, and on some days they see no light at the end of the tunnel. What is wrong with this type of thinking? While some (or all of these) thoughts could be true, if you keep thinking about them, you will not be motivated to work. Negative thinking leads to self-fulfilling prophesies; the more you tell yourself how unfortunate your circumstances are, the less driven you will be to work. Neil Fiore, author of *The Now Habit*, summarizes five common thinking patterns that distinguish procrastinators from producers:

1. **"I have to"**: This is very typical of "victim-thinking," and it will make you feel like you are forced to do something. It is true that you might not want to do every project, but going to graduate school was *your* choice. You decided to pursue a Ph.D. because you wanted to. Thus, while you might not enjoy every moment of it, replace "I have to" with **"I choose to."**

2. **"I must finish"**: For various reasons, many of us feel a rush to graduate. Some students really do need to graduate by a certain deadline, due to financial issues or family obligations. Other students, however, become fed up with disappointments and just want to "get out." Some professors believe that these feelings are normal, and even necessary as part of your "rite of passage" to the Ph.D. world. When you encounter these negative feelings, realize that they will make you angry, frustrated and non-productive. Instead, focus on the next project that needs to completed and ask yourself: **"When can I start?"**

3. **"This is so big"**: A doctoral dissertation is a big project, and to my knowledge nobody finished it in one day. A common reason that people procrastinate is that they perceive their project as too overwhelming to even start. Instead of focusing on how complicated your

project is, brainstorm about how you can break it down into small parts (small accomplishments can be as simple as reading a paper, asking your advisor some questions or organizing your lab notebook). Tell yourself: **"I can take one small step."**

4. **"It must be perfect":** This type of thinking immediately sets you up for disappointment. Instead, determine realistic expectations. What are the important things that must be accomplished in your thesis? Can these goals be accomplished within a reasonable amount of time? If you accomplish them, will you satisfy the requirements for a Ph.D.? When you realize that you are driving yourself beyond your limits, remind yourself that: **"I can be human"**

5. **"I don't have time to play":** I have discussed previously where this type of thinking can lead: exhaustion and possibly illness. Rita Emmett, author of *The Procrastinator's Handbook*, suggests that the best time to take a break is when you feel the most overwhelmed. I did not believe this advice initially, but later I realized that if we take some time to relax (a few minutes, maybe even an hour, if we can afford to) during the busiest times, our minds will automatically come up with solutions to resolve problems creatively and prioritize our work. Therefore, when you feel that you are too busy to take a break, remember that: **"I must take time to play."**

Besides dreading unpleasant or overwhelming tasks, people also procrastinate because of certain subconscious fears. The three most common fears are: 1) fear of imperfection, 2) fear of success and 3) fear of uncertainty. You can overcome these subconscious fears by changing your self-talk.

What is fear of imperfection? Outstanding students, such as those who go to graduate school, strive for excellence—and possibly perfection—in every aspect of their lives. They might drag out their studies because they are never satisfied with their results. Unfortunately, fear of imperfection can hinder you from finishing or even starting a task. Have you ever bought a beautiful journal and were afraid to write in it for fear that you would ruin it? Were you ever afraid of starting a project because you thought you were not adequately prepared for it? You can overcome this fear if you realize that you are not expected to do a perfect job. If you make mistakes, as you most likely will, you will have many chances to correct them. The important this is to begin somewhere, wherever it is easiest to make progress.

 Strive for excellence, not perfection. If you focus on having the perfect thesis, you will waste a lot of time on non-essential tasks.

Fear of success does not sound like a real fear. After all, why should one be afraid of being successful? Fear of success occurs if you are afraid that the completion of a current project will lead to another responsibility that you do not think you can handle. For example, you might be concerned that if you pioneer a new software in your group, everyone will come to you for help, and you will have no time for your own thesis. Margo, a biochemist, temporarily put off doing experiments, because whenever she did a good job, her advisor gave her more to do. In order to have time to complete her own thesis, she finally had to stand up to her supervisor and request that he limit the number of projects assigned to her. (This is a perfect example of practicing communication with your advisor. For more tips on this topic, see chapter five.) Occasionally, some students might even be *embarrassed* to be successful. June, a shy chemist, made an interesting discovery, but felt apprehensive about standing up in front of her department to present her work. While preparing her seminar, she confided that she did not like speaking in public, and was concerned that her advisor might even ask her to speak at a conference (gag!).

Fear of success can also result from uncertainty about handling personal issues. Sasha, a biomedical engineer, had developed a novel device, but hesitated to travel to other universities to present her work. Her underlying fear was that she did not know how she would arrange for the care of her young child while she was out of town. She eventually brainstormed about solutions, such as inviting her mother-in-law and arranging for extended daycare on the days she would be gone. Are there any underlying issues that prevent you from reaching your full potential?

Fear of success can also prevent you from striving for your dreams. You have probably been advised to move out of your "comfort zone" to grow intellectually, but this is particularly challenging in graduate school. Besides having to adapt to a new lifestyle, you are expected to learn project management, communication skills and the academic material related to your research. Thus, it is tempting to procrastinate when you have to move out of your comfort zone, because it means that you need to do things differently.

While you do need to move out of your comfort zone to grow intellectually, you do not have to do it in one day. The key to sustainable progress is to take one small step at a time. Every day, ask yourself: What can I do *today* to make progress? Remember that the hardest part of every task is the beginning; if you take small steps every day, you will be amazed at how motivated you will feel to complete your project.

 If you are intimidated by learning new things, move out of your comfort zone gradually, by consistently taking small steps every day.

Another common reason for procrastination is the fear of uncertainty. What will happen if I get this project done? Will I be able to handle the next step? Instead of fearing the uncertainty of the challenge, think of it as an exciting new opportunity for growth. Thomas applied for a fellowship in Germany, because it was important for his career development. He won the fellowship, but had a difficult time preparing for his trip. He procrastinated his studies, arranging his travel and finding accommodations. He had never been to Germany before, and did not know where to begin the planning. Thomas finally got organized after he talked to German graduate students and learned more about the country and the town he was moving to. Thus, to become more comfortable with the decisions you are making, gather more information about your situation.

Fear of uncertainty can also occur while you write your thesis. If you are in the last stages of your thesis, you might wonder: What *will* I do after I graduate? Kayla procrastinated the writing of her thesis, but had a jolt of energy when she was offered a position with a strict starting date. For three weeks, she dedicated herself entirely to writing—no coffee breaks and no movie nights—and she did finish her thesis by the deadline. Jackson, a mechanical engineer, was purposefully holding back his graduation, because he did not know what to do with his degree. He soon found himself in a vicious circle between procrastinating job interviews (because he did not know when he would graduate) and procrastinating his thesis (because he had no plan for his employment after graduation). Eventually, Jackson realized that his supervisor had limited funding, so he had to finish his thesis and schedule some job interviews. Fortunately, he had some savings to pay for bills during the few months that he was out of a job. (In chapter seven, I discuss job-hunting strategies; if you think fear of graduation is holding you back from completing your thesis, you might want to skip ahead to that chapter.)

 Have a financial plan, in case you will be unemployed for a few months after you graduate; that way, fear of uncertainty will not hold you back from finishing your thesis.

Do not despair if there is no job offer on the horizon; you just need to have a plan and something to look forward to after graduation. If you have no plan, time will melt through your hands. Days will morph into weeks, months and maybe even years, but you can turn this around with proper planning. Do not worry if your plan does not turn out exactly the way you want it to. After years of struggling with a difficult thesis, Dana finally made a commitment to finish her thesis by the end of the school year. She talked with her advisor and they agreed on some milestones. Dana worked diligently, but she could not complete her thesis by the deadline. Fortunately, she had made so much progress, that she was easily able to finish her thesis and papers within the following semester. Dana was not bothered by graduating six months later than planned, because once she made a commitment, she was on the right track to finish her thesis and develop her work into several publications.

Motivating yourself with internal and external rewards

Rewards can be very motivating and they do not have to be elaborate. I used to motivate myself by visualizing the pleasant walk I would have along the Charles River in Cambridge after I completed my work. If you can afford it time- and money-wise, you can plan bigger rewards for more significant accomplishments. After I passed my qualifying exam, I went out with a few friends to eat tiramisu, and the day after graduation, I traveled to the Berkshire Mountains for a five-day painting course. What an unforgettable experience! Looking forward to this trip was a big incentive during my last semester. Get creative with your rewards system. One former graduate student went surfing the day after he handed in his thesis, and another biked across America with her charity group. Is there any hobby that you have been putting off until after graduation?

 Rewards can motivate you to work, so plan something exciting that you will look forward to.

While rewards can be inspiring, I have now realized that the satisfaction from completing a task is an incentive in itself. To reward myself, I acknowledge my efforts after completing each assignment, no matter how small. I struggled while writing my first scientific publication, but I committed myself to spending an hour on it every day. Some days I made little progress, but I kept a positive attitude. By that time, I had realized that loss of motivation, and hence procrastination, was influenced by self-talk. If you recorded all the thoughts that went through your mind during the day, what would you hear? Would you hear empowering thoughts such as: "I have made progress on my thesis today and I am really proud of that"? Or, are your thoughts slightly more negative, such as "I was hoping to get more done today. I wish my research would go more quickly."

Most people consider themselves positive thinkers, yet the subtle negative thoughts that creep up in the backs of our minds can gradually dampen our motivation. It is hard to be motivated when you are dissatisfied with certain aspects of your life. Your negative thoughts could be about the weather, a bad hair day, apprehension about an upcoming presentation, your advisor or a particular study that is not going according to plan. Do not let these little setbacks get to you. Accept—in fact, *expect*—that your progress will be slowed down by unforeseeable complications.

Thomas Edison, one of the most prolific inventors ever, made the following statement: "Many of life's failures are people who did not realize how close they were to success when they gave up." Edison had to perform thousands of experiments to invent the light bulb. Can you imagine how the course of history would have changed, had Edison given up his quest for an electric light? Until that time, people used dim gas lights for reading, working, looking under microscopes, and performing surgeries. Most people went to bed when the sun went down, as they could not afford those gas lights. His light bulb, however, was brighter, safer and more economical than the gas lights used until then, and in this way, he revolutionized people's lives.

 Acknowledge your efforts every day, and give yourself praise for every little accomplishment.

Under what circumstances is it advisable to procrastinate?
While we all want to become go-getters and doers, I would also like to cite some examples of when it might be a good idea to procrastinate. I believe that being properly organized for completing a task is so essential, that it could be to your advantage to put off the task until you are properly prepared. Suellen, a biochemist, decided to analyze her samples with an instrument that she was not familiar with. Her colleague, who was the expert, was away on vacation for another week, and Suellen decided to run her samples on her own. Unfortunately, she did not read the manual, and the instrument was not properly calibrated. As a consequence, her samples, which took two weeks to prepare, were wasted. She probably should have taken the time to learn how to use the instrument with less valuable samples, or waited for her colleague to return from vacation.

 Make sure you are properly organized for a project before you invest time and effort.

It is also important to pay attention to signals from your body. If you feel chronically tired and unmotivated, rule out the possibility of an illness before trying to get work done. Some students go to work even when they are sick, because they feel compelled to be there, but they end up being unproductive and they also delay their recovery—not to mention possibly making other people sick, in the process. I used to think that I never got sick because whenever a cold or flu was going around I did not have any typical symptoms, but I realized that I was tired all the time. Normally, I could not sleep more than eight hours, but during flu season, I could sleep for 10 hours or more. Once I understood how my body handled an illness, I took off just one day to rest, and was usually ready to work the next day. If you feel unusually lethargic, it is essential to see a doctor. The best that can happen is that the doctor will tell you that nothing is wrong, and that will already make you feel much better.

 Take time to rest and seek medical help, if you feel that you are coming down with an illness.

CHAPTER SUMMARY AND ACTION PLAN

Becoming an independent researcher

Step 1: Establish a sustainable daily schedule.
- Determine your ideal work hours, based on family and social commitments.
- Incorporate regular breaks into your schedule, to help you stay sharp throughout the day.
- Set aside a few hours every week to pursue sports or hobbies.

Step 2: Construct your thesis proposal.
- Plan a thesis that can be completed in a reasonable amount of time with the given resources and expertise.
- Design a research plan that will give you solid training in your field and includes marketable job skills.
- Include several backup plans in your proposal, in case your current project goes awry.
- Network with professors and committee members who will give you constructive feedback on your thesis.
- Use electronic resources to stay on top of the literature.

Step 3: Learn to motivate yourself, regardless of your circumstances.
- Define the tasks that you are putting off.
- Realize that the most difficult part of getting anything done is starting it. Begin with the easiest part to fuel your motivation.
- Combine unpleasant tasks with fun activities such as listening to music or working with a friend.

- Change your self-talk by acknowledging all of your accomplishments, big and small.
- Determine whether there is an underlying fear (e.g., of imperfection, success or uncertainty) that is holding you back from completing your goals.

What is a high-risk thesis? *Victor's and Molly's stories*

A high-risk thesis is one where you rely on luck to bring you exciting results. It might be a project that is so novel, that very little is known about it. A novel topic might be advantageous, because anything that you discover could be publishable. On the other hand, the methodology for a "hot" project is frequently not established. Victor, a chemical engineer, chose a cutting-edge topic for his doctoral thesis. Very little had been published beforehand, and he struggled with the basic experimental set-up for three years without publishing any papers. In his fourth year, he considered quitting or at least changing his project. He was fortunate that an experienced postdoctoral fellow joined his group, and they were able to set up the experimental system. Once the methodology had been established, Victor could collect the necessary data, and he graduated within two years.

Another example of a high-risk thesis is one where you ask a "yes or no" question, but the answer is interesting only if it is a "yes." In her second year, Molly proposed to investigate whether the cells that she worked with produced a particular type of protein. Fortunately, she soon realized that if the answer came back as a "no," her research would not be publishable and her graduation would be delayed. Instead of her original idea, she proposed to characterize the types of proteins produced by the cells. This slight change in her proposal ensured that she would have a publication, because her group had already worked out the methodology for the proposed experiment. In other words, she changed her thesis topic from a closed-ended "yes or no" question (i.e. "Do these cells produce this protein?") to a more open-ended investigation with a high chance of success (i.e., "What types of proteins do these cells make?").

The lesson from Molly's story is that when you propose a question for your thesis, you need to consider all the possible answers that you might find. If you ask a "yes or no" question, will your research be publishable, either way? If not, think about asking a more open-ended question that will lead to an interesting paper, regardless of what your results are.

Using communication to overcome procrastination: *Rob's story*

Rob, a chemical engineering student, went through a "rough patch" in his third year after he earned his master's degree. His advisor, a hands-off professor, asked him to do a project that required programming. Rob was more interested in theory and had no prior experience with programming. For several months, he tried to force himself to work, but there was little progress. He was embarrassed to tell his advisor about his struggles, particularly because they had communicated very little previously. Finally, Rob realized that he would never finish his thesis at the current rate of progress, so he decided to tell his advisor about his difficulties. Rob expected his advisor to be condescending, but to his surprise he was very understanding and simply asked: "Why didn't you tell me about this earlier?"

In order to help Rob with his thesis, his advisor found him another project that included more theory. As he progressed with his work, Rob gradually incorporated programming into his thesis until he became an expert. In fact, programming is an essential part of his job now. "Once I spoke to my advisor, I felt motivated again to work on my thesis. We had a really good connection after that meeting, and our relationship definitely improved once we were able to communicate."

It is not unusual for students to experience a lack of direction after they finish their master's thesis. One Ph.D. has even called this period the "missing third year." Some struggling is normal during the Ph.D. process, but if you see no progress on your work for months at a time, it is time to think about alternative projects and discuss them with your advisor. Remember that results will motivate you to work more, so aim for a project you have experience with.

CHAPTER 3:
MAXIMIZE YOUR EFFICIENCY

"Have a bias toward action—let's see something happen now. You can break
that big plan into small steps and take the first step right away."
Indira Gandhi, Indian Prime Minister (1917–1984)

Like many other graduate students I was an overachiever and a worka-holic. I took on a bigger workload than I could comfortably handle, and everything that I did had to be perfect. As a consequence, I was always under stress, because no matter how much I worked, there was still more to do. As I was nearing my fifth year in graduate school, I began to wonder whether my project was ever going to end. Clearly, staying late in the lab and working every weekend did not speed up my progress as much as I had hoped and expected. What could I do to be more productive?

The answer came to me, surprisingly, through my recovery from repetitive strain injury (RSI). This injury, which significantly restricted the use of my hands, forced me to be more productive in spite of having limited time on the computer. Fortunately, you do not need to be injured to learn these skills.

In this chapter, you will learn how to:

- Increase your efficiency at work
- Organize your time and space

Challenge #1: Increasing your productivity at work
What is your current work style?
I once attended a project management seminar and was surprised to learn that most people could concentrate on work for only three to four hours a day. Where does the rest of the time go? Why can we not be productive all the time? If you observed yourself and others at work, you would notice that we all have peaks and valleys in our energy levels. You might sit down enthusiastically to read a journal article, just to find yourself dozing off half an hour later. Or, you might look forward

to devoting an entire day to your research and then be disappointed as you get continuously interrupted by phone calls or visitors. It is worth pondering how your productivity changes throughout the day, and whether there is any way to improve it. If someone were to cut your time at work in half, what tasks would be given priority? Or, if someone were to double your time at work (i.e., magically increased the number of hours in day), what other projects could you complete?

Most people can identify activities that they can cut out, and they can also think about projects they would like to complete if there were more hours in a day. Both of these components are important. It is necessary to have buffer time, which is extra time scheduled in your day in case a meeting crops up or an experiment needs more time than predicted. Without some down-time between commitments, you will be stressed and always running late. The other problem with not having down-time is that when you feel rushed, you begin executing tasks automatically, without having the opportunity for spontaneity.

Construct your daily schedule so that you have buffer time between commitments.

On the other hand, it is also not good to plan too little. Ambition is the driving force behind progress. If your meeting ends half an hour early, is there something productive you can do? When I was under significant time pressure during my last semester, I used the "parallel conveyor-belt" approach. I always had two or three projects running simultaneously. While I was waiting for my samples to run through the liquid chromatographer, I analyzed data from my previous experiments. To speed up my progress, I also had a small spiral notebook with a never-ending to-do list. If I had a free minute, I did not even need to think about what to do next—I just checked my notebook and started the next task. Carlos, an astronomer, always started his day by adding a few extra items to his to-do list. "I tried not to overwhelm myself with tasks, but I also found it helpful to plan just a little bit more than I thought I could do. I did not expect to get through everything, but on some days I did."

Plan a few extra to-do items, in case you make more progress than expected.

In order to assess your current work style, write down all the to-dos that are on your mind right now. You might be surprised at how many commitments you already have. For example, you might have plans regarding your money, organizing your new dorm room, calling your mom, arranging your summer vacation and losing weight, plus all the planning for your thesis and career! Once you have all your to-dos on paper, it will be easier to prioritize your time.

 Your Ph.D. is a series of many small challenges. Do not be intimidated by the breadth of your project and take care of each hurdle one by one.

The flexible schedule of graduate school, which allows students to pick up new hobbies and sports, can be a double-edged sword. I loved all of my hobbies, but when I dropped them to have more time to work on my thesis, I realized how overcommitted I had been. I belonged to several student groups and I organized barbecues, dinners, and dance parties. I was a resident tutor in a dorm, took drawing lessons at the fine arts museum, was a member of the MIT Masters Swimming Club, and I also had to organize my wedding!

 Write down your all your current commitments and worries to keep track of where your time and energy go.

When you are overwhelmed by extracurricular activities, ask yourself: "Which ones are the most valuable for me?" If you enjoy all your activities, it might be difficult to choose your favorite ones. Keep in mind that putting aside a hobby for the sake of completing your thesis does not mean you need to drop it forever. Jonathan was an enthusiastic resident advisor, but felt so overwhelmed by this extra obligation that he decided to quit his position during his final year in graduate school. Gerald, on the other hand, volunteered to be a teaching assistant for an intensive undergraduate course during his last semester. He enjoyed interacting with undergraduates, and he defended his thesis on schedule, in spite of this extra time commitment. It is up to you to decide what the right balance is between work and extracurricular activities, and you should not feel guilty about relinquishing extra responsibilities if you need to.

Some students claim that their hobbies (such as swimming, dancing or kick-boxing) re-energize them, and they work at their optimum when they include these activities in their lives. Know where to draw the line.

 You might need to put aside some extracurricular activities in order to finish your thesis, but remember that you can pick them up again after you graduate.

Many graduate students are at the other end of the commitment spectrum: They have enough time, but are not inspired to work. Days, weeks and months go by without any significant progress. If you are in this situation, you are probably wondering: "How can I give myself a boost of energy?" Maybe your advisor is knocking on your door constantly for results, or maybe she is so busy with her own schedule that you do not even get any guidance from her. You might just sit and wait for something to happen. Sometimes it does—maybe you had to wait for your grant money to come in, or for the test mice to breed—but more often than not, sitting around will not make your thesis happen. You have to *make* it happen.

What can you do to feel more motivated? Perhaps you have lost interest in your thesis, or your project is so complicated that you feel too overwhelmed to work on it. Did you talk to your advisor, to try to find a topic that is suitable for you? If you do not like the research in your group, why not change your advisor? Also are there any personal issues that are worrying you? Have you just been through a difficult experience and need time to adjust? Is there somebody whom you can talk to about these problems? If you talk to somebody, you might get ideas on how to solve academic or non-academic problems. Regardless of where your insights might lead you (e.g., change your project or your advisor), you will be motivated again by knowing that you are on the right track to achieving your research and career goals. (See chapter two for more details on getting motivated.)

 Remind yourself of the "big picture" of your thesis and your long-term career goals, whenever you feel unmotivated.

Increase your efficiency with the 80/20 principle

If you analyzed how much you accomplished each day, would you say that your productivity was evenly distributed across the week? Most people find that they have bouts of energy on some days, followed by more mellow days when they are not very productive. In his book *The 80/20 Principle*, Richard Koch describes how to increase your productivity with less effort. The 80/20 principle was first described by an Italian economist, Vilfredo Pareto, in 1897. This principle states that the majority of results are achieved by the minority of effort. Pareto observed that about 20% of the population in Italy enjoyed 80% of the wealth; he later noticed this imbalance in other countries and during different time-periods.

After World War II, American economists also realized the importance of the 80/20 principle. George Zipf at Harvard University observed that about 20–30% of resources—such as people or time—accounted for 70–80% of the results. The 80/20 principle was also applied in the 1960s and 1970s at IBM, when the company noticed that their computers were spending 80 percent of their time executing 20 percent of the code. Therefore, IBM rewrote the operating software, so that the most-frequently used 20% was efficient and user-friendly.

The 80/20 principle is also true in our personal lives: You probably wear 20% of your clothes 80% of the time, and 80% of your happiness occurs during 20% of your time.

How does the 80/20 principle apply to your thesis? If you assessed your accomplishments, you would probably find that most of your tangible results occurred within a small fraction of your time. Angela, a physicist, noted that in theory, her work should have been completed in one year, yet it took her three years to collect her data. Where did the rest of her time go? Troubleshooting her instrument took longer than expected, but she also worked on projects with no interesting results. In retrospect, Angela thought that she could have realized sooner that her side projects would not lead to publishable material—in other words, had she focused solely on the most fruitful projects, she could have graduated sooner. In the case of your thesis, how do you decide where to concentrate your efforts?

In order to incorporate the 80/20 principle into your work positively, keep track of your time for a week; at the end of the week, assess the progress on your thesis. Did you spend too much time on activities that did not contribute to your thesis (e.g., side projects, e-mailing, web-surfing)? After a few weeks of tracking your days, you will have a better sense of how you spend your time and energy. Expect progress to be slow (or none) on some days. There will be unexpected setbacks related to your research and personal issues. Some of your struggles and "wasted time" are parts of the learning process. Nevertheless, observe your daily agenda critically. Are you focusing your efforts on projects that will contribute to your thesis?

 Focus your energy on projects that will contribute the most to your thesis, and eliminate the activities that eat up your time and energy.

According to Al Secunda, author of *The 15 Second Principle*, you can speed up progress on your thesis by distinguishing "actions" from "activities." With an action, you take an important step towards achieving your goal. When you perform an activity, you keep yourself busy, but you are not contributing to your thesis. The definition of what constitutes an "action" or an "activity" depends on your individual circumstances. If you have not yet started the literature search for your thesis proposal, then reading recent publications in your field is an action. On the other hand, if you have already completed the literature search, and it is time to move on to constructing the figures, then skimming over papers for a second or third time is just an activity. As you observe yourself during the week, take note of your actions and activities. It is not always easy to distinguish between the two, because you might not be able to predict how each action or activity will contribute to your thesis. Nevertheless, if you rely on your intuition, you will probably know what you need to do to make the most progress.

 Distinguish actions from activities: Actions will bring you closer to your final goal, whereas activities will keep you busy without leading to tangible results.

You can also use the 80/20 principle to maximize your enjoyment of your free time. Ask yourself what you *really* enjoy doing. Preston, an electrical engineer, used to feel compelled to attend concert performances when his lab mates got discount tickets. He hoped that attending these performances would enhance his social life, but he did not enjoy the concerts, nor did he get to talk to his friends while the music was playing. He realized that he enjoyed sports more than music, so he decided to organize his own social events such as barbecues and basketball games. "I do not feel guilty anymore about not going to concerts with my friends. They know I am not into music and we have a blast at the barbecues and playing basketball."

The beauty of the 80/20 principle is that it allows you to maximize your productivity and your happiness simultaneously, because the happier you are, the more energetic and productive you will be. On days when you accomplish a lot, notice what was different. Maybe you got a few extra hours of sleep (that always helps), or you worked on a certain project that had exciting results ("Oh, maybe *this* is the project that I should work on!"). Maybe you had a focused discussion with your advisor or you got organized, and now you feel on top of your work again. The earlier you notice your patterns of productivity, the sooner you can begin to optimize your workflow.

 Use the 80/20 principle to maximize happiness in your personal life. Identify the hobbies that are the most exciting, and do not feel obligated to spend your precious free time on activities that you do not enjoy.

Of course, one challenge of working with the 80/20 principle is that habits are difficult to change. You might have realized that your mornings are not productive because you spend too much time e-mailing, or it takes you too long to get ready for work. Realizing the problem does not necessarily lead to a solution. You know that you would be more productive if you wrote two pages of your thesis before you checked your e-mail, but how do you implement this change into your routine? Habits are difficult to break, but they can be changed gradually. In the next section, I will discuss how to implement change permanently into your daily routine.

Move out of your comfort zone with ease
Moving out of your comfort zone is not easy, because it takes patience to break a habit. I would like to illustrate the power of perseverance by sharing the story of Mary, a friend of my family. Mary decided to

quit smoking after one of her relatives died from lung cancer. If you are familiar with anyone who has tried to quit smoking, you probably know that it is one of the most difficult habits to break. Mary tried to quit "cold turkey" many times, but the withdrawal symptoms were too uncomfortable. Her next approach was to resist cigarettes for just a few minutes at a time. As her time intervals for not smoking became longer, she preoccupied herself by reading books, and she also took notes to write her own book. After many months, these little notes added up to an entire book, which she successfully published—and she never smoked another cigarette again. Thus, her commitment to quit smoking also helped her realize her dream of becoming a published author.

What is the lesson from Mary's story? It is this: If you want to change a habit, you need to do it gradually. Changing your routine too suddenly can backfire and discourage you from trying again. For example, whenever you start an exercise program, you need to give your body time to get used to the new routine. If you run five miles on your first day, you might experience such muscle soreness that you end up quitting exercise altogether. In order to incorporate new habits permanently into your life, you need to *pace* your progress. Make small and gradual changes to your life, so that you do not feel overwhelmed or confused by your new routine.

 If you want to change a habit for good, pace your progress and introduce change slowly into your life.

How do the above examples relate to moving out of your comfort zone? Moving out of your comfort zone can be scary, because it forces you to change your habits. Most people are not comfortable with changing their lifestyles too quickly. You can work around this inner resistance by committing very short time intervals, every day, to your new habit. If you need to start writing your thesis, for example, can you commit to writing one paragraph a day? Or, if you need to learn how to use a new software package, can you spend 15 minutes each day on it? Such small time-contributions might not seem like they will lead to significant progress, but as mentioned, the toughest part of any job is *starting*. You might feel overwhelmed by trying to write the introduction to your thesis in one afternoon, but committing to one paragraph will probably seem more doable. As Al Secunda points out in *The 15 Second Principle*, you will be motivated to finish what you started, after just spending a few minutes—or even just 15 seconds—on your project.

So, what is the next step? Commit to spending a short time on your new project *every* day. Do not expect yourself to work for five hours on a paper; just begin with 10–15 minutes of writing. Some days, that will be all the time that you can commit to your writing (and you might be surprised at how much progress you can make in such a short time). On other days, these few initial minutes will motivate you to write for longer periods, and you will ultimately make more progress than you had expected.

Commit to spending a few minutes every day on an important project that you have been putting off.

Set effective external and internal deadlines

How do you tackle a large and possibly overwhelming project, such as a doctoral dissertation? With a deadline so far in the future (assuming your proposed graduation date is still years away), how do you motivate yourself to work? Abe, an electrical engineer, structured his research by setting deadlines for himself: "I always tried to work hard, but the truth is that nothing motivates you like a deadline. My advice is to send abstracts to every possible conference, because that will give you the extra push to work harder." External, "hard" deadlines—such as those associated with conferences, department seminars and committee meetings—will motivate you to put in a few extra hours to perfect your poster or your talk.

Most graduate students have only a few deadlines a year, and they prepare for these events just one month or a few weeks in advance. How do you motivate yourself the rest of the time?

Set up external deadlines for yourself, such as registering for conference presentations, to motivate yourself to make progress on your thesis.

The key to maintaining your motivation throughout graduate school is to set both external and internal deadlines. You can use external deadlines, far in the future, to help set short-term internal deadlines.

Let us assume that your next hard deadline is a poster presentation at a conference, in half a year. Given that the conference is six months away, how do you know what you need to do today? In order to set internal deadlines, you can use a strategy called the "reverse calendar," described by Neil Fiore in his book, *The Now Habit*. When you use the reverse calendar, you begin by defining your final goals. What do you hope to show on your poster? Imagine each panel on your poster in detail, and determine what you need to do to be able to present this data. Which experiments do you need to do? What type of data analysis will you need to carry out? What journal articles do you need to read? Once you have specified your goals, you can estimate the amount of time needed to reach all of your milestones. You will also need to make sure that you have set enough time for "administrative" duties, such as ordering supplies and printing your poster. Working backwards from your hard deadline, you might have a "reverse calendar" that looks something like this:

> Today's date: April 2
> Date of conference: October 15
> *Estimated time for preparing and printing a poster: two weeks*
> Deadline for analyzing data: September 30
> *Estimated time for data analysis: two weeks*
> Deadline for collecting data: September 15
> *Estimated time for experimentation: three months*
> Projected timeframe for data collection: June–August
> *Estimated time for ordering supplies and setting up workspace: one month*
> Projected timeframe for setting up workspace: May–June
> **Today's assignments:** order necessary supplies, begin literature search to determine appropriate experimental protocols

When you construct your to-do lists in reverse order, you will realize that you have immediate assignments, even though your conference deadline is still six months away. Projects usually take about three times longer than originally predicted, so use generous estimates, with lots of buffer time, when setting deadlines. Do not be disappointed if you do not complete all tasks by your predetermined deadline. Perhaps on the day of the conference, you will only be able to present data on a subset of your milestones, but you will know that your work is the result of the best possible planning.

While a reverse calendar is no guarantee that you will finish everything by the deadline, it is an excellent planning tool, for three reasons. First, it helps you set deadlines, so you know what you can realistically expect from yourself within a certain time period. Second, these deadlines will motivate you to work, because you will realize how much you need to accomplish by a certain date. Third, a detailed plan will also clarify what skills and resources you need to finish your project. Do you need to take a workshop to acquire more expertise in a particular topic? Will you benefit from collaborating with another professor? Do you need to request a new grant, so that you can purchase a particular instrument? Of course, your goals and deadlines will change as you go through your research, so revise this calendar at least monthly, or after you reach an important milestone.

 Break down long-term deadlines in reverse and into well-defined goals, so you can clarify your short-term milestones.

Develop a productive and sustainable workflow

You might have already heard that you should not compare yourself to other graduate students; your project is unique, after all, and it does not make sense to analyze who stays at work the longest, who spends the greatest number of weekends in the lab or who publishes the most papers. Unlike in college, where we all had the same assignments, progress in graduate school cannot be measured with conventional yardsticks. Some students publish just one paper (or perhaps none at all), yet they earn Ph.D.s by laying down the foundations for further research. Other students might be in a field where many papers can be published, but that does not mean that the breadth of their work is sufficient for a doctoral dissertation. I once met a famous chemistry professor whose entire laboratory published only three papers a year, yet they were so thorough that everyone else in the field looked forward to them. Comparing yourself to others is not only meaningless, but it can actually hinder your progress, by filling you with guilt and a sense of low self-esteem.

If you cannot compare yourself to others, how can you learn to do research? Through my interviews, I realized that regardless of your field, there is a logical order of steps in completing a research project. I have divided these steps into seven stages, as follows (see FIGURE 3-1):

1. Define your long-term thesis goals
2. Review the literature
3. Draft a plan using the literature and your ideas
4. Discuss your plan with your advisor
5. Get organized (e.g., obtain necessary supplies, borrow relevant books)
6. Do the work
7. Evaluate the results

These seven stages constitute your workflow, and it is most likely going to be an iterative process. Research is by no means a linear and straightforward process, and you will need to jump back to earlier steps as you work through your project. For example, have your goals changed as a result of reviewing the literature? Did a meeting with your advisor help you refine your central question or hypothesis? Did you get surprising results that changed the course of your thesis? Finally, you will probably need to reconsider your long-term thesis goals after you evaluate the results of your studies. In the figure, I show a "return" arrow only from steps 7 to 1 and 4 to 3, but it is likely that you will need to go back to earlier steps throughout your studies.

 Remind yourself constantly of your long-term thesis goals as you design your research plans.

Once you have chosen a general topic, the next step is to review the literature. How is your project making a significant contribution? Are there any competing groups? What are the latest findings in your field, and do they help you come up with ideas for your research? According to Calvin, an electrical engineer, his biggest surprise in graduate school was the length of time required to review the literature. "I used to spend hours reading papers—especially during my first two years, when I was not familiar with the jargon."

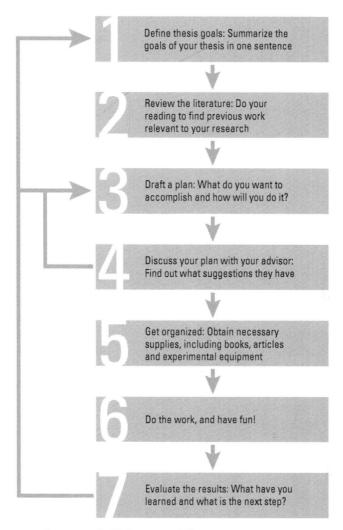

Figure 3-1: Stages of efficient workflow

 Literature searches are a time-consuming yet essential part of research. Expect reading and analyzing papers to take a significant portion of your time.

After your literature search, draft a written plan, regardless of whether your advisor expects one or not. A written plan can be a simple flowchart in your notebook that lists the different stages of your research. If you do experimental work, write your methodology in detail (with references), so that you can follow a straightforward plan. If your advisor expects regular progress reports from you, it is even more important to put your plans in writing and to attach references.

 Draft your research plan in writing, and assess whether your goals reflect the long-term vision for your thesis.

By the time you have a written plan, it is tempting to start working right away. It is important, however, to get organized *before* you begin your research. (It is the blueprint of your entire work, remember.) If you are an experimentalist, what materials do you need? If you are a theorist, what references or software are required? If you are in the humanities, do you need materials from the archives or a special collection? Foreseeing all your needs will save you a lot of time that might otherwise have been spent waiting for supplies or references to arrive. In addition to acquiring all the materials, you will also need to organize your space and time. If you are starting a new experiment, have you set up adequate lab space for it? Or, if your project requires a specific time commitment, have you revised your schedule accordingly? (See the next section for tips on efficient time management.)

 Organize your space, time and materials before you begin your research.

Step 6 is "do the work." This is the fun part that you have probably been looking forward to. Finally, you can get some work done and get one step closer to finishing your thesis. This part of the workflow might be a few days or possibly a few months. If it is a long period of time, you will probably experience several setbacks. It is unrealistic to expect everything to go according to plan, or to expect yourself to be sharp on all days. If you do experience a few "lows," just do as much of the work as you can. Even if you feel unmotivated in the morning, you might be inspired by the afternoon, if you have jumped over a few hurdles early in the day.

 When you feel uninspired, try to make a small and new dent in your work. Motivation increases with progress, and a slow

start will frequently turn into significant productivity later in the day.

In the last step of the workflow, you need to evaluate your results. Is this what you expected? How do the results of this study contribute to your thesis? Is it clear what you need to do now? If your advisor is hands-on, you probably will need to share your results with him or her before deciding what to do next. If you are more of an independent researcher, it is up to you where you will take your project next. Either way, it is important to analyze your results before beginning your next study. Some students make the mistake of rushing through experiments without evaluating the results of each study. Bernadette, a biologist, believes that her biggest mistake in graduate school was shortcutting the data analysis process. "After I completed a series of experiments, I just eyeballed the results," she said. "I did not take time to do in-depth statistical analyses, to determine whether my results were really significant." When her thesis committee asked for rigorous analysis, she found out that many of her results were not statistically significant. As a consequence, she had to repeat some experiments, and graduated a semester later than she had originally expected.

 Evaluate your results critically before beginning your next study.

In summary, a good workflow requires a routine—one that is unique to your needs. You will know that you have a good work flow when you feel that you have control over your project. In a good workflow, you are making daily—or at least weekly—progress (negative results count too). You *feel* organized, and you are excited about your work. Who could ask for more?

Challenge #2: Organizing your time and space

Ever met anyone whose desk appeared to be disorganized, yet they always knew where to find everything? Joseph, an engineering student, lived in a dorm room that was an incredible mess: There was absolutely no clear space on his floor, desk or bed. Yet, whenever he needed a band-aid or a screwdriver, he had it ready, almost instantaneously. He was also an excellent student and an officer in several campus organizations. For Joseph, a functional environment did not equal clear desk (or floor) space. He created a work environment and schedule that allowed him to strive for his personal and academic goals. In other words, being organized is not just about having a clear desk, but about having an environment that inspires you and helps you to find what you need, when you need it.

How do you start to get organized? I believe that effective organization starts in your mind, with creating well-defined long- and short-term goals. What do you hope to accomplish? How will you make time to do it? What resources do you need to accomplish your goals? I divided the process of getting organized into the following three categories: 1) managing your task list, 2) budgeting your time and 3) organizing your space.

FROM THE PH.D. SECRET ARCHIVES:

12 easy ways to get organized

How to maintain a reliable to-do list
1. Carry around a portable organizer.
As you go through your day, do you find that your mind jumps from one concern to another, such as financial worries, family issues, health problems and planning vacations? Is it difficult to focus on your thesis? A portable to-do list is a powerful tool for staying in control of your research and your life. Write down all your to-dos as they occur to you, wherever you are. Jot down reminders for your work and for your personal life. You do not need a fancy organizer or Palm Pilot; in fact a simple small spiral notebook will be sufficient. The key is to have a pen and paper handy whenever an idea comes to mind. If you write down everything, you will notice that your notebook gets cluttered quickly. I rewrite my list every few days when it becomes too long; as a consequence, the list ends up being shorter than expected, since many of the tasks are redundant, completed or no longer relevant.

2. Be specific about what needs to be done, before you can consider your tasks completed.

According to David Allen, author of *Getting Things Done*, one of the reasons that people feel overwhelmed is that they have not defined exactly what needs to be done, to consider their projects completed. When you review your list, make sure that you specify what you need to do to complete each task. For example, if your goal is "make progress on thesis proposal," have you determined what you want to accomplish? Do you want to finish the introduction, draw figures or write the bibliography? Be specific about each step required for your project. In the case of "complete introduction," you can have a numbered list, such as: 1) finish writing last paragraph, 2) proofread text and 3) format bibliography. If you know exactly what your final goals are, you will be more motivated to get through your task list.

3. Review your task list daily, either first thing in the morning or right before you go to sleep.

You now have a portable and well-organized to-do list. How do you make sure that all your tasks get completed? First, commit to a certain time of day when you will review your list. I prefer to read over my list in the evenings, so I can plan my day in advance. Another option is to look at your list in the morning before you do any work, even before you check your e-mail. Your task list will help you plan your schedule efficiently. If you have a dental appointment at noon, for example, you can optimize the use of the few hours you have before noon. Instead of coming to work wondering what you should do that day (and then realizing that the dental appointment cuts into your plans), you will have already clearly defined your goals for the morning.

After you have planned your daily to-dos, think about any long-term goals that you can start working on today. For example, if you want to apply for a faculty position, will you have an opportunity today to research a few schools? If you want to work in industry, will you have a few minutes to check out an upcoming career-fair on the Internet? Try to include a few actions every day to help you achieve your long-term goals. You might not get around to completing everything on your list; few people do. At the end of the day, prioritize your remaining tasks for the following day, so that you will be sure to get all the important work done.

Your planning sessions will also remind you to put deadlines into your calendar. For example, one item on your list might be to submit an abstract for a conference, but the deadline is still a month away. You are not ready to submit the abstract, and you are not even sure whether you want to go to the conference. You can write this deadline in your calendar, so that when the deadline comes closer, you can decide whether you want to attend the conference. Also, write down other deadlines such as due dates for library books, progress reports, and any bills you need to pay. If you set aside a few minutes every morning or evening to manage your task list, you will not only make consistent progress on your thesis, but also take care of high-priority personal goals.

In summary, in order to efficiently manage your to-do list:

- Carry around a portable organizer that you always have access to.
- Write down all tasks that must be completed.
- Review this list every day, preferably at the same time.
- Define your goals specifically, so you know exactly what needs to be done before you can cross off each item.
- Use your to-do list to plan your day, and write reminders in your calendar.

Manage your time wisely
4. Balance work and play by compartmentalizing your time.

One of the challenges in graduate school is setting boundaries between work and personal life. After you get home from work, how do you decide whether to watch television or read a journal article? If you have ever tried to read while watching television (and I believe many of us have to avoid feeling guilty), you probably found that it is difficult to enjoy leisure time and focus on your work at the same time. Judy, a microbiologist, "compartmentalized" her schedule to balance her time between work and family. Judy usually did not finish her work at her office, because she had to pick up her son from daycare by 5 p.m. She also found it difficult to concentrate on her work at home, because she wanted to spend time with her family. Trying to be the perfect mother, wife and researcher, she was frequently torn among her commitments. Instead of trying to multitask, she decided to "compartmentalize." She structured her schedule so that she was able to devote her attention to one and only one task at a time. She no longer tried to read while she watched her son, because she was not able to focus on her work, nor was she spending quality time with him. In order to resolve this dilemma, she committed one hour to her work every evening after her husband arrived home. When the hour was up (and she was surprised how much she could accomplish when there were no interruptions), she enjoyed guiltless quality time with her family.

5. Optimize the use of your down-time.

Many of us complain about not having enough hours in the day, but do you ever have five, 10 or 20 free minutes and not know what to do during that time? You might think that a few minutes will not make a difference in your thesis anyway, so it is tempting to spend this time reading e-mail or web-surfing. If you have devoted several hours to reading or writing, you have probably noticed that your concentration is best during the first few minutes. When you are focused, you can get a lot accomplished in a short time. Your to-do list will help you to optimize the use of these short fragments of time during the day. Perhaps 10 minutes before a meeting is not sufficient to start an experiment, but can you start writing a section of your thesis or complete a quick errand during this time?

Students who are parents or who have jobs do not have the luxury of long stretches of time to devote to their studies. They might have only short periods of time during the day and in the evenings to work on their theses. Sonia, an engineer and single mother, had to use every available minute to finish her work. "I was very focused during the day, just trying to cross things off my list before I had to pick up my daughter from daycare. I was usually tired by the time she went to sleep, but I still spent a little time in the evenings writing." Sonia's hard work and superb organizational skills paid off: A few years after graduation, she was a tenured faculty member at a well-known research university.

6. Commit to high-priority tasks during your productive hours.

Have you ever tried to work on your thesis but were too tired to concentrate? If you find that your energy waxes and wanes during the day, you can increase your efficiency by planning high-priority tasks during your most productive hours. After a few weeks of observing yourself, you will know whether you are most focused early in the morning, right before lunch, in the late afternoon or in the evening. Many students plan their day around their work, without realizing all of the other commitments that they have. Neil Fiore, author of *The Now Habit*, suggests organizing your day in your calendar by filling in only predetermined commitments, such as doctor's appointments, classes, seminars, sports, hobbies, meals and commuting. After writing down all of these extracurricular activities, you might realize that you have only a few hours each day to work on your research. Schedule your highest-priority tasks for the time of day when you think you will be most productive. Leave errands (e.g., making phone calls, writing e-mails, ordering supplies) for the periods when you expect to be least productive (e.g., after lunch).

7. Restructure your days if you have too much time.

If you have already finished your coursework and do not need to work or teach, you might have the unusual problem of having too much time to do research. You arrive at your office early in the morning and have the entire day ahead of you to do work. Does this sound like a lifestyle that you were looking forward to, when you were still juggling coursework and research? The possible disadvantage of having too much flexibility is that you might not feel the need to plan your days. I call this situation the "time trap," because you might be under the illusion that it is not necessary to plan your schedule. Unfortunately, without proper planning, weeks or months can go by without significant progress. Even though you have sufficient time to work on your thesis, you might try to cram a lot of work into the few days or weeks before a conference deadline or committee meeting. This work style results in stress, guilt and low-quality work.

In the previous chapter, I mentioned Jim, whose strategy for staying focused during the day was to alternate 45 minutes of work with 15-minute breaks. In addition to these small relaxation sessions, most students feel that they need longer breaks away from work. Herman, an engineer, started work between 8 a.m. and 9 a.m., and by noon he felt he needed some fresh air. Instead of eating lunch at his computer, Herman ate lunch with his friends at a nearby park. After lunch, he worked for a few more hours, but noticed that his productivity decreased by 5 p.m. He then headed to the gym, and worked out for an hour before he went home to eat dinner with his wife. When he had an impending deadline, he worked for a few hours at home too, but he usually relaxed in the evenings. "I tried to be very focused during the day, and I found that I was more productive when I had time off at night."

It is unrealistic to expect yourself to work 12 hours straight, every day, for months or years. What can you do to build more structure into your day? Once again, take out your calendar and look at all the commitments not related to your thesis: sports, hobbies, meals, meetings and the like. If you do not have any extracurricular commitments, add a few

MAXIMIZE YOUR EFFICIENCY

commitments that are relaxing, such as going out with friends for dinner, sports or a hobby class. Beth, an art history major, worked for two hours as a receptionist at a yoga center, every afternoon during her last year in graduate school. "I did not work just for the money, but also because these two hours helped me structure my days. This commitment forced me to get organized, because I had fewer hours in the day."

8. Assess your accomplishments at the end of every day.

If you do not get feedback from your advisor, it is difficult to determine whether you are making progress. For this reason, you might question your productivity: "Did I get enough done today?" To reassure themselves, some students try to work a few extra hours in the evening, even if they are tired and no longer productive. You can get around this sense of guilt if you take a few minutes at the end of every day to look over what you have accomplished. Perhaps you did not make significant progress on your work, but you did complete many errands. Or, you did work on your thesis, but you are not satisfied with your progress. It is tempting to beat yourself up, but that will make you even more frustrated. Instead, give yourself a pat on the back for what you *have* accomplished; doing so will motivate you to work more. Even the most productive students are rarely satisfied with their progress. They always wish that they had done more. If you believe that you could have accomplished more, where do you think you can make improvements in your daily routine? Do you feel that you are not organized enough? Are your goals too vague? Is it time to meet with your advisor, to refine your research question? Whatever your situation, assessing your accomplishments at the end of the day will help you realize where you could improve your efficiency. Keeping track of your daily accomplishments will help you to notice if you have been consistently tired and unmotivated. If so, talk to your advisor about finding a more exciting project, and also see a doctor to make sure you are not sick.

In summary, you can optimize the use of your time if you:
- Compartmentalize your schedule, to balance work and personal life.
- Use short segments of free time during the day to complete tasks.
- Get high-priority tasks done during your most productive hours.
- Structure your days by including time for leisure.
- Recognize your accomplishments at the end of the day and think about how you could improve your time management.

Organize a functional workspace
9. Create a functional working environment.
If you have taken to heart some of the aforementioned suggestions for managing your to-do list and budgeting your time, you are probably a very organized person already. There is, however, one more important component of your life that influences organization: your space. In college, every semester began with a fresh page and clean, crisp notebooks; new textbooks; maybe even a new dorm room. In graduate school, you usually have the same desk (and maybe the same dorm room) for several years. Initially, my filing cabinet just had a few lonely journal articles, but the same cabinet was overstuffed with bulging folders by my third year. I had to reorganize my folders continuously and recycle outdated papers. My desk also had to be reorganized as old textbooks became obsolete, and laboratory notebooks filled up one after the other. Is there a way to keep your desk organized *without* being continuously preoccupied with it?

Remember that your workspace is *yours*. Before you begin organizing your desk or room according to someone else's principles, visualize what *you* would like this space to look like when you are done rearranging it. The last thing you want is to have a space that just "looks" clean, with all the stuff tossed inside drawers, because that certainly will not inspire you. Question the purpose of your desk, lab bench, lab notebook, filing cabinet and even the different parts of your computer hard drive, because all of these "spaces" are meant to help you with your research.

As an example, ask yourself, "How do I wish this desk to be organized?" Perhaps on the right of your table, you would like all your stationery to be organized in a little bin along with a cup of (working) pens. On the left, you might want to have your current reading material and your lab notebook. For your filing cabinet, you probably want to organize your papers by topic so that you have easy access to them. If you like lists and diagrams, draw a picture of your ideal space, and then write down all the steps required to achieve this goal. In the case of your desk, your list might be: 1) clear everything off the desk and empty the drawers, 2) organize all stationery in a bin on the right side of desk (if you cannot fit all stationery into the bin, donate it to the office), 3) look through all personal items in drawers, and decide which ones to keep and which ones to discard, and 4) rearrange research notebooks and data CDs in your drawer chronologically.

10. Make your workspace inspiring.

You can make your environment more stimulating if you add something that will make this space your very own. What inspires you? Is it a calendar with motivational quotes? Pictures of nature? Julie, an engineer, could not concentrate on reading in her dorm room. She soon realized that her desk was in the darkest part of her room, so she rearranged her furniture and put her desk next to the window. She also added a more luxurious feel to the room by purchasing a soft navy carpet. With the added light and a plushy carpet under her feet, Julie actually looked forward to working at home.

If you have an office on campus, you are probably limited by what you can do with your space. Nevertheless, you still have many options available when you set up your space. Do you like clear space, or do you want to decorate your walls? If previous graduate students left behind lab souvenirs (e.g., old books and photographs), do you want to hold on to them or would you prefer to hand them over to your advisor? (You probably need to consult with your advisor before you discard anything.) Also, do not feel obliged to decorate your space with "stuff," just because others do it. I once visited an office where many of the workers had stuffed animals on their desks. It is a cute trend, but if it is in the way of your work, put the stuffed animals aside. If you like clear space, keep it that way.

11. When you get organized, tackle one part of your space at a time.

It is tempting to put off getting organized, because it seems overwhelming at first. You might have hundreds of files, stacks of notebooks and multiple bookshelves to put in order. Organizing an entire office could take an entire day, possibly even two. If you are a graduate student, I am guessing that your desk and office are probably not very big, but it can still seem intimidating to organize them. Julie Morgenstern, author of *Getting Organized from the Inside-Out*, suggests you organize your space by dividing it into "zones." A zone could be a bookshelf, your desk or even just one drawer in your desk. Choose the zone that needs the most urgent help or the one that is easiest to work with. Once you begin getting organized, you will probably be motivated to continue working on the other parts of your space.

As you work through your chosen zone, unpack everything and separate its contents into three separate piles: 1) items that you will keep in this zone, 2) items that you will keep, but not in this zone and 3) items that you will discard or recycle. Some of these decisions are not easy, and you might spend a few hours or an afternoon organizing a desk. After you re-pack your belongings, you should have only the items that you need in that zone. Pack your items in clearly labeled containers or folders, so that every item in your zone will have a home. As you rearrange your supplies, think about which items you use most frequently, and make those the easiest to access.

Avoid the temptation to "zigzag" from one zone to another. Focus on one part of your space at a time. When you are satisfied with the results of your first zone, you will probably feel motivated to transform the next zone: your filing cabinet, lab bench or computer hard drive, for example. Soon, you will impress your boss and friends with your well-organized workspace, and you will save time by having quick access to journal articles and experimental results.

12. Devote an afternoon every few months to reorganizing your space.

Separating your space into zones will help you remain organized. Nevertheless, it will also be necessary to rearrange your space occasionally, especially if there has been a change in your project or you have accu-mulated more "stuff." The power of zoning your space is that it simplifies cleanup: You no longer need to re-organize the entire area each time—just the zone that needs help. Consider these cleanup sessions as opportunities to reorganize your space as well as your thoughts. You might be surprised at how inspired you will feel once you have a clean workspace.

Sabrina, a biochemistry student who was fed up with the disorganiza-tion in her lab, initiated a group cleanup. Initially, she felt overwhelmed by the responsibility of being in charge of such a large project. As the cleanup progressed, however, she was surprised to see how having a common goal united the lab members. People who normally did not communicate, worked together to find a space for everything. In addition, many sought-after items suddenly appeared, and they did not have to be repurchased. At the end of the day, everyone had a sense of accomplishment and was satisfied with the results. One student even remarked, "We should do this again sometime!"

In summary, to get organized:
- Visualize the function of your space and determine how you want it to be organized.

- Divide your space into zones and decide what the function of each zone is.
- Organize your space one zone at a time before moving on to the next.
- Decide, for every item in the zone, whether you want to keep it, discard it or recycle it.
- Make the most frequently used items the easiest to access; store the rest in user-friendly and clearly labeled containers.
- Revisit the organization of your space occasionally and rearrange it according to your current needs.

CHAPTER SUMMARY AND ACTION PLAN

Maximize your efficiency

Step 1: Review your work style.
- Write down all your current commitments, both work-related and extracurricular.
- Determine whether there is a good balance in you life between work and relaxation.
- If you are overwhelmed, think about eliminating the activities that are least productive for you.
- If you are unmotivated to work, examine whether your thesis work supports your long-term career goals.
- Discuss any major changes with your advisor, such as starting a new project or changing your research plans.

Step 2: Prioritize with the 80/20 principle.
- Keep track of your accomplishments every day for a few weeks, and assess how you have made progress on your thesis.
- Distinguish "actions" from "activities," and focus on generating tangible results.
- Eliminate or reduce activities that waste your time and hinder progress on your thesis.
- Maximize happiness in your free time by pursuing meaningful hobbies and sports.

- If you need to change your habits, do so slowly, to give yourself time to adjust to your new routine.

Step 3: Develop a productive workflow.
- Strive to optimize your own workflow without comparing yourself to others.
- Keep on top of the literature, to ensure that your project will make a significant contribution to your field.
- Plan your project in detail and obtain all necessary supplies before you begin your work.
- Depending on how involved your advisor is in your research, finalize your plan with him or her before you get started.
- Evaluate the results of your current projects before moving on to your next study.

Step 4: Get organized.
- Record your to-do list in a portable planner and review it daily.
- Schedule your high-priority tasks for the times of day when you are most alert, and complete errands during pockets of time when you are not productive.
- Do not wait for a large block of time to start a new project; take advantage of "time fragments" during the day.
- Design a workspace for yourself that is both functional and inspirational.
- Divide your workspace into zones and arrange the most frequently used items in easily accessible areas.
- Reorganize your space every few months as your needs change.

Table 3-1: At-a-glance productivity booster

Many times, it is difficult to assess why we feel unmotivated or distracted. In the table below, I have summarized some common graduate student complaints and possible solutions.

Complaint	Tips for refueling your motivation
Feeling overcommitted in general	Write down all your thoughts, both those related and not related to your thesis. Just recognizing that you have a lot on your mind can loosen up your burden. What is the first thing that you need to get done?
Feeling overwhelmed by thesis project	Start working on a small part of your project. Once you have momentum, you will find the motivation to keep going. Determine the easiest task, no matter how small, and do it. Continue breaking down your to-do's into very small, manageable parts.
Stress due to upcoming deadline/presentation	Accept that you have an upcoming deadline and expect less from yourself in other areas. Once the deadline/presentation passes, you will feel relieved and you will be able to focus on your other commitments.
Disappointment due to feelings of failure	Recognize that research is not a linear process and that productivity usually comes in bursts. Many students collect a significant portion of their data in the last six months of their program.
Thesis has no direction	Focus on what you have already accomplished. Decide in which direction you would like to go. Talk to your advisor or committee members and negotiate a direction that is acceptable to all of you.

Table 3-1: At-a-Glance Productivity Booster *(continued)*

Complaint	Tips for refueling your motivation
Frustration due to conflicts with your advisor	Realize that the most likely reason for a conflict is miscommunication. Advisors are very busy, and your project is a very small part of their overall work. Take charge of your project and brainstorm about creative solutions. (See chapter five for tips on effective communication.)
Feeling that a lot of your work has been in vain: your new data is contradictory, your advisor changes your project or someone publishes "your" findings before you	Determine how much work/time you lost. Some of your data might still be valuable and could be adapted to your new project. Even if you need to completely abandon your project, you have gained experience by learning an experimental technique or familiarizing yourself with a specific research area.
You lost your data/report!	Assess how much information has been lost. You might still be able to salvage some of your data from a notebook or a computer printout. If your computer crashed, a computer administrator might be able to restore your hard drive. If you have a hard copy of your work, you might be able to scan it in and use character recognition software to turn it into an electronic file.
Constantly obsessed with thesis, yet disappointed with progress	You might need a distraction to loosen up the stress. Join an exercise group, socialize with friends, or go on a short vacation. These commitments will cut into your research time, but a satisfying hobby will relax you and ultimately make you more productive at work.
Anger: feeling like you have had enough already!	Remember that many students feel the same way, yet they eventually graduate. While your thesis might take longer (or much longer) than you had originally planned, enjoy this time as much as you can. Listen to music while you work, talk to supportive friends, and enjoy a few hours of your favorite hobby every week.

Table 3-1: At-a-Glance Productivity Booster *(concluded)*

Complaint	Tips for refueling your motivation
Uncertainty about life after graduation	Focus on getting your thesis completed. It is always possible to add more detail later if you need to stay in graduate school a few extra months before you start your job. Ask your advisor, thesis committee, and career office about job opportunities. (See chapter seven for job-searching resources.)
Non-academic distractions taking away your time	Allow yourself to take care of your personal life issues (e.g., wedding or family emergency) and give them the attention they deserve. If there is an issue that needs continuous attention (e.g., child care), reorganize your priorities to meet your new needs (e.g., get a part-time job or save money for child care).
Having "writer's block"	Writing for just a few minutes might inspire new ideas. If you are still blocked, use a journal to open up about your ideas. (See chapter six for suggestions on the writing process.)
Muscle strain, fatigue	Ensure that your workspace is ergonomic and that you keep an ergonomic posture at your desk. (See chapter four for treating and preventing repetitive strain injury.)
Sleep deprivation/feeling ill, unmotivated	Even if you go to sleep early every night, your quality of sleep might not be good. Try relaxation techniques (see chapter four) and exercise. Sometimes, taking a personal day can help to relax you. If you see little or no improvement, see a doctor to make sure there is no underlying illness.

Getting organized through leadership: *Chris' story*

Chris was in a biochemistry program with an advisor who was very hands-off. He was excited about his project, but he needed additional outside motivation to make progress on his work. Chris also liked working with other people, so he decided to mentor an undergraduate who wanted to work in his group. "I became really organized after he started to work with me. He was an enthusiastic student, and kept asking me for more work. After I hired him, I made really good progress on my thesis. I think that having somebody work for you really helps to get you motivated and organized." Chris' story exemplifies how we can make progress on our project through leadership. It is important to realize, however, that hiring an undergraduate is a big responsibility. Do not expect them to get data for your thesis, although some talented undergraduates might make significant contributions. If you hire an undergraduate, you are a mentor, not a boss. Always double-check their work—or better, yet repeat it yourself, if you want to include it in your thesis. Remember that you are ultimately responsible for your doctoral dissertation, and you want to make sure that everything that goes into it has been researched properly.

Increasing motivation by assessing progress: *Ethan's story*

Ethan, a chemical engineering student, used the "page-a-day" approach to keep track of his achievements. He purchased a three-ring binder, and at the end of each workday he summarized his major accomplishments of that day, including interesting lessons from his coursework. He organized these pages in the binder by topic: theory, modeling, programming, and so forth. After just one year, he had 365 pages of accomplishments. Ethan noted that even during his fifth year, he found himself looking at his notes from his coursework and early research experience, to find out how to solve challenging engineering problems. "It was very useful for me to keep a binder of all of my accomplishments. Some days it was not easy to write a page about what I had accomplished, but I usually found that even on "non-productive" days, I did make some progress on my thesis. Knowing that I would need to write a summary at the end of every day motivated me to work harder. It is very important to be consistent with this journal. If you skip a day because of a holiday or illness, just continue writing as soon as you are back at work."

"If I had eight hours to chop down a tree,
I'd spend six hours sharpening my ax"
Abraham Lincoln, American president (1809–1865)

Claire, a microbiologist, struggled for eight years in graduate school before she earned her Ph.D. She expected to graduate in six years, but there were two major challenges that she had not anticipated before starting her program: 1) extreme anxiety that interfered with her concentration, and 2) repetitive strain injury (RSI). "I was very stressed in graduate school, because there was a lot of uncertainty in my project. I think that one of my biggest challenges was dealing with my anxiety when I reached a dead end." She also added, "I worked long hours every day, which is probably the reason that I developed repetitive strain injury. My arms hurt so much that I had trouble solving a crossword puzzle." Claire had to take time out to recover from her injury, and when she returned to work, she changed her habits. She set up a more comfortable workspace, bought ergonomic pipettes and worked reasonable hours. Could Claire have prevented anxiety and RSI *before* her symptoms had become severe?

As a graduate student, you are your own supervisor, and you will probably drive yourself harder than any other boss would. With so much flexibility in your schedule, it is difficult to judge when to take a break, so you might choose to err on the side of working harder than necessary. You might be fresh out of college, or have just a few years of working experience, yet you are expected to manage a research project, become financially independent and take care of your health on your own. It is no small wonder that many graduate students struggle with stress, anxiety, depression and RSI.

In the first part of this chapter I will describe why so many graduate students experience anxiety, and how you can overcome your

Increasing motivation by assessing progress: Ethan's story   121

worries, and even make them work to your advantage. In the second section, I will discuss how nutrition affects your thinking ability, and how you can incorporate a healthy and affordable diet into your lifestyle. The third section of this chapter focuses on recognizing and preventing RSI, and where to seek help if you have been injured.

In summary, this chapter will show you how to:

◆ Let go of stressful and unproductive thinking patterns
◆ Incorporate healthy meals into your diet that will keep you sharp throughout the day
◆ Prevent and alleviate RSI

Disclaimer: The suggestions in this book are not meant to substitute for medical advice. If you experienced symptoms of anxiety, depression or RSI see a medical professional immediately. Also consult with a professional nutritionist before changing your diet.

Challenge #1: Overcoming stress and anxiety

Although most students begin graduate school enthusiastically, a few years down the road, many students ask themselves questions such as: "What if my studies don't make any sense? What if everything I did was a waste of time? What if it takes longer than I anticipated?" Interestingly, most students found the middle years of graduate school to be the most challenging. At the beginning, you are preoccupied with courses and qualifiers, and at the end you are writing your dissertation and preparing your thesis defense. During both of these periods, your assignments are well defined. In the middle, however, you might experience the "glass is only half full" syndrome. You know you have made some progress already, but it is not clear what you need to do to graduate.

Many students worry when faced with such uncertainty, and they consequently develop stress-related conditions such as anxiety, depression, RSI, backaches and insomnia. You might even believe that you need to work so hard for your degree, that there is no way to avoid stress or injury to your body. This is not the case. Many graduate students have been able to complete their dissertations while maintaining a healthy schedule and never experiencing RSI. If they did not know how to be efficient, how could they become famous researchers, professors and doctors after graduation? One of my favorite quotes is from an electrical engineer who claimed he never worried about his dissertation: "I don't worry, I do." (He did finish his thesis in less than four years.)

One difficulty with trying to follow such advice is that you might not know *what* you need to do to avoid worrying. The reason that I call this section, "How to make worry work for you" is that worry is your body's way of telling you that there is a particular issue that you need to take action on. If you learn how to pay attention to your body's signals, you can turn worrying into action-oriented thinking. In the next section, I summarize the most popular strategies in dealing with worry.

FROM THE PH.D. SECRET ARCHIVES:

12 ways to beat worrying

1. Recognize that worrying is a signal from your body to take action.

If you are worried about something, you have two choices: 1) build up more anxiety or 2) think about how you want this problem to be resolved. Many people choose the first option. There is some comfort in feeling like the victim, when something does not go according to plan. When you are a victim, after all, you are not at fault. If you choose the second option, however, you will save yourself the time you would have spent worrying, and you will come up with a solution to your problem.

2. Define the real problem before you get caught up in your worries.

Let us assume that you are worried because you and your advisor disagree on the direction of your thesis, and you wonder whether you will graduate on time. At this moment, you have two choices. You can continue worrying, or you can ask yourself what the real problem is. Are you worried that your advisor is expecting you to complete a project that will take six months? Or is s/he asking you to work on a boring project? You will have made significant progress in conquering your worry, if you can define in one or two sentences what is *really* bothering you. One possibility might be: "I am worried because my advisor is asking me to reanalyze my data and now I might not meet the deadline for graduating this year." Now that you have clarified that you are worried about not graduating this year, you can think about how to solve the problems associated with this situation (e.g., finding funding for another semester).

3. Mentally accept the worst-case scenario and think about how you could improve upon your situation.

Dale Carnegie, author of *How to Stop Worrying and Start Living*, points out that many people worry because they have not examined their options, nor the consequences of the worst-case scenario. In the above example, the worst-case scenario would be that your graduation would be delayed because your advisor asked you to complete another project. Mentally accept this scenario by visualizing your classmates lining up for their diplomas while you are sitting in your office crunching numbers. Imagine further that you will have to live on a graduate student stipend for another semester. You might even need to turn down a job offer or at least postpone your starting date. While this scenario might not be ideal, would you consider it truly catastrophic, or merely inconvenient?

When you mentally accept the worst that could happen, you might realize that 1) it is not necessarily a tragic outcome and 2) there could be some advantages to the worst-case scenario. For example, with an additional six months in graduate school, could you finish another publication? Could you volunteer to write a review article? Would you have more time to transition into post-graduation life? You can also brainstorm about ways to prevent the worst-case scenario. If you think that having to repeat all of your calculations will delay your graduation, can you speed up your work by asking a statistician to help you? Is there software that can process your data faster? Is it possible that you might be able to get an extension from the registrar's office for handing in the final version of your thesis? As you can see, this type of thinking helps you weigh your alternatives, rather than build up your anxiety.

4. Turn worry into action-oriented thinking by brainstorming about desired outcome(s).

Graduate students commonly worry about their theses not having direction. If you are in this situation, contemplate how *you* would like things to turn out. The reason that I wrote "think about the desired outcome(s)," in plural, it is that you probably need to consider several alternative projects. You will most likely run into a few dead ends, before you find a project that will turn into your dissertation. Write down a few ideas for your thesis, and research them before the next meeting with your advisor. Have concrete reasons to explain why you chose these particular options for your thesis.

Your desired outcome does not necessarily have to be related to your thesis. It could be a non-academic goal such as, "I wish my advisor and I could agree on what the next step should be." In this case, your goal is to reach an agreement, rather than complete a specific project. If this is your goal, try to see the situation from your advisor's point of view. Why does she disagree with your opinion? What are her priorities for this project? At your next meeting, make it clear that you have redesigned this project so that it meets with both of your needs. (See chapter five for tips on effective communication.) As you can see, when you determine what your desired outcome it is, you will also come up with ways to reach these goals.

5. Strive for excellence, not perfection.

In spite of your careful planning and hard work, you might not be satisfied with your results, if you always want to do more and you want everything to be perfect. While your intentions are understandable, perfectionism will lead to never-ending stress. When you are dissatisfied with your work, ask yourself: "What will make this project complete?" It is best to set goals for your project when you begin your research. Ask your advisor early on: "What do I need to do, to graduate?" If you are in the experimental sciences, for example, it might not be necessary to reproduce your results exactly. Many of the sciences allow up to a 20 percent-error between data sets. Clarify what constitutes an acceptable thesis, rather than trying to make every detail perfect. Since research is unpredictable, the goals for your thesis will change. Communicate with your advisor and your committee members frequently, to find out what you need to do to produce an excellent (but not necessarily perfect) thesis.

6. Beat chronic worry with meticulous planning.

Some students might superstitiously believe that the more they worry, the more productive they will be. I used to be one of these students, but now I realize that worrying eats up my mental stamina and leaves me with no energy for productive planning. What is the difference between planning and worrying? Sometimes when we are worried about something, we might fool our minds into thinking that we are planning for the future. You might be nervously brainstorming about how to complete your doctoral dissertation or what precautions to take to avoid another fight with your roommate. The truth is that when you are worrying, you are *not* planning. How can you distinguish worry from planning? The answer is simple: worrying causes anxiety and planning does not. In fact, planning usually calms you down, because it gives you a chance to design a strategy to achieve your goals.

Nina, an engineer and postdoctoral fellow, claimed she had the best thesis advisor one could have. Her advisor was an untenured female professor with young children, who did obtain tenure eventually. When I asked her why she liked her advisor, she replied, "She never worried about any issue in the lab. We could always calmly discuss my thesis, and focus on how to make things work better. She was a great planner. I rarely saw her get upset about her work."

Unfortunately, many people do get emotional about their research. They worry about solving conflicts with coworkers, fixing instruments and analyzing unexpected results. It is understandable if you are concerned about these issues, because they could affect your thesis. On the other hand, it is not worth wasting energy over issues that you have little control over. Sometimes it is not possible to make your research go faster or to please everyone in your group. You are in graduate school to complete a doctoral dissertation, and your job is to plan your research as meticulously as possible. In other words, when you find yourself worrying, think about what it is that you are trying to accomplish and brainstorm about solutions to solve the problems. (See chapter three for suggestions on planning and prioritizing.)

7. Use your breaks to let go of worries.

In previous chapters, I have emphasized the importance of taking breaks during work. What can you do during your breaks? Former graduate students suggest cleaning up your space, stretching, drinking water and taking a walk. Regular breaks can also serve another purpose: relaxation and letting go of tension. Did you ever take a break from work (e.g., to eat lunch or dinner) and then realize how tense you had been during the day? Sometimes you might not realize how worried you have been all day, until you try to go to sleep at night.

According to Herbert Benson, author of *The Relaxation Response,* you can consciously let go of tension anytime and anywhere: in a library, at your desk or in your laboratory. Begin by focusing on your breathing: Is it rapid or slow? To begin relaxing, take a deep breath and then breathe normally, taking care not to breathe too shallowly. Relaxing breaths should affect your abdomen as your diaphragm expands to take in more air. Try this: Put your hands on your abdomen. When you breathe in, your abdomen should expand, and when you exhale, your abdomen should go down. After breathing this way for a few moments, shift your awareness to other parts of your body. Where do you feel tension? Can you relax those muscles? (If not, try slightly tensing each of them separately for five seconds, and then relax the muscles fully.) Next, shift your awareness to your thoughts: What are you worried about? If you take just a few minutes out of your day for relaxation, you will probably realize why you are feeling anxious. As I will discuss in the next section, RSI and some types of muscular tension are more likely to occur when your body is tense. If you are worried because of your thesis, a difficult boss or a personal issue, give yourself the gift of a few minutes of relaxation. In their book *Five Good Minutes at Work,* Jeffrey Brantley and Wendy Millstine list 100 simple meditations, each of which can be done in five minutes.

8. Set aside a few hours every week to connect with your spouse, friends or support group.

The number one piece of advice for beating stress in graduate school is to socialize with friends or members of a support group. Plan at least one afternoon or evening every week to connect with your friends. It easy to get caught up in your worries (e.g., "I wish I had done a better job at the group meeting."); talking to friends will relieve you of many of your concerns. You are also less likely to worry about work when you are having fun.

While socializing in a supportive environment is a good way to beat stress throughout your life, it is especially important in graduate school. As a doctoral student, you are your own boss (yes, your advisor is your boss too, but in the end, *you* need to make the project come together). There is little feedback, unless your advisor is very involved with your thesis. Some days you are the *only* one who can give yourself praise, but many students are self-critical. Unfortunately, being strict with yourself might make you more anxious and eventually tire you out. If you have supportive friends, they will probably give you a pat on the back when you are dissatisfied with the presentation you just gave ("Oh, I don't think you seemed nervous at all."), or you think that you will never graduate ("I know how you feel, but I am sure things will work out.").

9. Conquer your inner negative voice.

At one point or another in graduate school, many students doubt that they will ever graduate. Your self-confidence will probably wax and wane, depending on the status of your work. When your project goes well, you will get a sense of accomplishment, but other times you might feel low and think, "I *knew* this study would not work out. Maybe I am not meant to be a Ph.D." If you have ever experienced self-doubt, think back to the time you were accepted to your doctoral program. Did you envision graduate school as a series of successful studies without any setbacks? Whether or not you had prior research experience, you probably knew that not every study would go well. Nearly every student has setbacks, and some have more than others. Rather than putting yourself down, ask yourself what you have learned this time and what you could do to make progress on your thesis. Sometimes it can take years to develop an appropriate protocol. If you are still doubtful, recall the story of the graduate student from chapter one, who was in school for six years but collected most of her data in the last six months. Bear in mind that "slow and steady wins the race."

The problem with being negative for long periods of time is that it can tire you out. When I was struggling with my thesis, I would recall the summer when I learned how to drive. My instructor told me that a common problem among novice drivers was that they had trouble controlling the speed of their vehicles. They had a tendency to go too slow on the highway and too fast in the city. Similarly, many of us are tense when we should be relaxed and tired when we need to focus. When you build up anxiety through negative self-talk during the day, you will feel stressed in the evenings and have trouble sleeping at night. This pattern can lead to sluggishness in the morning, and low productivity during the day. You can turn this vicious circle around, by listening to the subtly negative messages you give yourself during the day. Instead of worrying about what you did not accomplish, recognize what you have done. The more positive messages you give yourself, the more motivated and energetic you will feel in the mornings and at work. Furthermore, after a day of feeling good about yourself, you will also feel more relaxed in the evenings and probably sleep better at night. It is common to have trouble sleeping during periods of stress, and it is very important to see a doctor if your energy level and your quality of sleep are not satisfactory.

10. Take initiative and make decisions.

Ella, a biologist, claimed that indecisiveness was one of the major sources of stress in graduate school. "I hesitated a lot regarding the direction of my thesis. It took me seven years to finish, and I think it would have been faster if I had chosen a project more quickly and not tried to do everything perfectly," she said. Louise, a geologist, had a similar experience. "I did not expect to have to be so independent in graduate school. I had to make a lot of decisions myself and it was difficult to have the courage to do so initially." If you worry about going in the wrong direction, think about the possible outcomes. What will it cost you if you make a mistake? Can you get more information about the different options? If you need to make a decision based on incomplete information, at least have an "exit plan." How will you know that you have reached a dead end? Making mistakes is part of your learning process, and yet you will feel frustrated if you try to have the perfect thesis. The consequences of reaching a dead end are rarely catastrophic. Remember that your job as a researcher is to make the most educated decision based on the available information.

Sometimes indecisiveness is the result of fear or guilt. Betty, an analytical chemist, hesitated spending her savings on a trip to China, but her real fear was that taking a few weeks off from her work would ruin the flow of her experiments. Objectively speaking, it is hard to imagine how one trip could significantly affect her dissertation. She worried so much about her work, she canceled her trip twice before she allowed herself to take time off. If you find yourself going over and over the same issue, take a moment to think about the reason for any indecisiveness. Most of the time, you will find that the risk you take with making the wrong decision is small compared to the inner turmoil caused by indecisiveness. In a way, indecisiveness is similar to the fear of imperfection—we want to optimize everything, but that is an unrealistic goal. You can find comfort in knowing that you have made the decision using all the information that was available to you at the time.

11. Indulge yourself with small luxuries.

As graduate students, we frequently live on the edge and we hesitate about allowing ourselves to enjoy luxuries. Do I deserve this trip to Spain? Should I postpone this vacation until I have a "real job"? First, let me point out that when you have a real job, your disposable income might not be significantly more than it is now. Jake, a chemist at a pharmaceutical company, put his finances in perspective: "Now that I have a job, I bought a house and a car, and again I have no money." As academics, we are not wealthy, but we are not poor, either. Alice saved only $100–$200 a month, but over the course of two years she saved enough money to travel through Europe for a month. She had no trouble refusing shopping sprees, because she was saving up for her dream vacation. No matter what your budget is, it is essential to treat yourself occasionally to something special. If you continuously deprive your life of fun, you are—intentionally or not— sending negative messages to yourself: I am poor, I am not worthy and I do not deserve this. These subtle feelings of deficiency can eventually lead to chronic feelings of poverty—financially and emotionally.

The truth is, no matter what your budget is, you can spoil yourself, at least occasionally. A senior scientist mentioned that he was so poor as a graduate student that he could never afford a six-pack of beer. He could only buy beer one can at a time, and usually just once a week. He would, however, look forward to treating himself to that one can of beer—and he likely savored it more than most people would. Janice, a biologist, discovered that as a student she could get free admission to the fine arts museum; it was just a matter of making time. Thus, she set aside one afternoon every month to visit the latest exhibits, and she would indulge fully in the experience by relaxing afterwards on a bench in the nearby park. What is your luxury? Is there anything that you could afford time- and/or money-wise, that you have been denying yourself?

Allowing yourself to enjoy luxuries can lead to dilemmas, whether it is about spending money or making the time to enjoy a hobby. On the one hand, you might believe that you have no time or money; on the other hand, you do need to make yourself feel special. Interestingly, you are more likely to experience inner turmoil when you *can* afford something but deny it to yourself. For example, I never met a graduate student who pined over whether to purchase himself a yacht or a mansion on a beach, because these items are so expensive that most students on stipends would never consider them anyway. I did meet many students, however, who wavered when deciding whether to go out for dinner ("Do I have the time?") or whether to take a weekend ski trip ("Can I afford it?"). These are luxuries that we can afford (at least some of the time), and deep inside we know it. If you find it difficult to allow yourself to have fun, the best solution is to determine a budget for your free time (many students set aside one or two evenings a week) and for your disposable income. That way, if you reach your limit and have to refuse a dinner with friends, you will have a clear conscience.

With a predetermined budget, your subconscious mind will realize that you are not purposefully denying yourself fun, but that the objective reality is that this particular month, you have already surpassed your budget and can no longer afford any more fancy dinners. There is the hope, however, that next month you can once again indulge in such a luxury.

As an aside, be realistic when you set financial goals. Financial planning is beyond the scope of this book, but talk with other graduate students about managing money. Inquire about discount airfare tickets, sales at department stores and specials at restaurants. I also discussed resources for financing your graduate education in chapter one. The more ideas you have, the easier it will be to eliminate the stress that comes with financial worries.

12. Seek counseling and medical advice if anxiety becomes too difficult to handle.

Lena practiced meditation and yoga regularly, but she still experienced significant anxiety. "I benefited a lot from cognitive therapy, but I also had to take medication sometimes. I think there was just too much pressure to handle on my own." Lena continued going to yoga, meditation and even art classes throughout graduate school. While the cognitive therapy and medications helped to ease her anxiety, she still felt that the other stress-relieving approaches were essential to her recovery.

As a doctoral student, you might try to do everything on your own, but it is a challenge to handle several life changes simultaneously (e.g., becoming independent, managing a dissertation, possibly getting married or having children). Counseling deans at your school or your personal physician can probably recommend therapists who work with doctoral students and are familiar with the challenges of graduate school.

Coping with personal problems: *Ron's story*

Ron, an electrical engineer, had a positive experience in graduate school. He was enthusiastic about his project, and his mentors were also supportive. He did experience anxiety, however, because of his relationship with his girlfriend. Ron decided to attend support group meetings, where graduate students had the opportunity to discuss both academic and non-academic difficulties. "I did not have any problems with my thesis, I went to these sessions primarily for personal reasons," Ron recalled. At the support group meetings Ron opened up about the difficulties between him and his girlfriend, and learned ways to cope with his personal problems. Anxiety, whether caused by academic or non-academic issues, can interfere with your concentration. Support groups can help you deal with these problems, because other graduate students probably face similar challenges. Ron learned about his support group through his physician; you can find supports groups by consulting with your doctor, graduate student association or counseling dean.

Challenge #2: Enhancing your thinking ability through your diet

Most of us think about our diet only when we want to lose weight, but good nutrition is also the cornerstone of a healthy mind. It might seem like a challenge to follow a healthy diet in graduate school, especially when you are short on time and money, but eating habits can significantly affect self-confidence and academic performance. "My weight fluctuated in graduate school, sometimes by as much as 40 pounds," said Shelley, a mathematics major. "When I did not eat well, I gained weight and felt drowsy—and my research did not go well, either." Robin, a chemistry major, spoke enthusiastically about her diet in graduate school. "I love to cook and I usually invited people over to enjoy a good dinner. Overall, I ate very well in graduate school, and I still try to follow good eating habits. In general, I think that students who cooked usually ate healthier." Some other Ph.D.s mentioned that they tried to follow a healthy diet, but it was too expensive or too much work. I have always believed that a healthy diet was essential for your thinking ability, so how can you improve your diet in graduate school, when you have limited time and money?

NURTURE YOUR MIND AND BODY

To answer this question, I researched the literature and consulted with Dr. Ann Yelmokas McDermott, a nutritionist and Associate Professor at Cal Poly State University. Dr. McDermott explained the four principles of a healthy, balanced diet:

- Complexing, or including carbohydrates, proteins, and fats in each meal and snack
- Consuming fruits and vegetables of a variety of colors at every meal (ten servings a day is optimal, five is the bare minimum)
- Ensuring that your proteins, carbohydrates and fats are from healthy sources
- "Going back to nature," or choosing foods in their most natural form (e.g., a whole orange instead of orange juice), which will often increase your intake of fiber

While incorporating a good diet into your busy lifestyle might seem like a daily chore, there are many inexpensive and quick shortcuts to ensure that you eat well at every meal. I offer ideas for monthly and weekly shopping lists at the end of this section, so you can stock your pantry with healthier food choices. In the long run, having a well-stocked pantry will save you time and money, because you will no longer need to go to vending machines, convenience stores or the university cafeteria. As with academia, planning is crucial to success.

Fuel your brain through nutrition
THE IMPORTANCE OF COMPLEXING

Have you ever been hit by a mid-afternoon low, when you feel that you still need to work for a few hours, but are too tired to do so? Most of us will turn to a cup of coffee or a pastry to regain our energy. Some graduate students even have regular coffee breaks around 3 p.m. as a way to awaken themselves during the day. As much as I loved browsing through the pastries at the local coffee shop, I soon realized that the energy I gained from these snacks was short-lived. In fact, just an hour or two after consuming a chocolate croissant, I felt tired, and I was craving sugar again. What was going on? Why was I feeling drowsy so shortly after my snack?

As I began looking into these questions, I was surprised to learn that the answers were based on simple principles that I had learned just a few years previous, in my biochemistry class. If you are not a biochemist, do not worry; you need only remember the following simple principle: glucose (which is the breakdown product of carbohydrates) is the preferred fuel source for your brain[1-3]. Therefore, your mind will function best when you maintain a steady level of glucose in your blood. So, what is wrong with eating a snack, such as a pastry, that is high in carbohydrates?

Rather than helping to maintain a steady blood-glucose level, the consumption of processed carbohydrates by themselves leads to a quick increase in your blood-glucose, stimulating the production of the hormone insulin. Insulin signals the body to store excess glucose in the liver and muscle as glycogen, which removes glucose from the bloodstream. Hence, my high-sugar snack stimulated insulin to remove glucose from my bloodstream, paradoxically leading to fatigue and drowsiness. To make matters worse, the excess calories from glucose are usually stored as fat, a consequence that most of us probably do not desire.

What can you do to keep your blood-glucose levels constant? The answer is "complexing," or eating mixed meals. A mixed meal includes a balanced combination of proteins, fats, and carbohydrates. Unless you are on a special diet, however, it is not necessary to precisely calculate the amounts of proteins, fats and carbohydrates for each meal. Simply try to include some amount from each nutrient in every meal, including your snacks. Instead of a pastry, for example, I now eat a cup of yogurt and sprinkle just a few pieces of walnuts on top, to keep me satiated longer. (Incidentally, walnuts are a good source of fiber and also contain a lot of omega-3 fatty acids, which are thought to be important for brain function.)

 Combining proteins, carbohydrates and fats in every meal and snack will keep you satiated for longer than if you ate only one type of calorie source.

WHAT ARE HEALTHY FOOD CHOICES?
While "complexing" will maintain your blood-glucose levels better than eating only one type of food, it is still important to get your calories from healthy sources. Not all carbohydrates are created equal, and it is best to get foods in their most natural form. Healthy carbohydrate

NURTURE YOUR MIND AND BODY

choices include oatmeal, whole grain breads, whole wheat pasta, high-fiber cereals, brown rice and fresh produce. Fruits, vegetables and whole grains are important parts of mixed meals, because they have high amounts of fiber. Foods with fiber will keep you satiated for longer, and increase your alertness after meals[4]. Another reason it is beneficial to include many fresh fruits and vegetables into your diet is that they have high water content, which will keep you hydrated throughout the day.

If you eat carbohydrates other than fruits and vegetables, you can read the nutrition label to determine how "close to nature" they are. The higher the fiber content, the less processing they went through. Cereal bars, for example, vary significantly in their fiber content; if you want to choose the best for your digestive system, choose a cereal bar that has at least 4 grams of fiber. You can also make your sandwiches healthier if you choose a bread that has at least 3 grams of fiber per slice. If you use high-fiber bread, your sandwich will have 6 grams of fiber, which is about 20% of the daily recommended allowance. (The American Heart Association (www.americanheart.org) recommends 14 grams of fiber per every 1,000 calories consumed.) On the other hand, processed foods such as pastries, doughnuts, cakes, white bread and bagels usually have no fiber, and will fill you with calories without satiating your hunger.

 Consuming foods with high fiber content will keep you satiated for a longer period of time.

I usually expected a sigh when I asked my interviewees whether they had had at least five servings of fruits and vegetables a day in graduate school, but I got a surprising answer when I asked Meryl, a biochemist. "Oh yeah, it is not that hard to get your five servings. I just had a cup of juice for breakfast, one or two fruits during the day, and then vegetables with my dinner. I think a lot of people have their five servings a day, but they do not know it." Meryl was right: One serving of fruit or vegetables is not that much. A medium-sized fruit such as an apple (equivalent to the size of a tennis ball) is considered one serving, but it can be difficult to squeeze five of those into one day. How else can you get your servings of fruits and vegetables? If you like to drink your fruits and vegetables, remember that just 4 ounces of juice equals one serving (though juices do lack fiber). Furthermore, if you eat dried fruits such as cranberries or raisins, you need only eat one quarter-cup to achieve a serving. For small vegetables such as peas, a serving is just half a cup, and for larger or loose vegetables such as broccoli and lettuce, one serving equals one cup. If it is inconvenient or too expensive to eat fresh fruits and vegetables, consider the frozen ones, as they still contain a significant portion of their antioxidants.[5;6] In fact, flash-frozen vegetables and fruits, which are frozen quickly after harvest, might contain even more vitamins and minerals than fresh produce. The packaging will usually tell you whether your fruits or vegetables were flash-frozen.

You might lose some of the vitamins if you cook your vegetables[7], but certain micronutrients such as carotenes[8;9] and lycopene[10;11] become more bioavailable with cooking[8]. Furthermore, adding some vegetable oils to your leafy greens will increase the bioavailability of fat-soluble vitamins (e.g., vitamins A, D, E and K) and alpha and beta carotenes.[12;13]

In order to make it more convenient to get your fruits and vegetables every day, include dried, frozen, cooked and fresh produce in your diet. If you drink fruit or vegetable juices, remember that one serving equals 4 ounces.

If you include fats in your meals, you will be satiated for longer, but it is important to pay attention to the amounts and sources of fat in your meals. For a balanced diet, the American Dietetic Association recommends that no more than 30% of your calories come from fat. (For more information on dietary guidelines, see the homepage of the American Dietetic Association at www.eatright.org.) Eating low-fat meals helps to maintain a healthy weight and also a better nutrient profile.[14-16] In addition, there is evidence that a low-fat breakfast, supplemented with proteins and carbohydrates, will satiate you longer than a high-fat breakfast.[17;18] If your meal does not have a nutrition label (or you cook your own meals), keep in mind that one gram of fat has more than twice as many calories as one gram of protein or carbohydrates (9 calories per gram from fats, versus 4 calories per gram from carbohydrates and proteins). Therefore, you might only need a sprinkling of nuts or a tablespoon of olive oil to add sufficient fat to your meals. The sources of your fats are also important to consider, especially if you or your family have a history of cardiovascular disease. "I was very surprised that my blood pressure and cholesterol were elevated after I graduated with my Ph.D.," said Oliver, a geologist. "I did not pay attention to my diet back then, but now I try to eat better, and my cholesterol level has improved."

What are healthy fat sources? In general, fats from plants are unsaturated, and so they are considered healthier than the saturated fatty acids from animal sources. Trans fatty acids are found, to some extent, in animal fats, but most of the trans fats we consume are produced industrially in order to increase the stability of oils and shortenings. Trans fatty acids, also known as partially hydrogenated oils, are considered deleterious for cardiovascular health, and their consumption should be avoided altogether. Healthy fats come primarily from plants such as soybeans, canola, olives and nuts. You can incorporate plant fats easily into your diet by spreading hummus or peanut butter on your sandwich instead of butter or cream cheese. Fish, particularly salmon and tuna, are also an excellent source of omega-3 fatty acids. Fresh fish might be too expensive when you are a graduate student, but canned tuna and salmon, as well as flash-frozen fish, are more affordable and available at most supermarkets.

 Choose your fats from plant (e.g., soybeans, olive oil, and walnuts) and fish sources (e.g., tuna and salmon).

In addition to including healthy carbohydrates and fats, it is also important to have some protein at every meal. It is not necessary to have animal protein, particularly since plant-based protein sources usually have less fat and no saturated fats. Beans and lentils, for example, provide a very lean source of protein and also contain significant amounts of fiber. Soy products, such as soy milk and tofu, also contain added calcium and omega-3 fatty acids. Interestingly, some Ph.D.s recalled eating rice and beans to save money in graduate school, but they were actually eating healthier than if they had consumed fast foods at the local restaurants. If you eat animal protein, consider lean cuts of beef, poultry, fish and low-fat dairy. Eggs are also an inexpensive source of protein, but they also contain fat, so you probably do not need to add extra fat (e.g., cheese) to satiate your hunger.

Include low-fat proteins in your meals, such as lean cuts of meat, poultry, fish, beans, soy, and dairy.

Snacking between meals is not a bad habit, nor does it necessarily increase your overall calorie intake.[10] It does take some planning to ensure that your snacks are healthy, but in the long run, you will save money and also eat better. Examples of healthy and relatively inexpensive snacks include a high-fiber cereal bar, a yogurt with nuts and fruits, and whole wheat bread with low-fat cheese and sliced vegetables. It might seem like a chore to try to eat healthy in graduate school, especially when there is so much else to do. Putting a little bit of effort into your meals and snacks, however, can keep you focused throughout the day.[19] It is common for eating habits to deteriorate when students are under stress, but this trend can be turned around with planning. A nutritious diet and a sharp mind go hand-in-hand: The healthier you eat, the more energy you will have—and the better your academic performance will be.

 Healthy snacks throughout the day can satiate your hunger and maintain your blood-glucose level.

See the end of this section for ideas on weekly and monthly shopping lists, so you can keep your pantry, fridge and freezer stocked with nutritious and low-fat foods.

What should you drink?
Your health is influenced not only by what you eat but also by what you drink. When asked for the number-one piece of advice for people trying to lose weight, a nutritionist replied, "Don't drink your calories." My friend, Juliet, gained almost 10 pounds during the three months of writing her thesis, even though her diet had remained the same. I noticed, however, that she was treating herself regularly to a fruit and soy shake. While examining the bottle, I saw that one serving had over 200 calories, but that the whole bottle itself had nearly 500. Most days, she drank just one bottle, but on days when she had to stay at work later, she consumed a second drink. Thus, she was drinking an extra 500 to 1,000 calories every day for three months, in addition to maintaining her previous diet. When you consider that 1 pound of body fat

comprises approximately 4000 calories, it is easy to see why she gained weight. I am not suggesting that you eliminate all sugary drinks, but you might be surprised to see how many calories some beverages have. What *can* you drink, then?

Water is a beverage that many of us take for granted, unless we have no access to it. Katie, a biologist, was frustrated because the water fountains in her department looked unsanitary and she was frequently thirsty. She tried to get hydrated from the coffee machine, but too much coffee made her cranky. Katie and her lab mates decided to invest in a water cooler, and paid for water to be delivered every week. When Katie became a postdoctoral fellow, she was thrilled to tell her lab mates that her new department had a clean water fountain on every floor.

Samantha, a biochemist who struggled with her weight, noticed that whenever she began drinking sodas and juices regularly, she gained 3–5 pounds in two weeks. To lose the weight, she decided to drink primarily water, and after a week she did not miss her soft beverages at all. She still treated herself occasionally to fruit juices, but she diluted them with water or seltzer two- or three-fold. Water and diluted juices were more thirst-quenching than concentrated juices, and she was able to keep the extra weight off. As an added bonus, her dental health also improved: Her teeth were no longer stained from fruit juices, and she had no cavities at her next check-up.

I saved the discussion about caffeine for the last part, because it is a sensitive subject for many people. Some students had been advised by their doctors to cut down on caffeine, but this can be a challenge if you like to drink coffee regularly. "I like to drink coffee, because it is nice to sip on a warm liquid while working on the computer," said Misha, a chemist. "I was advised to avoid coffee in the afternoons, because I had trouble sleeping at night. It was difficult to cut down on coffee, because I experienced headaches and fatigue. Eventually these symptoms disappeared, and now I drink tea in the afternoons."

Doug, another chemist, eliminated his consumption of caffeine when he was diagnosed with heart palpitations. He quit "cold turkey," and was unable to work for three days. "In retrospect, it was not a good idea to quit so suddenly, because I could not get out of bed the entire weekend. My doctor actually recommended cutting down on it gradually, maybe eliminating a cup every few days. Occasionally, I still have a cup of coffee in the morning, but only if I have time to eat breakfast with it. If I drink coffee, I make it with half decaf, so I reduce the caffeine content even more. Fortunately, my heart palpitations disappeared."

 Talk to your physician about gradually reducing or eliminating caffeine intake, if you experience insomnia or anxiety.

Not every Ph.D. that I interviewed was sensitive to caffeine. Some claimed that they could go to bed right after drinking a cup of coffee. Others tried to avoid it in the evening or maybe all afternoon. There were also a few Ph.D.s who were so sensitive to caffeine that they stayed away from it completely. If you feel anxious, unable to concentrate or have difficulty sleeping, it might be worth lowering or eliminating its consumption. If you drink specialty coffees and chai teas, you can find out their caloric content on the store website or at www.calorieking. com. Some caffeinated beverages contain 400–500 calories, especially if you get the large sizes.

Caffeinated sodas and teas also have notable levels of caffeine, and so they could affect sensitive people. Unfortunately for people with a sweet tooth, chocolate has significant levels of caffeine as well. An 8-ounce cup of coffee has between 80 and 170 mg of caffeine (with the average being around 130 mg), and 1 ounce of dark chocolate has 20 mg of caffeine.[20] Thus, if you eat a 3-ounce bar of dark chocolate, it is the equivalent of drinking half a cup of coffee. Being a chocolate lover myself, I have never been able to (nor did I want to) eliminate chocolate from my life; however, I do try to avoid eating chocolate (especially dark chocolate) close to bedtime, and I also combine it with other foods to decrease the rate at which it gets absorbed into my bloodstream. Dark chocolate is believed to have cardiovascular benefits, so consuming dark chocolate in small quantities could be beneficial.[21-23] Candy bars, however, have high concentrations of fat and sugar and can lead to jitteriness when consumed by themselves. Feelings of lightheadedness and anxiety might fool you into thinking that you are craving sweets, but they are actually indicators that your blood-glucose level is not balanced. If you begin feeling drowsy or irritated, consider a healthy snack before grabbing a pastry or another cup of coffee. Remember that a diet that is good for your brain is also healthy for your body, and it can help you stay in shape.

NURTURE YOUR MIND AND BODY

With all of the commitments in graduate school, it might seem difficult to eat healthy foods on a consistent basis. Fortunately, a healthy diet does not need to be complicated or expensive. Just remember the following simple principles:

- You can achieve steady blood-glucose levels by eating mixed meals that are balanced in terms of healthy proteins, fats, and unprocessed carbohydrates.
- Consuming fruits, vegetables, and whole grains as part of your mixed meals will satiate you for longer than eating processed carbohydrates, because they contain more fiber. Aim for 10 grams of fiber in the morning, 10 grams in afternoon and 10 grams in the evening.
- Select low-fat sources of protein, such as lean meats, poultry, fish, soy, low-fat dairy and legumes.
- Choose healthy fats from plant sources and fish.
- Eating high-fiber meals will keep you satiated for longer periods of time. Stock up on nutritious foods and prepare snacks ahead of time, so that you do not need to rely on vending machines and convenience stores.
- Sugary drinks are high in calories, and will not quench your thirst as well as water.
- If you want to eliminate caffeine, reduce your consumption gradually to avoid unpleasant withdrawal symptoms.

In the next section, I list some ideas for monthly and weekly shopping lists, so that you will always have access to nutritious foods.

Shopping list ideas
If you know that you will not have time to shop for a while consider buying foods that will keep for over a month:

- Frozen vegetables and fruits (aim for flash-frozen)
- Dried fruit
- Canned fruits (in juice rather than syrup), vegetables, and beans
- Fruit and vegetable juices (also consider the small containers you can bring with you for lunch)
- Low-fat cheeses, such as sliced mozzarella

- Hummus
- Peanut butter
- Chopped nuts
- High-fiber cereal
- High-fiber cereal bars
- Instant oatmeal without sugar (also consider the individual packets you can prepare at work)
- Frozen entrées that are high in protein and low in fat (check the nutrition label for total calorie content, as well as breakdowns of fats, proteins and carbohydrates)
- Lean cuts of meat, poultry or fish that you can freeze
- Tofu (sometimes you can buy it pre-sliced and pre-marinated)
- Canned fish, such as tuna or salmon
- Canned beans
- Dried beans and lentils
- Whole wheat pasta
- Brown rice

Each time you shop, look for fresh foods such as:

- Fresh fruits
- Fresh vegetables
- Pre-washed and pre-cut fruits and vegetables (usually more expensive than whole fruits and vegetables, but you might be more likely to eat them)
- Low-fat dairy products, such as milk, yogurt and cottage cheese
- Lean cold cuts such as turkey, chicken breast and ham
- Whole wheat bread with at least 3 grams of fiber per slice (bread will keep longer in the refrigerator, and even longer in the freezer)

Challenge #3: Preventing and alleviating repetitive strain injury (RSI)

Have you ever felt back pain, tense shoulders or fatigued arms after typing for a long time? I was experiencing these symptoms for years before I was diagnosed with RSI. Now I realize that had I recognized my body symptoms earlier, I could have avoided injury to my hands and arms.

I will never forget the day I was diagnosed with RSI. I woke up at my usual time of 5:30 a.m., to get ready for my workout with the MIT Masters Swim Club. I limped across my apartment in a morning daze to prepare my breakfast. As I poured corn flakes into my bowl, I sensed a sharp pain in my right elbow. This pain was not a surprise, because I had already been sensing some discomfort in my arm for a couple of weeks. I suspected that I was typing too much, but I was hoping that the pain would subside within a few days. As I looked at my elbows, however, a sense of panic went through my body. Both of my elbows, particularly the right one, were swollen and extremely sensitive to even the slightest touch. Needless to say, I skipped my workout that morning and scheduled an appointment with a doctor. Thus began my journey with RSI, an experience that not only transformed the way that I type, but also forced me to become more organized and efficient.

What is RSI, and who is at risk? RSI is a blanket term for injuries resulting from repetitive motion. The term "RSI" refers most commonly to injury of the hands, arms, and shoulders that can result from excessive typing, pipetting, playing an instrument or participating in certain sports. In its worst form, RSI can prevent you from typing, writing by hand, drawing, cooking or any other activity that involves your hands. With proper therapy, you can usually restore function to your hands, but injury could recur if you do not pay attention to early signs of discomfort. Carpal tunnel is the most well-known type of RSI, but this condition is relatively rare among computer users. Most former graduate students who developed RSI suffered from tendonitis (inflammation of the tendons), particularly in their elbows.

During graduate school, I attended a support group for RSI. I had been told previously that I had a high chance of suffering from RSI, because I was a small-boned woman. The audience at the support group suggested otherwise. About half of the participants were male, and many of the women were also taller than average. Two of the men, in fact, were quite muscular, and probably taller than 6' 2". Unfortunately, both of them were unemployed, on account of RSI caused by excessive typing. One of the women was a housewife, but her RSI worsened to the extent that she had trouble doing chores. Her arms hurt while lifting the laundry basket, and she felt pain when playing with her children. RSI is a condition where prevention is infinitely better than treatment; if you are feeling pain in your arms, you might have already been injured. The good news is that with a little bit of attention, this injury can be prevented.

In this section, I will share with you some strategies for preventing and recovering from this devastating condition. Fortunately—or perhaps unfortunately—there is a lot of information about RSI, because so many people have suffered from it. If you experience any discomfort while typing, I urge you to see a doctor and revise the set-up of your computer and workspace. If you feel no discomfort at your workspace make sure it stays that way, by paying attention to your posture at the computer. Later in this chapter I will give suggestions for setting up a proper station. RSI has few warning signs and even if you are not experiencing discomfort you might be tensing your wrists and shoulders. Therefore, it is essential to stay aware of your posture and your comfort during typing.

Proper ergonomics of typing

Though it may not seem like it, typing is exercise. Each keystroke requires minimal effort, but each day you probably type hundreds or maybe even thousands of characters. It all adds up. (One page of double-spaced text is 250 words, which is more than 1,000 characters.) Just as you maintain proper posture while exercising, you also need to pay attention to your alignment when you type.

I was recently approached by my friend, Michelle, who began exhibiting some typical symptoms of RSI. Michelle noticed a dull pain in both of her forearms, which was exacerbated by typing, yoga and even biking (due to the pressure from holding onto handlebars). When I looked at her workspace and her posture during typing, I noticed that she had made many common mistakes, which I will discuss below. I will show you how you can correct your posture and typing habits in this chapter, but you should always discuss your program for recovery (or prevention) with a health professional. Michelle, for example, had a wrist injury, and she suspected that improper healing could have also contributed to her pain; therefore, her recovery program included exercises to ensure proper healing of her wrist. Only a doctor can decide what the best treatment is for you. There are, however, universal precautions that can be practiced during typing that will help prevent injury to your arms.

NURTURE YOUR MIND AND BODY

When I examined Michelle's desk, I noticed that there were several problems with her set-up. First, her keyboard was towards the middle of her desk, so she had to lean forward to type. Her keyboard was also propped at an angle, so her wrists were hyper-extended, restricting blood flow to her arms. Another problem was that her chair was too low, so she had to hunch her shoulders up towards her ears so she could reach the keyboard. Furthermore, her monitor was flat on her desk, and she had to bend her head downwards to read it (see FIGURE 4-1).

Be proactive about preventing RSI: Set up a comfortable workspace where you can work for long periods of time.

Michelle felt overwhelmed with suggestions while I critiqued her set-up, but I told her that by keeping just two main points in mind, she

Figure 4-1: Incorrect body posture in front of computer. Notice the following strains on the body: a hunched posture with the head forward, a hyperextended wrist, reaching far for the keyboard, and putting the weight on the toes, rather than on the full feet.

Challenge #3: Preventing and alleviating repetitive strain injury (RSI)   145

would significantly reduce tension in her body: 1) maintain a healthy posture and 2) keep everything (keyboard, mouse, pen, etc.) as close to her body as possible. Most of us have seen a picture of how to set up an ergonomic workstation, as shown in FIGURE 4-2. Whether you are reading, writing by hand or typing, always keep your feet flat on the floor. Some physical therapists suggest crossing the feet at the ankles in case you do want to cross them, but keeping your feet flat on the floor will give you the best posture. Also remember to have your back flat against the chair and the *top* of your monitor at eye level. As you read the text on your screen, your head should be either straight ahead or slightly tilted down. Michelle was able to adjust the height of her monitor by putting it on top of some books. To keep your arms and wrist relaxed, position the height of your chair so that your arms and wrists are horizontal (or bent slightly *downwards*), rather than bent

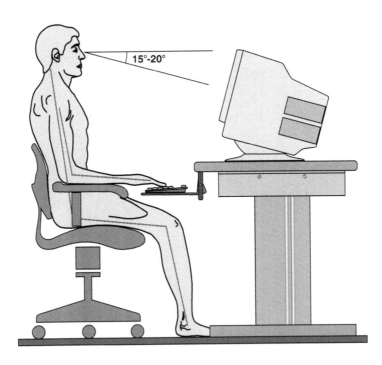

15°-20°

Figure 4-2: Correct body posture in front of computer. This person has a straight back against the chair and the monitor is placed such that the user does not need to strain their neck. Furthermore, the elbows are kept close to the body and the feet are flat on the floor.

NURTURE YOUR MIND AND BODY

upwards. You probably spend a lot of time sitting, so invest in a chair appropriate for your body type. If you are tall, for example, you might want a chair with a high backrest. Conversely, small people might be more comfortable in chairs with shorter seats, so they can bend their knees properly. I tried out several chairs in an office furniture store, and I just *felt* it, when I found the right one. Make sure the height is easily adjustable, because you might prefer a different height for typing than for writing by hand. It is usually not possible to change the height of your desk, although there are some tables (found in computer clusters, for example) where you can raise or lower workstations with the push of a button. These tables are very expensive, however, so I invested in a table where the height could be adjusted upon assembly, and since I am the only person using it, the height does not need to be readjusted. (See the appendix for places where you can purchase ergonomic chairs and tables.)

Laptops, unfortunately, are difficult to set up ergonomically, and I believe that my RSI worsened when I began typing on a laptop. One option for using a laptop comfortably is to attach a keyboard drawer to the bottom of your desk. This way, your laptop will serve as a monitor (and you can stack it on a couple of books until it is at eye level) and you can have a separate keyboard and mouse at the right height underneath your desk. If you have RSI, it can be a burden on your hands and wrists to carry around a laptop. I decided to invest in a desktop system for my home and my work. I was sad to see my laptop go, but I realized that I could transfer files easily between the two computers. It is a personal choice whether or not to use a laptop, but I found that the risks outweighed the benefits for anyone who has a high chance of developing RSI.

 If you must use a laptop, set it up ergonomically by attaching a separate keyboard and mouse to help you stay upright.

Another challenge for people suffering from RSI is to use shared computers. You might need to type on a computer attached to an instrument, or do research on a library computer. Even if you have some symptoms of RSI, you might not feel pain in these cases, because you will not need to type on shared computers for extended periods of time. Remember to try to work in as ergonomic a posture as the workstation will allow, and to take a break as soon as you feel tension. If you need to use a shared computer on a regular basis, think about alternative options. Can you transfer files from a shared computer to your own? Is there special software that you could purchase for your computer? Once you have developed RSI, the university might provide you with additional funding to set up an ergonomic workstation and buy necessary software, thereby preventing further injury.

Warning signs of RSI: How do you know you have it?

RSI is a frustrating condition, because it is difficult to assess how much you have injured yourself until you are experiencing significant pain. There are, however, early signs of this condition; if you pay attention to them, you will not only prevent RSI but you will also improve the quality of your work. According to Emil Pascarelli and Deborah Quilter, authors of *Repetitive Strain Injury*, warning signs of RSI include the following sensations in the hands and arms: pain, fatigue, lack of endurance, weakness, tingling, numbness or loss of sensation, heaviness, clumsiness, stiffness, lack of control or coordination, heightened awareness, hypersensitivity and coldness. Not surprisingly, these symptoms can worsen during times of stress, because you might hold more tension in your body. A graduate student who is writing a thesis is at high risk of developing RSI, because he or she is typing a lot, sometimes for 10–12 hours a day. In addition, graduate students might be experiencing more stress than usual, due to concerns of finishing their theses by a certain deadline. Even if you have not developed RSI, it is essential to pay attention to how you sit in front of the computer and whether you experience any discomfort. During severe stress, a mild backache or pain in your hands can quickly aggravate into a more serious condition, which could prevent you, for weeks, from typing. If you are unsure of whether you have developed RSI, see your doctor. The best-case scenario is that you do not have RSI, but your doctor will likely suggest some stretches that you can do at your desk to keep your muscles healthy.

 Contact your primary care physician if you begin experiencing fatigue, pain, numbness or tingling in your hands or arms. RSI can quickly deteriorate into a debilitating condition.

NURTURE YOUR MIND AND BODY

Interestingly, many of the Ph.D.s I interviewed had not suffered from RSI, but still experienced tension in their backs, necks and shoulders. They felt uncomfortable while typing, and had to take anti-inflammatory drugs to relieve pain. For Kelly, a biochemist, the pain was so severe that she sometimes woke up in the middle of the night with excruciating backaches. "I was very stressed about some personal issues, and I also had to submit a thesis proposal at the same time. I probably did not have good posture in front of the computer, and I was likely tensing my whole body while typing." Kelly actually visited her orthopedist, who suggested a variety of stretches during her typing breaks. "The stretches encouraged me to take breaks from typing and release tension in my body. My back pain has become much less frequent since I started paying attention to it." Fortunately for Kelly, the symptoms improved when the stressful periods were over.

For others, tension in their backs, shoulders and necks were warning signs of future development of RSI. Lance, a chemist, struggled with back pain during graduate school, but developed RSI only after he started his job. Amber, a geologist, did not develop RSI, but she noticed that her eyesight worsened from excessive computer use. It is important to recognize deteriorating eyesight, because if you cannot properly see the screen, you might tense your neck and shoulders, and possibly develop RSI from typing in this awkward position.

 Extended hours in front of the computer can deteriorate your eyesight, and lead to an awkward posture as you strain to see the screen.

Healing yourself from RSI

The road to recovery from RSI is a bumpy one. If I had to plot my pain as a function of time during my recovery, it would not be a straight line going downwards; instead, the plot would move in a general downward direction, but with several relapses along the way. Thus, it is very difficult to assess how much progress you have made. What makes the recovery process even more challenging is that you need to wait for the acute inflammation to subside before beginning physical therapy. Relapses can be frustrating, because you might suddenly feel pain, even after paying attention to your posture and limiting your time at the computer. If your hands or arms hurt, it does not mean that you have to start your recovery program from the beginning. You might have injured yourself on a particular day (e.g., typed too long, did not take a break, lifted a heavy object or twisted a hard-to-open jar of spaghetti sauce); if you take a rest, however, your arms might feel better the next day.

 If you have RSI, be patient about your recovery. There will be many bumps along the way, but with proper treatment, most people recover from this condition.

There are several types of RSI, such as carpal tunnel, bursitis, tendonitis and Raynaud's disease. There is also an injury called cervical radiculopathy, which is caused by holding a phone between your head and shoulder. Staying in this uncomfortable position for long can compress disks in your neck, and cause pain as you move your neck. (Although I never developed this type of injury, I always use a headset if I need to be on the phone for an extended period of time.) Only the doctor can make a proper diagnosis regarding your condition; *your* job is to recognize early warning signs and seek help when necessary.

 If you experience a relapse in your recovery, it does not mean you are back to square one, or that your arms will hurt again the following day. Continue with your stretching program and typing breaks, and remain in an ergonomic posture while typing.

When I developed RSI, I did not know what I needed to do to recover. I followed the traditional path of taking anti-inflammatory medications, doing stretches and icing the inflamed areas. Unfortunately, the pain in my arms persisted despite physical therapy, acupuncture, massage and yoga. I was fortunate, however, to live in a community were I had the opportunity to learn about alternative therapies for RSI. Stress, for example, is one of the leading risk factors for RSI, and regular relaxation is one of the most powerful therapies for relieving muscular tension. In the previous section, I described how relaxation can alleviate habitual worrying; here, I am emphasizing the importance of relaxation as a way of preventing or treating tension in your body. You can practice relaxation in meditation and yoga classes while listening to

NURTURE YOUR MIND AND BODY

music, or during relaxing activities such as dancing or eating dinner with your friends. During relaxation, people experience warm sensations in their bodies, particularly in their backs, hands, arms and shoulders. These warm sensations are signs of increased blood circulation, which will encourage the healing process.

Another common therapy for RSI is strength training. In fact, many physical therapy exercises involve small weights, to strengthen the wrists and shoulders. One gentleman from my support group even picked up weightlifting as a serious sport during his recovery from RSI. It is important, however, not to lift too much, because that can re-injure you and perhaps render you in a worse condition than you were before. If you do decide to try weightlifting, begin by using the small weights suggested by your therapist. With the aid of a personal trainer, you can gradually move on to slightly heavier weights and other types of exercises, to strengthen your back, legs and core abdominal muscles. While doing weightlifting, my focus was usually not how much I could lift, but to exercise the major muscle groups so that I could increase circulation in my body and improve my posture. My friend Marianne, who was also struggling with RSI, did not have access to a weight room, but she found that her RSI symptoms improved from simple household tasks such as cleaning out closets and rearranging bookshelves, which were activities that helped her exercise her arms without straining the muscles.

 Exercise on a regular basis (3–5 times a week) to strengthen your body and relax your mind. The time invested in exercising has a high return in terms of keeping you healthy, energetic and relaxed.

People with RSI frequently find relief through aerobic exercises, because they are simultaneously relaxing and increasing circulation in their bodies. Ask your therapist whether you are ready for aerobic activity, because what helps some people can actually re-injure others. Yoga, for example, has helped me stretch my muscles, but others have hurt their wrists while doing strenuous poses. If you have a good yoga teacher, he or she can help you to get into the correct pose, and even suggest modifications to lessen burdens on your wrists and shoulders. Swimming can also be therapeutic, because it stretches out your back and arms, but some competitive swimmers develop RSI in their shoulders from their strenuous training program.

 Reach out to as many resources as you can, to recover from RSI: personal physicians, orthopedists, physical therapists, acupuncturists, massage therapists, RSI support groups, and Feldenkrais and Alexander technique practitioners.

A less well-known type of therapy that has helped many people recover from injury is the Feldenkrais method. The Feldenkrais method was named after its founder, Moshe Feldenkrais, a nuclear physicist in Israel. During the 1940s, Feldenkrais had an accident that left him unable to walk. Determined not to let this injury disable him, he developed a method by which we learn new ways to use our bodies and decrease tension. Feldenkrais is unlike any other type of exercise. Rather than pushing you to work your body to its limits, this method trains you to pay attention to yourself and to decrease unnecessary effort. Once I began practicing Feldenkrais on a regular basis, I noticed positive changes in my posture and in the way I sit at my desk. I also realized how often I tense my muscles unnecessarily and how frequently I hold my breath when I am nervous.

I was initially attracted to Feldenkrais because the practitioner in my area learned this method to overcome his own RSI. (You can find practitioners in your area by using the references I list in the appendix.) Feldenkrais can be time-consuming and expensive, but I have saved money by practicing Feldenkrais in my own home using CDs from Feldenkrais resource centers (see the appendix). It would be beneficial, however, to do these exercises initially with a practitioner, to learn how to pay attention to your body.

Another method, which is similar to the Feldenkrais method, is the Alexander technique. F.M. Alexander was a Shakespearean orator who developed chronic laryngitis. He was able to cure himself of this condition by observing himself in a mirror and noting where he was carrying unnecessary tension in his body. His method has helped others, including those with RSI, to change the way they carry themselves and overcome pain. (See the appendix for resources.)

If you choose to pursue any non-traditional routes for recovery, make sure that you keep in touch with your physical therapist.

NURTURE YOUR MIND AND BODY

Although most non-traditional therapies are not covered by insurance, physical therapists are usually familiar with them and can give you references. Once the acute inflammation subsides, massage can also be helpful for relieving tension and increasing circulation to your muscles. It is very important, however, that you find a trained therapist to perform the massage, and your physical therapist or doctor can probably refer you to someone appropriate.

Ergonomic typing and pipetting aids

Many manufacturers claim to have developed ergonomic keyboards and computer mice, but the only way to know whether they are right for you is to try them out. (See the appendix for resources on ergonomic devices.) It usually takes at least a few days to determine whether a device is appropriate for you. A person with small hands would probably prefer a small mouse or keyboard, whereas someone with a larger build may be more comfortable with a larger keyboard. Some universities have offices that lend ergonomic keyboards and mice; if you do not have access to such a facility, make sure that you keep all the necessary documentation and packaging, so that you can return your devices if they are not comfortable.

Lauren, a geology student, experienced significant pain in her hands and arms while writing her dissertation. "We didn't have a lot of money, so I had a very small and crowded desk. I had to turn my head to the left to look at my monitor while typing, and I had very poor posture. At my new job, they purchased me a nice desk and I am set up ergonomically. I no longer experience symptoms of RSI." Jonathan, a chemical engineering major, commented that his university was very proactive about preventing RSI. "Most of our work consisted of modeling and programming, so we had an ergonomically set up computer cluster. We typed for many hours a day, but I do not think anybody suffered from RSI."

 Regardless of whether you have developed RSI, experiment with different keyboards and mice to make sure that you can be comfortable at your workspace.

Voice-activated software has come a long way since it was first developed. In order to lessen the amount of typing I had to do, I tried a few different types of software (see the appendix for resources) and was generally satisfied with the results. Once you have trained the software, the recognition is quite accurate; you can also train the software to understand scientific terminology. There is a learning curve at the beginning, but if you are unable to type, it might be the only way to write your thesis. After you learn the software, you might even be able to write faster by dictating than typing. Voice-activated software can also be used to surf the Internet and to work in Excel. Some people find it difficult to rely exclusively on voice-activated software. You can use the software if you need to type text for long periods of time, but sometimes it is easier to do the editing manually. You can save yourself time if you familiarize yourself thoroughly with the manual before you begin using the software. The programs today have more features than one would expect, and there are also ways to increase the speed and the accuracy of the text generation. (I talk more about writing your dissertation with voice-activated software later, in chapter six.)

If you decide to continue typing, the best strategy is to work for short periods of time, because you might only feel the pain after you take a break. Your goal should be to stop typing before you feel any discomfort. I began my recovery program by limiting my typing to 30 minutes a day, and only a few minutes at a time. I typed only a few paragraphs every day, but most of what I wrote made it to the final version of my thesis. In other words, this condition forced me to become more organized before I sat down at the computer, and I no longer allowed myself to become distracted by e-mails or the Internet.

 Limiting your time at the computer can make you more productive by forcing you to focus on your work, rather than becoming distracted by e-mails, the Internet or instant messaging.

If you are in a biology- or chemistry-based laboratory, you probably need to pipette to complete your experimental work. Repetitive pipetting does not always lead to RSI, but some people do injure their arms, hands and fingers. "My thumbs hurt a lot when I pipetted," said Dave, a chemist. "I convinced my postdoctoral advisor to purchase electric pipettes, so I would no longer feel pain." Elisa, a biology major, also experienced significant pain while finishing her dissertation. "My

NURTURE YOUR MIND AND BODY

lab purchased a set of ergonomic pipettes, and now I am much more comfortable doing experiments. I don't think they are that much more expensive than regular pipettes, so I recommend them to people whose hands hurt." (See the appendix for resources to purchase ergonomic pipettes.) If you do not have access to more ergonomic pipettes, you can still decrease strain on your arms by working in a comfortable position (e.g., sitting rather than standing for long periods of time) and taking frequent breaks. You can further reduce tension in your body by holding the pipettes close to your body (i.e., keep the elbow of your pipetting arm near your waist).

 If you experience pain while pipetting, switch to ergonomic pipettes, take frequent breaks, and keep the pipettes close to your body as you work.

Manuel, an electrical engineer, typed for many hours a day, but typing was not the reason he developed RSI. He worked in a laboratory and strained his forearms by pulling apart and twisting optical tubes on a daily basis. Manuel was able to prevent a more serious condition by recognizing mild pain and taking a break from work when his arms began to ache. He also tried to be more ergonomic by using his larger muscles, to lessen the strain on his forearms. Furthermore, he noticed that when he cut down on typing, he decreased the overall strain on his arms, and he experienced less pain from his laboratory work.

 Laboratory work, especially if it requires repetitive twisting and wrenching, can lead to pain in your arms and hands. A good way to relieve discomfort is to take frequent breaks and to lessen strain on your arms by cutting down on typing.

How to optimize your typing breaks

It is easy to tell ourselves that we will take a break every 15 to 20 minutes; it is much harder to actually stick to this schedule. Most of the time, we are so immersed in what we are doing, that we either forget to take a break or we do not want to. It is essential to take breaks, however, because you might not feel pain until you have stopped typing (sometimes just hours later). Therefore, instead of relying on your memory, you can set up break-timer software, which has the following advantages (see the appendix for resources):

- The software can be programmed to remind you of a predetermined break schedule (typically every 10 to 15 minutes), and you can also choose the length of the breaks (for example, two minutes). Sometimes you can also enable a "micro break" feature, usually every 5 minutes for 10 seconds, to remind you to release tension from your body as you work.
- Some programs will suggest stretches, to help you increase circulation in your fingers, wrists, arms and legs. For some of the stretches, you will need to stand up (which is a good idea every 15 minutes anyway); they will help you decompress your back. You should not feel self-conscious if you need to stretch in a shared office. When I opened up about my injury, I was amazed at how many other people also felt discomfort while typing. Many of the stretches are also discreet, and your office mates will not even know you are taking a typing break. Do not feel compelled to follow the stretches suggested by your software. Use the exercises recommended by your therapists or any other stretches that are comfortable.
- Your break schedule depends upon mouse and keyboard usage rather than clock time. During my recovery, I had to be very careful not to exceed a certain amount of computer usage each day. Sometimes I sat in front of the monitor for many hours proofreading my work and planning my thesis, but the actual time spent typing was very limited. Thus, you can use the software to track how long you typed each day.
- During the breaks, your keyboard and mouse will be disabled, although you do have the option of skipping the breaks. If you suffer from RSI, do not postpone the breaks. I found that the most important components in my recovery from RSI were: 1) taking regular breaks, 2) maintaining proper ergonomics while typing and 3) standing up and stretching every 15 minutes.

 Take regular typing breaks, because you might not feel pain until a few minutes or even hours after you have stopped typing.

Overcoming the psychological aspects of RSI: Kurt's story

Kurt, an electrical engineer, suffered from RSI during the completion of his Ph.D. thesis. He attributes the development of his symptoms to excessive typing, strenuous lab work with his hands and stress from personal issues. "It took a long time to overcome this condition. I sought help from doctors, physical therapists and acupuncturists, and I also reorganized my workspace to be more ergonomic. All of these changes helped me, but the most difficult part of my recovery was to overcome the psychological aspects of this condition. Some days I would walk to the lab and my hands began hurting, even before I entered the door. That's when I understood how much my general stress level must have contributed to my pain." Kurt's observation was not unique. Several others at my RSI support group also seemed to experience pain at the mere thought of work. One strategy that worked for some people was to practice relaxation techniques when the pain ensued. In other words, some RSI sufferers were able to relieve their pain by slowing down their breathing and consciously relaxing different parts of their bodies. "I think stress contributed significantly to my RSI," commented Kurt. "Now that I am out of graduate school, I only have transient symptoms, which are easier to manage."

CHAPTER SUMMARY AND ACTION PLAN

Nurture your mind and body

Step 1: Overcome your worries:
- Define what you are worried about and how you would like the problem(s) to be resolved.
- Set aside a few hours every week to socialize with friends and pursue hobbies.
- If you have trouble sleeping, practice relaxation on a regular basis—especially in the evenings.
- If you notice excessive anxiety or tension in your body during the day, take a break for a few minutes to determine what is really bothering you.

- Do not get discouraged if you experience self-doubt about your ability to earn a Ph.D. These are normal thoughts for many doctoral students. If you cannot resolve thesis problems on your own, discuss them with your advisor and committee members as soon as possible.
- Do not try to construct the perfect thesis or research project; it is more important to keep working and to make informed decisions along the way.
- Indulge yourself in small luxuries on a regular basis, as a way to appreciate yourself.
- If your feelings of anxiety or depression become overwhelming, contact your doctor immediately.

Step 2: Fuel your brain through your diet.
- Consume "complex" meals and snacks, which are comprised of healthy proteins, fats and carbohydrates.
- Eat fruits, vegetables and whole grains instead of white breads and pasta as your carbohydrate sources.
- Choose healthy fats from plant and fish sources, and try to limit your fat consumption to no more than 30% of your daily calorie intake.
- Include low-fat protein sources in your diet, such as lean cuts of meat, poultry, fish, beans, soy and dairy products.
- Choose breads, cereals and cereal bars with a high fiber content, to keep you satiated for longer.
- Limit your intake of sugary drinks or dilute them with water or seltzer to quench your thirst.
- Reduce or eliminate caffeine if you experience insomnia or anxiety.

Step 3: Prevent or alleviate RSI.
- Invest time and money (if necessary) to set up an ergonomic workspace. See the appendix for resources on ergonomic devices.
- Pay attention to your posture during typing and place frequently accessed objects close to your body.
- See your doctor if you experience chronic tension in your body or notice sharp pains in your arms, hands or shoulders.

- If you have already developed RSI, be patient with your recovery, as there may be many small relapses along the way.
- Discuss alternative therapies, if necessary, with your doctor (e.g., acupuncture, massage, yoga and Feldenkrais or Alexander techniques).

Reference List

1. Benton,D., Owens,D.S., and Parker,P.Y. (1994) Blood glucose influences memory and attention in young adults. *Neuropsychologia*, **32**, 595-607.

2. Benton,D., Ruffin,M.P., Lassel,T., Nabb,S., Messaoudi,M., Vinoy,S., Desor,D., and Lang,V. (2003) The delivery rate of dietary carbohydrates affects cognitive performance in both rats and humans. *Psychopharmacology (Berl)*, **166**, 86-90.

3. Owens,D.S. and Benton,D. (1994) The impact of raising blood glucose on reaction times. *Neuropsychobiology*, **30**, 106-113.

4. Holt,S.H., Delargy,H.J., Lawton,C.L., and Blundell,J.E. (1999) The effects of high-carbohydrate vs high-fat breakfasts on feelings of fullness and alertness, and subsequent food intake. *Int.J.Food Sci. Nutr.*, **50**, 13-28.

5. Lester,G.E., Hodges,D.M., Meyer,R.D., and Munro,K.D. (2004) Pre-extraction preparation (fresh, frozen, freeze-dried, or acetone powdered) and long-term storage of fruit and vegetable tissues: effects on antioxidant enzyme activity. *J.Agric.Food Chem.*, **52**, 2167-2173.

6. Mullen,W., Stewart,A.J., Lean,M.E., Gardner,P., Duthie,G.G., and Crozier,A. (2002) Effect of freezing and storage on the phenolics, ellagitannins, flavonoids, and antioxidant capacity of red raspberries. *J.Agric.Food Chem.*, **50**, 5197-5201.

7. Agte,V., Tarwadi,K., Mengale,S., Hinge,A., and Chiplonkar,S. (2002) Vitamin profile of cooked foods: how healthy is the practice of ready-to-eat foods? *Int.J.Food Sci.Nutr.*, **53**, 197-208.

8. Veda,S., Kamath,A., Platel,K., Begum,K., and Srinivasan,K. (2006) Determination of bioaccessibility of beta-carotene in vegetables by in vitro methods. *Mol.Nutr.Food Res.*, **50**, 1047-1052.

9. Unlu,N.Z., Bohn,T., Francis,D., Clinton,S.K., and Schwartz,S.J. (2007) Carotenoid absorption in humans consuming tomato sauces obtained from tangerine or high-beta-carotene varieties of tomatoes. *J.Agric.Food Chem.*, **55**, 1597-1603.

10. Lawton,C.L., Delargy,H.J., Smith,F.C., Hamilton,V., and Blundell,J.E. (1998) A medium-term intervention study on the impact of high- and low-fat snacks varying in sweetness and fat content: large shifts in daily fat intake but good compensation for daily energy intake. *Br.J.Nutr.*, **80**, 149-161.

11. Gartner,C., Stahl,W., and Sies,H. (1997) Lycopene is more bioavailable from tomato paste than from fresh tomatoes. *Am.J.Clin. Nutr.*, **66**, 116-122.

12. Hedren,E., Mulokozi,G., and Svanberg,U. (2002) In vitro accessibility of carotenes from green leafy vegetables cooked with sunflower oil or red palm oil. *Int.J.Food Sci.Nutr.*, **53**, 445-453.

13. Mulokozi,G., Hedren,E., and Svanberg,U. (2004) In vitro accessibility and intake of beta-carotene from cooked green leafy vegetables and their estimated contribution to vitamin A requirements. *Plant Foods Hum.Nutr.*, **59**, 1-9.

14. Sigman-Grant,M., Warland,R., and Hsieh,G. (2003) Selected lower-fat foods positively impact nutrient quality in diets of free-living Americans. *J.Am.Diet.Assoc.*, **103**, 570-576.

15. Ledikwe,J.H., Blanck,H.M., Khan,L.K., Serdula,M.K., Seymour,J.D., Tohill,B.C., and Rolls,B.J. (2006) Low-energy-

density diets are associated with high diet quality in adults in the United States. *J.Am.Diet.Assoc.*, **106**, 1172-1180.

16. Ledikwe,J.H., Blanck,H.M., Kettel,K.L., Serdula,M.K., Seymour,J.D., Tohill,B.C., and Rolls,B.J. (2006) Dietary energy density is associated with energy intake and weight status in US adults. *Am.J.Clin.Nutr.*, **83**, 1362-1368.

17. Stubbs,R.J., van Wyk,M.C., Johnstone,A.M., and Harbron,C.G. (1996) Breakfasts high in protein, fat or carbohydrate: effect on within-day appetite and energy balance. *Eur.J.Clin.Nutr.*, **50**, 409-417.

18. Cotton,J.R., Burley,V.J., Weststrate,J.A., and Blundell,J.E. (2007) Dietary fat and appetite: similarities and differences in the satiating effect of meals supplemented with either fat or carbohydrate. *J.Hum.Nutr.Diet.*, **20**, 186-199.

19. Kanarek,R.B. and Swinney,D. (1990) Effects of food snacks on cognitive performance in male college students. *Appetite*, **14**, 15-27.

20. Caffeine Content of Foods and Drugs (Access Date: June 2008). www.cspinet.org/new/cafchart.htm . 2007.
Ref Type: Electronic Citation

21. Keen,C.L. (2001) Chocolate: food as medicine/medicine as food. *J.Am.Coll.Nutr.*, **20**, 436S-439S.

22. Engler,M.B. and Engler,M.M. (2006) The emerging role of flavonoid-rich cocoa and chocolate in cardiovascular health and disease. *Nutr.Rev.*, **64**, 109-118.

23. Engler,M.B., Engler,M.M., Chen,C.Y., Malloy,M.J., Browne,A., Chiu,E.Y., Kwak,H.K., Milbury,P., Paul,S.M., Blumberg,J., and Mietus-Snyder,M.L. (2004) Flavonoid-rich dark chocolate improves endothelial function and increases plasma epicatechin concentrations in healthy adults. *J.Am.Coll.Nutr.*, **23**, 197-204.

CHAPTER 5:
MASTER YOUR PEOPLE SKILLS

"A sense of humor is part of the art of leadership, of getting along with
people, of getting things done."
Dwight Eisenhower, American president (1890–1969)

Angie, a chemist, had many arguments with her advisor regarding the direction of her thesis. To make matters worse, one of her committee members also had a strong opinion, and he frequently disagreed with the thesis advisor. During committee meetings, Angie found herself in the middle of heated discussions between her thesis advisor and the other professor. All she wanted was to finish her thesis, but she first had to resolve the conflicts that arose between her advisor and the other committee member. After one of her committee meetings, she made the following comment to her friends: "If I'm able to pull my thesis together, I should also get a Ph.D. in people skills." Frustrated with the lack of focus in her project, Angie wrote a proposal that addressed the issues that the professors were concerned about. She then approached them individually and explained how recent research in the literature supported her revised proposal. After the individual meetings, she incorporated the new comments from each professor and continued with her research. At her next committee meeting, the professors still argued, but she was more confident defending her proposal. Her committee finally agreed to her plan, and she completed her thesis on schedule. Angie found out the hard way that in order to graduate, she had to learn how to resolve conflicts at committee meetings.

Not surprisingly, one of the most popular pieces of advice from former graduate students was "Choose your advisor wisely." About half of the Ph.D.s I interviewed described their advisors as being excellent and supportive mentors. They set aside time to meet with their students, gave them constructive advice on their dissertations and helped them with the job-searching process. One-quarter of the Ph.D.s found it difficult to get along with their advisors and to reach agreements with them on research plans. The remaining one-quarter got along with their advisors personally, but complained about insufficient guidance. In this chapter, I will describe the invaluable people skills former graduate students learned in order to communicate effectively with their advisors and complete their projects.

If you believe you already have good people skills, consider the following questions:

- Are you intimidated by the thought of causing conflict?
- Do you always want to be right? If you disagree with someone, do you feel a need to prove them wrong?
- Are you uncomfortable with giving or receiving criticism?
- Do you get upset because you believe that you have been treated unfairly?
- Do you believe that some people are difficult (or outright jerks) on purpose?
- Do you spend a lot of time roaming over past conflicts, or being anxious about future encounters with a difficult person?

If you answered "yes" to any of the above questions, you have probably been frustrated by conflicts with other people. Our self-confidence is strongly influenced by both how we stand up for ourselves and the respect that we get from others. Effective people skills do not come naturally to most of us, and we usually have a tendency to be either too passive or too aggressive. Passive people like to please others and avoid conflict, while aggressive people are focused on achieving only their own goals, without consideration for other people's needs. A happy medium between these two extremes is called assertiveness. An assertive person is able to communicate their ideas confidently, without stepping on other people. In this chapter, I will show you how to:

- Communicate your ideas assertively
- Give and receive criticism confidently
- Build good relationships
- Deal with difficult people

Why do we need people skills in graduate school?

As most of us prepare for graduate school, we rarely think about the challenges of getting along with people. If your advisor and coworkers are easy to get along with, you will only need good research skills to complete your dissertation. Most students, however, encounter several obstacles along the way, which can be resolved only when they call upon their assertiveness skills. Many people acknowledge that their lives would be easier if they were more confident, but for Angie, assertiveness was *essential* for completing her dissertation. In order to graduate, Angie had to confidently defend her ideas, while incorporating suggestions from her advisor and committee. Assertiveness is not something that should be learned for its own sake, but because it will make your life easier in the long run. When you collaborate with someone, you want to make sure that the project is completed properly. If you fail to communicate your ideas effectively, the other person might not do his or her part correctly, and you might need to repeat the entire study. What if you could collaborate so effectively that the two of you could create a project that is *better* than what each one of you could have done alone?

Effective people skills are not only important in graduate school, but they are also a vital component of your contribution to the workplace. Whether you go to a company and work in a team to bring a product to market, or follow an academic path and collaborate with other professors, you will find that assertive behavior will help you achieve your goals and gain respect from other people. Once you learn the principles of assertiveness, you can apply them to school, work, or getting along with friends and family members. Remember that you cannot control how other people behave; you can only control your own attitude towards that behavior. If you change yourself, you will be amazed at the positive changes in your relationships with those around you.

 Do not be afraid to express your ideas assertively to your advisor and thesis committee.

Challenge #1: Learning assertive communication

Communicating your ideas effectively with the three-step method
Assertive behavior is the foundation of effective communication. Through assertive communication, you will be able to voice your

opinions confidently and negotiate with others to achieve mutually beneficial goals. Easier said than done?

Dale Carnegie, whom I mentioned in the previous chapter, was one of the first people to study the principles of human interactions. Interestingly, the strategies described by the Dale Carnegie training session called "The Five Essential People Skills" are very similar to the suggestions of former graduate students. Ph.D.s who got along with their advisors attributed their success to being able to focus on solving problems, rather than on emotions. In order to communicate your ideas assertively, consider the following three-step method:

1. State the facts. Make sure that you do not let personal feelings get in the way of research. Focus only on work-related issues, and state the objective reality that concerns you.
2. Clarify your thoughts about the situation and why it bothers you. Are you concerned that the project is not being completed properly? Is it taking too long? Is it too expensive? Is it difficult to get along with someone on the project?
3. Explain what your goals are and how you would like the situation to be resolved. Before the meeting, draft a plan that will be beneficial to everyone. If you cannot accommodate everybody, what plan do you think makes the most sense?

CASE A: DISAGREEING ON A RESEARCH PROJECT

Let me illustrate this three-step method with an example. Assume that your advisor is asking you to complete a project that you find burdensome. If you are a passive person, you might decide to say nothing and do the task while feeling bitter. Conversely, if you are an aggressive person, you might storm into your advisor's office angrily and tell him that it would be a waste of time for you to work on this project. As you can guess, neither of these approaches is ideal. In the first case, you might feel like you are being taken advantage of, and you will probably not get much out of doing the project. In the second scenario, you might anger your advisor and jeopardize your relationship with him. How can you communicate your disagreement without offending your advisor?

As an assertive person, you can express your ideas confidently, while being sensitive to the needs of others. At your next meeting, remind your advisor that he has asked you to do this project, and ask whether he has time to talk about it now. You should always begin every conversation on a positive note, either by sharing some good news about your research or thanking your advisor for taking a few minutes to meet with you.

 Begin each meeting on a positive note (e.g., thank your advisor for their time), and focus on reaching a mutual agreement.

You can apply the three-step assertiveness the following way.

1. State the facts.
   Example: "Thank you for setting aside time to meet with me. I wanted to talk to you about the project you asked me last week to do. Just to clarify, you want to develop a more sensitive method to analyze our samples, right?" (It is important to define the scope of the project first, to avoid misunderstandings later on.)

2. Clarify your thoughts about the situation and why it bothers you.
   Example: "I think that a more sensitive method would allow us to use less sample, but I just do not think our instruments are suitable for this purpose. You might remember that I tried to develop a new method last year, but after months of work, I was not able to get better results."

3. Explain what your goals are and how you would like the situation to be resolved.
   Example: "The way I see the situation, we have the following options. Professor Daniels downstairs has a newer instrument, and we could start a collaboration with her. My preference would actually be to focus on my other project, which we could easily do with our own equipment. In fact, I already have some preliminary data to show you...."

Even if you have good preliminary data, your advisor might be set on doing the unpleasant study that you are trying to avoid, but at least you have clarified your own goals. If your advisor insists that you do that project, spend a minute to visualize the possible benefits. Will this project teach you a new skill that might be useful in the future? Also try to see the situation from your advisor's point of view. This project might be very important to him or her, perhaps because it will bring in more funding. Frequently, if you agree to do a study just for your advisor's benefit, you will earn their respect and appreciation. At the end of this discussion, you might have been excused from the project or perhaps talked into it; either way, you will feel more confident because you had the courage to speak up and clarify your own goals.

 At the end of every meeting, summarize what you have agreed upon and how you will proceed with the project.

CASE B: ASKING FOR FUNDING FOR TRAVEL
Spending money on research and travel can also lead to disagreements between students and their advisors. In the scenario below, let us assume that your experimental results are inconsistent, and you would like to spend a week at another university to learn some specific research techniques from your collaborator.

1. State the facts.
   Example: "I wanted to meet with you to discuss my progress, particularly the details of my last study. Do you have a minute now?"

2. Clarify your thoughts about the situation and why it bothers you. Are you concerned that the project is not being completed properly? Is it taking too long? Is it too expensive? Is it difficult to get along with someone on the project?
   Example: "You probably know that I have been working on this project for a year now, but my data has not been reproducible. I have called our collaborators in Pennsylvania, and we went over the protocol, but my results are very different from theirs. For example, in my last study, my numbers were 50% higher than theirs..." (Show your data.)

3. Explain what your goals are and how you would like the situation to be resolved. Before the meeting, draft a plan that

MASTER YOUR PEOPLE SKILLS

will be beneficial to everyone. If you cannot accommodate everybody, what plan do you think makes the most sense? *Example*: "I think that the best solution would be for me to spend a week in Pennsylvania and to do the experiments with them. I might be missing a technical detail that is confounding our data. I know money is tight, and that this trip would be expensive. On the other hand, I think I have tried everything already, and I cannot figure out where our mistake is."

Remember that assertive people are able to convey their own ideas while also being sensitive to the needs of others. If at any point during this conversation your advisor interjects, listen and paraphrase what you heard. If he or she does not let you talk, interrupt with something like this: "I think your idea makes sense because..., but do you think we could get better results if we tried to...?" Let your advisor know that you understand his or her concerns. For example, you can say, "Yes, I understand that a cheaper solution would be to send our samples to them, rather than trying to analyze them on our own. However, I think we will have more samples soon, so in the long run, it would be more cost-effective if we analyzed them ourselves."

You can make this meeting more productive by doing some research in advance. For the above example, you can have an estimate of the cost of your trip. Show him or her that you have researched airfares and hotel prices, and ask whether he or she could afford this trip. At the end of the meeting, summarize what the two of you have agreed upon. For example: "Sure, I can call Professor Johnson one more time to go over my protocol. If we cannot find the mistake, I will call our travel office to see if they can find a better price for this trip. If we decide to go ahead with this, I would probably travel during the first week of March."

 Make meetings with your advisor more efficient by brainstorming about solutions in advance.

Giving and receiving criticism

Criticism is a sensitive subject for many people. You might be intimidated to criticize your advisor who has more experience than you, or you might not know how to receive criticism without feeling offended.

Some students screen out all the positive comments and focus only on negative feedback. The principles of giving and receiving criticism effectively are similar to the principles of assertive communication. How do you handle criticism professionally?

 Do not feel intimidated giving criticism to a superior, such as your advisor. Explain the problem succinctly, and offer alternatives. (See Case C below.)

Giving constructive criticism

Case C: Discussing corrections to a manuscript

Publishing manuscripts is a common source of disagreement between students and their advisors, and it is great practice for learning how to give and receive criticism. What data should we include? How do we correctly interpret this data? Where should we get this published? Is it really necessary to do all this data analysis? During your discussion, use the three-step method to resolve your conflict.

In this example, you recently submitted a manuscript to your advisor. You hope to send the manuscript for publication soon, but your advisor wants you to add another section—one that you think is beyond the scope of this study. You can use the three-step method to give constructive criticism to your advisor.

1. State the facts.
   Example: "Good morning, I just received your corrections to this manuscript. I had some questions about your comments; do you have a few minutes now?"

2. Clarify your thoughts about the situation and why it bothers you.
   Example: "I noticed that you wanted to add another section about our latest results. I think the new data is beyond the scope of this paper, and I am also not confident about these results yet."

3. Explain what your goals are and how you would like the situation to be resolved.

MASTER YOUR PEOPLE SKILLS

Example: "I think that we should wait until I have confirmed my results and collected more data on the new project. If the results are as interesting as we think they will be, we could include them in a new paper. This would also give me more time to analyze my results and see whether they are statistically significant."

You can also ask for feedback in step 3:
Example: "Why do you think we need to include these results in this paper? As we discussed, we will have another manuscript on the follow-up study. Do you think we can include my latest results in that paper?"

It is common for some students to get emotional, especially when they want to publish their first manuscript. In the above case, your advisor might insist that you include your new results, even if it means delaying the submission of your paper. You can try to dissuade him by letting him know how much longer it would take, or that you cannot be confident of your results until you repeat the study. Most likely, you will be able to reach a mutual agreement. Whichever the outcome, you can be confident that you communicated your ideas clearly. If you think that you have a particularly difficult advisor, skip ahead to the section entitled "How To Communicate Effectively With Difficult People."

If there is a disagreement, let your advisor talk first. He or she is more likely to listen to you if they already had a chance to express their opinions.

Receiving criticism professionally
CASE D: DISCUSSING A PUBLIC PRESENTATION
Many former students attributed improvements in their public-speaking skills to incorporating suggestions from advisors into their talks. Some advisors were tactful, and others were critical. In this example, you have just practiced a conference presentation with your supervisor, and you received a lot of criticism, both positive and negative.

Supervisor: "Well, I think your talk needs improvement. First, I think you give too much information. Your slides are crammed with data, your font size is too small and there is too much color on your diagrams. I liked your presentation style—you spoke clearly and confidently—but I think you went too fast to cover all your points adequately. You need to cut out some information, so that you can go at a more reasonable pace."

How can you respond to criticism professionally? First, do not screen out the positive comments. Your advisor liked your presentation style; he is just suggesting changes to the content. Nevertheless, the negative criticism might overwhelm you. You might have spent weeks practicing this talk, and with the conference just one week away, you are not sure you will have time to restructure your talk. In order to handle this criticism professionally, focus on one problem at a time. Your advisor's primary complaint was that you had too much information, so let us try to resolve that.

Your response

1. State the facts/paraphrase criticism.
   Example: "Well, thank you for listening to my talk. I did take over 20 minutes, so I probably discussed too many of my results. Perhaps if I cut down on the length of the presentation, I could go slower and have less information on my slides."

2. Clarify your thoughts about the situation.
   Example: "I included a lot of data, because it was difficult to decide which studies to present. I thought the audience would need all the background from our earlier studies, to understand why our latest results are so exciting."

3. Suggest alternatives/explain how the situation could be resolved.
   Example: "I think that I could eliminate a few slides, if I summarized our preliminary results in one table, rather than in separate diagrams. The audience probably does not need to hear all the details of our earlier studies—just the key points.

Then, I could focus more on our latest study, which is what they want to hear about anyway."

You can also ask for suggestions in step 3:
Example: "How do you think I could cut down on the length of the presentation? Which part of the talk should I eliminate?"

 When you receive criticism, do not take it personally or screen out the positive comments. Focus on the goals of your project and what improvements it needs.

FROM THE PH.D. SECRET ARCHIVES:

Assertive behavior in practice: common mistakes

In the previous sections, I outlined the principles of assertive behavior. I would now like to illustrate how these principles apply to common situations in graduate school.

Mistake #1: "If I openly disagree with someone, they will dislike me." Students who think that they must agree with others in order to avoid conflict are heading in the direction of a passive attitude, because they put the interests of others before their own. A passive person's main priority is to get along with others, rather than possibly cause conflict. If you learn the principles of assertiveness, you will be able to communicate your ideas without offending the other person. It is possible for two people to disagree on many ideas, and yet still maintain a friendly relationship. Use the three-step method for assertiveness outlined in the previous section to communicate your ideas or resolve conflicts. Remember that at the workplace, your primary goal is to build collegial relationships, rather than agree with your coworkers on every issue.

It is also a mistake to think that in order to be a "good" graduate student, you need to agree with your advisor on everything. Your advisor has more experience than you, but by the time you have been in graduate school for a few years, *you* will be the expert on your thesis topic. In fact, most professors expect their students to know more than they do about their dissertations. Keep in mind that you are responsible for your own research, so remain assertive as you go forth with it. If there is a disagreement between you and your advisor, listen calmly to what he or she has to say and explain your own reasoning afterwards. Use examples from the literature or your own data to strengthen your arguments. Professors usually have respect for students who have confidence in their ideas.

> *Example*: "I understand that you no longer want to work on this project, because of the disappointing results from Professor Williams' group. I think that we should still go ahead with it, because we have not explored every option. In fact, I just read a paper that shows that…."

Mistake #2: "If I am right and the other person is wrong, I have to make them see my point until I win the argument." According to Dale Carnegie's philosophy, the best way to win an argument is to avoid one. Think about a situation in the past where you disagreed with someone. Were you tempted to keep repeating your point until you convinced the other person to see the situation from your point of view? It is very unlikely that after a heated argument, the other person will suddenly shrug his or her shoulders and say: "You know, you are right and I am wrong." Everybody wants to walk away having saved their face. The other person will also voice their own opinions and pour out their line of reasoning. In summary, everybody wants to be right, and they also want everybody else to know that they are right. You can put an end to such circular arguments if you realize that *it does not matter who is right*. Instead, focus on your goals. What would you like to achieve? How can this other person help you? How can you develop a plan that is beneficial to both parties? Our instincts dictate a more straightforward approach, such as direct arguing, so it might take time to learn how to be more sensitive the needs of others.

It is also important to choose your battles wisely and remain flexible. If the other person suggests something that is not exactly what you wanted, think carefully about how much a change in plans would matter to you. Is it worth arguing about what time the experiment should be started, which article to present at a group meeting or which restaurant to go to? If it is important, say so, and be clear about your reasons. If it is not important, adapt to the situation and go with the flow.

Example: "Let me see if I understand your point. Are you saying that we can skip step 2 of this protocol, to save ourselves time? I have not really thought about how that would affect our results. If you like, we can set aside a few samples and process them, without step 2. Then we can compare the results of the two experiments."

If your colleague turns out to be wrong, just say, "Well, it was worth a try...."

If she is right, acknowledge the idea: "You were right. It does seem like step 2 is not important. How about we try the new protocol with a few more samples, before deleting step 2 for good?"

Mistake #3: Accusing or labeling others without knowing the facts.

"My advisor is such a jerk," one student said angrily. "He keeps changing my project, so I never get to make real progress on it."

"Did you try talking to him about it?" I asked.

"No, he's impossible to talk to," she replied. "He only cares about his own goals."

In the next section I will discuss how to deal with difficult people—and I mean *really* difficult people. These are the people who are resistant to your attempts to resolve conflicts. Most people however, will respond if you try to communicate with them assertively. It can be intimidating to stand up to our superiors, but it will come more easily with practice. Before you label someone as "difficult" or "impossible," attempt the three-step method mentioned in the previous section. At that point, one of two things will happen. You will either be amazed that the other person will actually listen to what you have to say, or you will discover that they truly are a difficult person (see the next section for the typical characteristics of difficult people). If the latter is the case, you will at least have identified what kind of difficult people they are, and you will now know what you need to do, to deal with them effectively.

Example: "I am having a really tough time getting along with my advisor. It seems like he changes my thesis topic every month. I really should decide which project makes the most sense, and then discuss the options with him in detail. I need to make it clear that if I want to graduate within the next year, we need to finalize my thesis topic."

Mistake #4: Discussing sensitive issues over e-mail. E-mail has become a substitute for face-to-face communication. E-mail is ideal for sharing recently published articles and for distributing important announcements. If you have a delicate issue to discuss with your advisor, however, it is better if you communicate in person. Many miscommunications have resulted from e-mail, because you cannot sense the tone of voice or body language from an e-mail message. Jenna submitted a copy of her thesis to her advisor and a few days later she received an e-mail from him that simply said, "See me." Jenna panicked, and thought that her thesis had major problems. She only had a few days before the deadline, so she was concerned that she might not graduate that semester. She immediately went to his office, but he had left for the day, and she could not speak to him until the following morning. She spent the rest of the day worrying, and wondered what she would do if she could not graduate that year. The following morning, when she went to see him, his face lit up as he saw her. He said, "Good morning! I just wanted to tell you that I think your thesis is excellent. There are just a few minor errors that I think you should correct...." (It is usually to your advantage to assume that an e-mail has a positive tone, because if you go to see the person afterwards, you will start out on friendly terms. A positive attitude will also help to resolve disagreements should any arise.)

Sometimes, it is impossible to avoid communication over e-mail. Matt, an electrical engineer, recalled that his advisor was away on sabbatical the year that Matt had to finish his dissertation. They exchanged ideas about his thesis over e-mail, but they also discussed important issues during a teleconference. While you cannot read the other person's body language over the phone, at least you can get a sense of the tone of their voice and understand how they feel about certain issues.

Example (over e-mail): "I have some questions about the corrections you made to my thesis. Would you have a few minutes tomorrow afternoon to discuss them?" (i.e., ask for a time to meet, instead of e-mailing your questions directly).

Mistake #5: Expecting your advisor to solve your problems for you. Your advisor is a busy person and your thesis is just one of the hundred things on his to-do list. Cole, a chemist who now works in industry, said that whenever he walks into his manager's office with a problem, he also has a solution for it. The only reason that he goes to see his boss is to keep him updated on what is going on in the department. If you walk in to your advisor's office complaining about problems, he will probably not know what to do at that moment, and will tell you to think about it. A much better alternative is to sit down before you see him and define how you would like things to turn out. Is there another study that you would like to pursue? Or perhaps another professor that you would like to collaborate with? If you go into your advisor's office with a suggestion, he will be relieved that the problem is already (possibly) solved and he will most likely agree with your solution if you have good reasons for it. If he disagrees with you, at least you have the advantage of having thought about the problem so you can discuss the various alternatives with expertise.

> *Example*: "As you know, I have been having trouble getting along with our new technician. Perhaps because she has more experience than me, she refuses to follow my protocols. Right now, I am under a tight deadline, and I need to finish some experiments before I go to the conference next week. I would prefer to do these experiments by myself, to get them done quickly. If you still want me to train her, I can try again when I return from the conference."

Mistake #6: Being shy about asking questions or making comments at meetings. If you are invited to a meeting, it is because your contribution is considered important. Many students are shy, shaky or even trembling when they begin speaking in front of people. This nervousness eventually passes, and soon you will be the senior graduate student or the postdoctoral fellow asking all the questions. Remember that there is no such thing as a stupid question. Sometimes the most senior professors ask the basic questions, such as: "Why are you doing this type of research?," or "Why did you choose this method for your work?" The only way to learn is to ask questions, so do not be afraid to speak up. Most professors actually expect their students to be interactive during meetings, so do not worry if you disagree with someone. In fact, the best meetings result from lively discussions where multiple sides of a story are presented.

Assertive behavior in practice: common mistakes

Example: "It seems like you decided to use liquid chromatography to analyze your samples, even though there are more sensitive methods now. Can you explain why you decided to do your experiments this way?"

Mistake #7: Assuming that you and your advisor are "on the same page." Alan needed a recommendation letter from his advisor, to renew his fellowship. He had reminded his advisor a few months in advance, but as the deadline was nearing, he had not received the letter from her. When he approached her, the advisor said that she had no recollection of the request to write the letter. He had assumed previously that his advisor was just busy, but actually she did not know she was supposed to write a letter.

Mona assumed that she was nearing the end of her thesis research and began her job search. She had not met with her advisor for several months, so when she asked him about scheduling a thesis defense, she was crushed to hear that her work was not sufficient for a doctoral dissertation.

After a relaxing trip to California, Marie's good mood was immediately ruined as she realized that some important decisions about a project were made in her absence. She later found out that her advisor did not know that she would be going on vacation, so he did not ask for her opinion beforehand. Marie did tell him about her vacation two months in advance, but she did not remind him during the week before she left.

In the above cases, the source of frustration was the lack of communication. It is usually incorrect to assume that the other person is aware of your needs or that the two of you are on "the same page." If you need a recommendation letter, ask your advisor as soon as you find out, but remind him or her again a few weeks in advance. If you think that you are nearing graduation, keep discussing your plans with your advisor. You will need his or her input regarding your committee meetings and thesis defense. Make sure that you both have the same idea of how much longer you have in graduate school and what you need to do to graduate.

Also, keep your advisor informed of your vacation schedule or an extended sick leave. Sometimes your advisor might need a progress report for a grant, or would like to speak to you about an important meeting. Do not assume that he or she knows when you will be away, even if you told him or her months in advance. Remind him or her again, a few days before you leave, in case there is something urgent you need to finish beforehand. It can be very frustrating to find out during your vacation, or right after you return, that you were supposed to write up a report or complete an experiment (which you forgot about during the rush before you left).

> *Example*: "As you might know, I am applying for a fellowship and the application is due in two weeks. I have forwarded you the form for the recommendation letter. Will you have time to write it?" (You can remind your advisor the following week, and maybe even provide him or her with an addressed and stamped envelope.)

Mistake #8: Taking criticism personally, or becoming defensive and emotional during a meeting. Carl, a computer programmer, said that the toughest part of his Ph.D. was dealing with his advisor. His advisor always played "the devil's advocate." No matter how much Carl worked, his advisor kept criticizing his research and told him why it was not enough to graduate. Carl was persistent and kept elaborating on his work, until finally his advisor agreed to let him go. Carl already had three years of industry experience and was more assertive and confident than most graduate students. (Of course, even if you do not have industry experience, you can still have confidence in your work, as long as you have a thorough knowledge of the literature and have done your studies properly.) It is a mistake to think that you are not doing a good job if your advisor criticizes your work. Many advisors "turn up the heat", or purposefully use harsh criticism as part of their training, because many of them were also criticized by their colleagues before their ideas were accepted.

If you are criticized, resist the urge to become defensive or emotional. Some students make the mistake of trying too hard to prove themselves. I saw one student being very aggressive about a making his point during a meeting. His advisor finally became irritated and said, "Will you please just listen to what I have to say?" There is no need to interrupt people or be aggressive to convey your message. If you are a good researcher, your results will speak for themselves. Your professor will probably have more respect for you if you listen to his ideas first, and then speak up assertively about your own suggestions.

> *Example*: "Yes, I do understand that we still need one more piece of the puzzle before I can graduate. It will probably take me three

months to complete that study. Why don't we go ahead and schedule a tentative thesis committee meeting for the end of March? It is hard to find a time convenient for everyone, so we might as well set a date now, and cancel it later if need be."

Mistake #9: Assuming that you know what your advisor's expectations are. If you have worked in industry, this assumption could be based on prior experience because you might think that you know what supervisors expect from their employees. If you had a prior boss who was very hands-off and only wanted to see your results when the experiments were completed, do not assume that your current advisor has the same expectations. This advisor might want to be more involved in your research. He might want to know how well your protocol is going, even if you are just in the beginning stages. Or, you might come from a company where you had to give weekly progress reports, yet your current advisor is not interested in the minute details of your work. She might be a busy person and might actually become annoyed if you want to discuss every step of your research. The best approach is to ask your advisor up front: "What are your expectations? Do you expect weekly or monthly progress reports? How often do you meet with your students? Are there regular group meetings?" You can also get answers to these questions if you talk to more senior students in the group.

Many of us think that we know how other people want to be treated, because we grew up with the golden rule: "Do unto others as you would have others do unto you." While the golden rule emphasizes consideration and politeness towards others, it is based on the assumption that other people expect the same treatment as ourselves, which is not necessarily true. The modern-day version of the golden rule, known as the platinum rule, is as follows: "Treat others the way *they* want to be treated." This concept was developed by Tony Alessandra, an entrepreneur, business author, and a Ph.D. himself. He published this concept in his book *The Platinum Rule*, after realizing that there are fundamental differences in behavioral styles among people. He divided these behavioral styles into four categories: directors, socializers, relaters and thinkers. When you "design" the way you will be treating another person you will be more effective if you consider this "typology." If you do not have time to read this book, you can still work effectively with others if you are proactive about understanding their expectations. Talk to others in the group and watch for clues that your advisor gives (" It would be great to have this data by the time the sponsor visits us next week."). If you are still unsure, ask her directly when she expects the work to be done.

> *Example*: "I will have to try many different experimental conditions to develop this protocol. Would you like to see the results along the way, or just a summary at the end? It will probably take me two months to go through all the parameters."

Mistake #10: Trying to resolve all conflicts on your own. In this chapter, I have outlined strategies for how to communicate effectively with other people. This does not mean, however, that you need to resolve all conflicts by yourself. Samuel, a biologist, had a particularly difficult advisor who did not allow him to schedule his thesis defense, even though he had already completed the necessary work. No matter how much Samuel did, his advisor expected him to do more. Samuel approached his committee members and told them that he already met all of the milestones that they had agreed upon at the last meeting. With the support of the other professors in the department, as well as a counseling dean from the university, Samuel's professor finally agreed to let him graduate.

Most conflicts do not escalate to the point where you need to seek assistance from counseling deans. Begin with friends, particularly other graduate students, who can understand your situation. If you still have no solution, turn to committee members and other professors whom you trust. As a last resort, do approach a counseling dean and possibly your department head.

> *Example* (approaching a committee member): "Professor Michaels, thank you for meeting with me. I was hoping that you could help me explain some experimental results. My advisor agreed to fund the research for another semester, but I am not really an expert in this field yet. I was wondering whether you had any ideas on how to explain the results of this last study…."

Building professional relationships

In the previous section, I described the principles of assertive communication that will help you resolve conflicts. These skills will be essential for achieving your goals while still being sensitive to the needs of others. Recent Ph.D.s have also emphasized the importance of a good support system consisting of family, friends, committee members and other professors in the department. For some students, building relationships comes easily; they socialize with their classmates on weekends and even pursue hobbies together. Others might feel isolated, especially if they are shy or experience cultural differences.

How do you connect with other people at your workplace? The principles of relationship-building have been described by Dale Carnegie in his book *How to Win Friends and Influence People*, which was first published in 1937. Dale Carnegie's principles are not based on how to win each battle one by one; instead, he focuses on how you can build a positive *relationship* with others so that you can work together successfully. In other words, you need to learn not just how to communicate, but how to *connect* with other people. If you have a conflict, it will be much easier to resolve when your relationship is built upon mutual respect. The best way to connect with people is to listen to them and to become genuinely interested in them and their opinions. While Dale Carnegie described these principles more than 70 years ago, they are still valid in the workplace, graduate school and personal relationships.

Mira, a biologist, recalled that during graduate school, she worked with a postdoctoral fellow who came from another country. The postdoctoral fellow was difficult to work, with because she was introverted and did not communicate readily. During one of the group lunches, Mira sat next to the postdoctoral fellow and casually asked her about her family background. The postdoctoral fellow was excited to recount her early days in her native village and her parents' struggles to send her to a bigger city to study. The student listened attentively and told the woman how impressive it was for her to earn a Ph.D. and work in the United States, after having grown up in a small village were many people could not even read. The postdoctoral fellow felt incredibly flattered and thanked Mira for her interest. Their relationship improved after that day, as the postdoctoral fellow opened up about herself and she was also more willing to talk about her research.

Zack, an electrical engineer, participated in an industry internship during graduate school. During his internship, he worked on developing a product for the company, and he had to collaborate with several people to complete the project. One of the challenges of the collaboration was recognizing the cross-cultural differences among the researchers on the team. "Most people expressed their opinions readily, but there was one guy who walked away when he was angry. He later explained to us that in his culture, it was impolite to show strong emotion, and when he walked away it was a sign that he had disagreed with us."

Recognize cross-cultural differences among your coworkers and try to understand their styles of communication.

Do not confuse genuine interest in another person with dishonest praise. If you work with someone, such as your advisor or a lab mate, for several years it is normal to be curious about them. What kind of a person are they? Are they focused exclusively on work or do they also have hobbies? Do they like to go out on Friday night for a beer? Casual conversations can lay the groundwork for building effective relationships with colleagues. First, it is easier to work together with someone if you have a personal connection. Second, some very important decisions are frequently made during informal chatting. For example, one postdoctoral fellow recalled receiving a raise while she was talking with her advisor near the water cooler. I have also witnessed the birth of many brilliant research ideas during casual conversations in a hallway or in a lunchroom. Third, casual relationship-building will help you understand your advisor's personality and expectations. Is she a very organized person who likes to get everything done as soon as possible? Or does she usually wait until the last minute to meet a deadline? Does she like to be updated on your work frequently, or only when there is a very important finding? It is also important for your advisor to get to know you as well, so she can help you finish your thesis and find a job.

Also remember to show appreciation for support staff. Administrative assistants, lab technicians and facilities workers can all be very helpful in times of need. Many of them have been at the university for a long time, and they know how to get things done. Leann, a chemist, dropped her keychain down the drain in the bathroom during a rush to get back to her experiment before her timer beeped. She lost the keys to her lab, her apartment, and her bike. The facilities person thought that it would be difficult to retrieve her keys, but Leann explained that she would be fined if she lost the keys to her dormitory room. She also told him how much she appreciated that he came on such a short notice. "All right, young lady, let's see what we can do," he replied. He disassembled the plumbing and after some work, he was able to return her keys. At the end of this experience, both of them were happy: the student because she was able to get her keys back, and the facilities person because he received honest appreciation for his work. Unfortunately, support staff are frequently underappreciated, so they will be very flattered if you acknowledge their hard work. Thank them for organizing department events, ordering supplies and taking care of your paperwork.

Another one of Dale Carnegie's astute observations was the power of remembering other people's names. A person's name is the most wonderful sound to them in the world. By remembering and addressing people by their names, you are showing your respect and appreciation for the other person.

 Show honest appreciation for others, including your advisor, committee members classmates, and support staff.

Challenge #2: Communicating effectively with difficult people

"No one can make you feel inferior without your consent."
Eleanor Roosevelt, US First Lady, diplomat and reformer (1884-1962)

Sometimes even the most skilled communicators have trouble when they need to work with so-called "difficult people." Difficult people are those who repeatedly resist the assertiveness skills that I outlined in the previous section. I once attended a seminar on how to deal with difficult people. At the beginning of the seminar, the speaker asked the audience, "How many of you here ever had to work with difficult people?" Almost everybody raised their hands. A moment later, however, when she asked, "How many of *you* are difficult people?" the audience members glanced at each other, not knowing how to answer. The speaker smiled and said, "Of course, *nobody* in here is a difficult person. The difficult people are all outside, in your offices and your homes." The audience began to laugh, because this comment made it clear that all of us have a tendency to be difficult people sometimes.

While most of us have difficult moments once in a while, there are people who are chronically difficult to work with. This can become a particularly acute problem if the difficult person in your life is your thesis advisor. According to the book *Coping with Difficult People* by Robert Bramson, difficult people can be divided into the following seven categories: 1) hostile-aggressives, 2) complainers, 3) silent unresponsives, 4) super-agreeables, 5) negativists, 6) know-it-alls and 7) indecisives. Through my interviews, I heard stories of advisors in all of the above categories. In addition, students encountered two more types of difficult advisors: 1) extremely hands-off, or super-busy types and 2) excessively hands-on micromanagers. In this section, I present coping strategies for all the difficult personality types, and how to handle typical scenarios in graduate school.

When we are dealing with a difficult person, we also need to be aware of our own behavior and recognize any of these characteristics in ourselves. Remember that it is much easier (or at least more realistic) to change yourself than to change somebody else. Most likely, if you practice assertive communication skills on a regular basis, your "difficult person traits" will begin to diminish and possibly disappear altogether. If you need to work with a truly difficult person, keep the following rule in mind: *difficult people respond to the same assertive communication skills as other people, but they might need more assertiveness on your part.* In order to deal with difficult people, you will need more self-confidence, more preparation, more patience, better listening skills and probably a lot of persistence. Which one of these tactics you will need to apply depends on the type of difficult person you need to work with. It is possible that your advisor—or another difficult person in your life—exhibits more than one type of "difficult person" personality trait. As you will see in the examples and chart below, the coping skills with the different personality types have a lot in common. Use the skills that are most appropriate for each particular situation, and remember to remain polite instead of becoming emotional.

Always begin by assuming that the other person is reasonable and will respond to basic assertive communication skills. If your first attempt is unsuccessful, it does not necessarily mean that the other person is a fundamentally difficult person. They might be having a bad day or this situation could be particularly upsetting to them. A truly difficult person, by definition, is someone who repeatedly resists your attempts at communication. The strategies that I describe in this section are a combination of the strategies from Robert Bramson's book and advice from former graduate students.

Always assume that the person you are dealing with is reasonable and will respond well if you communicate assertively. If you do have to work with a difficult person, you will need more assertiveness and patience to get your point across.

Types of difficult people (See Table 5-1 for a summary.)

HOSTILE-AGGRESSIVES

When most people think of a difficult person, the hostile-aggressive personality type comes to mind. Hostile-aggressive people, as their name suggests, are notoriously antagonistic and impolite. They will crush all your ideas and make you feel like a fool. Your job, as Eleanor Roosevelt said, is to not let them do so. Give the hostile-aggressive person a chance to calm down and stand up for yourself by assertively speaking your own point of view. Avoid fighting, because that can provoke them even more. If the difficult person is too much to handle on your own, seek the support of committee members, department heads and deans. Julian, a biologist, was repeatedly humiliated by his advisor for not collecting as much data as his lab mates. "I struggled a lot, trying to please my advisor, but no matter how much I did, she was always unsatisfied. I felt like a failure, and I considered quitting. Once I began to focus on my project rather than my relationship with my advisor, my thesis came together."

Snipers, also known as "covert" hostile-aggressives, will not openly criticize you, but might make sneering remarks during a meeting or talk about you behind your back. The general strategy, as Bramson put it, is to "smoke them out." If they make comments during the meeting, confront them politely. "Did you have a question about what I just said?" If you suspect that they are being passively aggressive behind your back, bring this behavior to light. Remain friendly and offer alternatives if applicable: "I heard that you are considering discontinuing this research project. Were you unhappy with the results from last week? I think that if we tried the approach that we discussed yesterday, we might get better results." Open, friendly and assertive communication can bring you a long way in dealing with both open and covert hostile-aggressive people.

 Do not get emotional if you are humiliated by a passive-aggressive person. Let them calm down, acknowledge their opinions and direct the conversation towards solving problems.

COMPLAINERS

You might also be one of the unlucky students who needs to work with a "compleat" complainer, who does nothing but moan about their troubles. If you need to collaborate with such a person, listen and acknowledge their complaints, but guide them in the direction of problem-solving. Mark, a chemical engineer, had an advisor who was the mother of two young children and was struggling with balancing the responsibilities of work and family. During meetings, she talked primarily about her personal problems, rather than her research. Mark tried repeatedly to get help from her for his dissertation. "Eventually, she did help a little bit, but it was difficult to get her focused. During my last two years I collaborated with another professor and that helped me to wrap up my thesis."

 If you have to work with a complainer, listen to the complaints for a few minutes, and then direct the conversation towards solving the problem.

SILENT OR UNRESPONSIVE CLAMS

Judy, a literature major, had an advisor known as the silent or unresponsive "clam," who responded to her inquiries with a grunt. He seemed to ignore Judy when she talked to him, even when there was nobody else around. "I approached him several times, with no success. Finally, I sought help from other professors in the department.

I still kept him in the loop by updating him on what I was doing. Occasionally, I received a nod if he agreed, but there was no significant input from him on my thesis." Although her advisor did not contribute verbally to her thesis, it was important to get his "nod" on her project. He was a well-respected professor, and she needed his approval to graduate. "I had to be really assertive with him, by informing him of my progress on a regular basis. I definitely gave him a chance to comment, but I had to do most of my thesis on my own."

Peter, an electrical engineer in a research laboratory, told me the following story about another "clam." Peter was looking to hire a master's student into his group, and he had pre-selected several qualified candidates for an interview. He was particularly looking forward to interviewing a woman who had a perfect GPA. She probably would have been accepted for this position, except that she had what Peter called "the worst interview I have ever seen." Peter began the interview by asking her why she wanted to join his group. The woman just shrugged her shoulders and quietly said "I don't know." He made another attempt by asking her what her future career goals were, but she seemed to ignore his question and just fidgeted in her chair. Just like Judy's advisor, this woman was not the classic example of what most people normally consider a difficult person—because she was not hostile—but her unresponsiveness made it impossible to communicate with her. If you need to deal with "clams," your best strategy is to keep asking questions, followed by silent stares, and to let them know how you will handle the situation on your own without their input.

 You can sometimes get clams to talk if you ask them open-ended questions. If they refuse to communicate, let them know what your plan is. Seek the support of your committee members if your advisor is a clam.

SUPER-AGREEABLE FRIENDLY TYPES

Another type of difficult person is the super-agreeable friendly type. Such a person will tell you all the things you want to hear and make empty promises. You might initially think that she is very easy to get along with, because she is so agreeable. If she just makes empty promises (or worse, makes important decisions without consulting you), however, she is a difficult person and you need to confront her.

Sometimes, you might need to take control of the situation yourself, rather than rely on help from a super-agreeable type.

Marla applied for a fellowship and she needed her advisor to write a recommendation. Her advisor promised to write it, but as the deadline approached he made no progress on it. "I reminded him several times, and he kept saying he was on top of it. I even asked him if he wanted me to write the recommendation, so he could just make corrections and sign it. He told me not to worry, and that everything would be taken care of. On the day of the deadline, I found out he had not written anything yet." At that point, Marla took matters into her own hands. She wrote the recommendation, and her advisor signed it. She was lucky to get an extension, and she also received the fellowship. "In retrospect, I waited too long. I should have written the recommendation earlier, so we could have sent it out by the deadline, rather than rely on an extension from the fellowship committee."

 Do not rely on super-agreeables to help you with your work. Complete as much of the work as you can on your own, to make it easy for them to do their part.

WET-BLANKET NEGATIVISTS

Vivian, a chemical engineer, had a good advisor, but she had to collaborate with a "wet-blanket negativist" professor. Negativists can bring the morale of an entire group down (hence the term "wet blanket"), because they believe that *nothing* can be done to improve a situation. "During meetings, he kept bringing up reasons as to why the project would not work. There was no encouragement from him, just a lot of negative feedback." Fortunately, Vivian's advisor was focused on the project and did not worry about the negative comments from the collaborator. If you need to work with a wet-blanket negativist, avoid getting drawn into their arguments. Acknowledge their concerns, but channel your energy towards the project and alternative solutions, and seek the support of coworkers and professors who can truly help you.

 Focus on the problem and alternative solutions, rather than the pessimism of negativists. If the negativists is your advisor, get help from your coworkers and other professors.

Challenge #2: Communicating effectively with difficult people

A know-it-all expert is someone who believes that his or her way is the only right way. Know-it-all experts fall into two categories: bulldozers and balloons. Bulldozers really do have expertise, and if it were not for their difficult personality type, others would enjoy working with them. Balloons, as their name suggests, are just full of hot air. Know-it-all professors usually, but not always, belong to the bulldozer category; they will not listen to what you have to say, and they believe that their way is the only right way. If you need to work with a bulldozer, it is essential that you do your homework before a meeting, so that you can demonstrate your expertise on the subject. Do not be aggressive about proving your knowledge; rather, build your ideas into the conversation. If he or she still will not listen to you, let him or her be the expert. Bulldozers enjoy being listened to, and you might even get some respect from them if you acknowledge their expertise.

Dena's advisor was a know-it-all expert and bulldozer; he was only interested in getting the projects done his way. "He was really pushy, and he dismissed all of my ideas. I was finally able to have input into the project by doing a literature search and discussing the alternatives with him. He was very impressed when he saw all the research I had done."

Rupert's advisor was a young assistant professor in computer science. As a classic balloon, he tried to hide his lack of expertise in his student's projects. "He wanted to help us with our projects, but he frequently seemed like he did not know what he was talking about. I ended up doing most of the work on my own, without his guidance." Georgia, a biologist, had to work with a technician who was also a balloon. "He did not really have any expertise in microbiology. We all sat there, looking at each other during meetings and raising our eyebrows." The best way to deal with balloon-style know-it-all experts is to acknowledge their comments, but avoid embarrassing them. Everybody wants to walk away from a meeting having saved their face. Know-it-all experts appreciate being listened to, even if you do not follow their advice. In the case of Georgia's technician, it was up to the principal investigator to manage this person's duties, and to decide whether to keep him in the group.

If your advisor is a know-it-all bulldozer, it is very important to be prepared for meetings, so that you can discuss your work with expertise. If you have to work with a balloon, listen and suggest your own ideas as well, but avoid creating embarrassment.

INDECISIVE ADVISORS

Indecisive advisors can be particularly frustrating to students, because as soon as some progress is made, the topic of the dissertation changes. "Every day I would come to the lab, not knowing what my thesis topic would be," said Tiffany, a biochemist. "My advisor was brilliant, but she had so many good ideas that she had difficulty settling on one project." How can you cope with such an advisor? If you have an indecisive advisor, it is essential that you take responsibility for your own thesis. A good way to deal with indecisive advisors is to read the literature and engage in in-depth discussions during meetings. Your focus should move from "Why do you always keep changing my topic?" to "How can we make this project more successful?". Your advisor might hesitate to make a decision, for fear that it will not be perfect, but you can cope with this indecisiveness by emphasizing the advantages of one particular project. It might not be perfect, you could say, but there is a good chance that you will get a very valuable publication out of it. "After five years, I told her that I wanted to graduate the following spring, and I laid out what I was going to do for my thesis. My thesis committee agreed, and she also went along with it," Tiffany recalled.

If your professor keeps changing your topic, you might want to think about other reasons for his or her indecisiveness. Trouble with funding? A need to complete certain projects, to acquire more grant money? Or, perhaps he or she truly is not satisfied with your progress, and wants to change the project to suit your skills better? If you realize that the work that you have been doing is the problem, acknowledge the weaknesses and propose a plan on how you will improve your research. Be realistic, however, and remember to design a study that can be completed within a reasonable amount of time.

Be assertive about your ideas if your advisor is indecisive, but also find out his or her reasons for being reluctant to make a decision.

Extremely hands-off or super-busy types

Super-busy advisors were usually described by their students as "she would have been a really great advisor if she had had time to meet with me." Students with super-busy advisors had to be particularly self-motivated to complete their dissertations. They had to review the literature on their own and consult with committee members and other professors regarding the direction of their theses. "When I did meet with my professor, he was very helpful. The rest of the time, I was on my own, and I had to learn how to become independent," recalled Brendan, a physicist. A super-busy professor is not necessarily a difficult one if you are comfortable working on your own. If you meet with your advisor infrequently, prepare thoroughly for these meetings. Be efficient by having all of your work organized and easy for your professor to look over.

It can be particularly challenging to work with a super-busy advisor, if he or she is also a difficult person. If this is the case, apply the strategies described above for dealing with difficult people. Also, seek the support of committee members and other professors, if it becomes too challenging to complete your thesis on your own. "My advisor was too busy to help me with my dissertation," said Mariana, an English major. "Fortunately, one of my committee members was very supportive; she helped me get ideas for my thesis, and she also reviewed it along the way."

There is also another type of hands-off advisor: one who does not care about his or her students. "My advisor was not that busy, but he did not seem to care about my project," said Miriam, a mathematics major. "I worked primarily on my own, and occasionally sought help from other professors. In retrospect, I probably should have switched advisors, and found someone who was interested in my project." It was difficult for Miriam to be motivated, because her advisor gave her no support during the process. She was able to complete her dissertation by setting her own deadlines and seeking support from other students and professors.

 Get support from coworkers and other professors if your advisor is extremely hands-off. Consider this challenge an opportunity to learn how to become an independent researcher.

EXCESSIVELY HANDS-ON MICROMANAGERS

Students with micromanager advisors complained of getting "too much attention." "My advisor was focused on the small details, but did not see the 'big picture.' For example, she wanted to save money by buying lower-quality gloves, but otherwise she was a bad money manager," recalled Tara, a biochemist. Micromanager advisors frustrate their students by trying to control every aspect of the research, and an excessively hands-on advisor can be very frustrating to work with. "My advisor expected me to work long hours every weekend, and sometimes he even called me at home to check on the status of my experiments," said Rose, a chemist. "Eventually, I had to set boundaries with him, so that he would give me more independence and not call me at home." Some professors might not be aware of their unrealistic expectations, unless you bring it to their attention. It is in everybody's interest that the project succeeds, and if you work for a micromanager professor, let him or her know the conditions for productivity. For example, discuss reasonable hours, time off on the weekends and the need for more independence. Also, listen to their needs, such as the need to complete a particular project or meet a strict deadline.

 Set reasonable boundaries if your advisor is a micromanager, but also listen to his or her needs and opinions.

Table 5-1: Strategies for dealing with difficult people

Type of difficult person, and associated personality traits	Approach for communicating effectively
Hostile-aggressives disruptive, disrespectful and impatient; frequently make others feel inferior. *Example: "What do you mean the concentrations were not detectable? Have I not explained how to do this experiment properly?"*	Stand up for yourself and do not let them intimidate you. Let them calm down if they become emotional. Be respectful and assertively communicate your goals. If you suspect covert hostile-aggressiveness, bring this behavior to light by asking the person specific questions. *Example: "I agree that these results are disappointing. I have followed the protocol exactly, so I think it is time to change our methods. I would suggest switching to...."*
Complainers a tendency to complain about everything. *Example: "Forgive my tiredness, my back was bothering me all night. I spent all morning at the doctor's...."*	Listen to their opinion, acknowledge their problems, and switch into problem-solving mode as politely and quickly as possible. *Example: "Wow, that does sound upsetting. You must be going through a difficult time. Speaking of difficulties, do you have any advice on how to resolve the following problem with my last study...."*
Silent and unresponsive close down (or clam up), and seem to ignore your presence. *Example: "Hmm..." or just a nod.*	Get them to talk by asking open-ended questions, followed by a friendly but silent stare. If they remain silent, ask them more specific "yes" or "no" questions. If they talk, listen and acknowledge their opinions. If they refuse to talk, let them know how you will resolve this issue on your own, and give them another chance to give you input. *Example: "I e-mailed you my presentation for the conference. I am leaving in 10 days, so if you have any comments, I still have time to make changes."*

Table 5-1: Strategies for dealing with difficult people *(continued)*

Type of difficult person, and associated personality traits	Approach for communicating effectively
Super-agreeables always say what you want to hear; make promises, but do not follow-through. *Example: "Sure, I will have it ready in two weeks," but after six weeks and several reminders, nothing is done.*	Be specific about your goals, and make it easy for them to give you what you want, or to be honest with you if they cannot keep their promises. Before you ask for their help, do some of the work on your own, so it will be easy for them to help you. *Example: "With spring just around the corner, I think we need to contact our collaborators in Germany and ask whether they could accommodate me for a summer internship. I know you have been very busy, so I wrote the letter. Would you like to look it over before I send it?"*
Wet-blanket negativists think that your project will not work out, and there is nothing that you can do about it. *Example: "There is no way you can do this in six months. Plus, funding is tight, so you will be out of money, too."*	Avoid getting drawn into negativism. Do not argue or try to prove them wrong. Acknowledge their concerns and politely suggest your ideas as alternatives. *Example: "It is possible that the study will take longer than six months, but according to the staff it can be completed on time. I also have some ideas on how to find more funding, if necessary."*
Know-it-all experts believe that their way is the only right way, and everybody else is wrong. *Examples:* *Bulldozers: "This method has to work. It is the golden standard, so you have to do it this way."* *Balloons: "I don't think your method will work. I think you just need to use Professor Green's method to get better results." (Professor Green's method is actually irrelevant to your study.)*	Bulldozers: Do your homework, so you can discuss your research with authority. Do not argue with them, but do communicate your ideas with confidence. *Example: "Yes, I agree that this is how it has been done for 10 years. However, I have repeated the experiment twice, and this method is not sensitive enough for these samples. Based on my literature search, I think it is worth trying…." (Show data and be very specific about what you want to do and why.)* Balloons: Listen and suggest your own ideas as alternatives. Do not embarrass them; give them an opportunity to save face. *Example: "Yes, I have thought about Professor Green's method, but he works with a different organism. I would suggest trying the protocol developed by…." (Strengthen your argument with data from the literature or another group.)*

Table 5-1: Strategies for dealing with difficult people *(concluded)*

Type of difficult person, and associated personality traits	Approach for communicating effectively
Indecisive stallers stalls on major decisions as long as possible, or until they are no longer relevant. *Example: "I am not sure this paper is ready to go out yet. We need to confirm our results one more time."*	Help them solve problems by finding out the blocks to decision-making. Is the problem with the project, or with the person doing the work? Suggest ideas that address their concerns. Once a decision is made, make sure that they follow through. *Example: "I understand that you want to make sure that our results are reproducible. I think that the standard is four data points per condition, and we already have that. Why do you think we need to collect more data?"*
Extremely hands-off types give you little guidance on your project, either because they do not have time or do not care about your dissertation. *Example: "I'll be traveling a lot this semester. Maybe we can meet in a few months to discuss your progress?"*	You have to take charge of your own dissertation. Choose a project that you can complete on your own. Be proactive about setting deadlines, and seek support from other professors in the department. Be very prepared for the few meetings you have. *Example: "Wow, that does sound like a busy schedule. Given that you will be away a lot, I was wondering whether you could look over my progress report. If you have a few minutes now, I can explain the different sections."*
Excessively hands-on mimicromanagers want to control every aspect of your research, including your hours at work. *Example: "I did not see you at work over the weekend. I thought you were trying to get this project going."*	Set boundaries and let them know which aspects of their managerial style are disruptive to your work. It might be necessary to put your requests in writing. For example, you might need to clarify your hours at work, and how frequently you think there should be meetings. *Example: "Yes, this project is a high priority for me. I have been working very hard for the last month, so I need the weekends to rest. If you want, I can show you my results so far."*

MASTER YOUR PEOPLE SKILLS

Master your people skills

Step 1: Learn the principles of assertive communication.
- Make your meetings more efficient by preparing for them in advance.
- Begin each meeting on a positive note.
- Use the following three-step method to communicate your ideas:
  - State the facts.
  - Clarify your thoughts about the situation, and explain the problem.
  - State your goals and how you would like the situation to be resolved.
- Listen to the other person if they insist on talking first, and paraphrase their opinions to let them know you understand their concerns.
- At the end of the meeting, summarize what you have agreed upon and what the plan of action is.

Step 2: Give and receive criticism constructively.
- Do not take criticism personally or become emotional.
- Concentrate on your goals, and let the other person explain their point of view.
- Address the criticism according to your professional opinion, or commit yourself to exploring the question further.
- If you want to criticize constructively, focus on what you want to accomplish and also include positive feedback.

Step 3: Build positive working relationships.
- Become genuinely interested in other people and their opinions.
- Recognize cultural differences among coworkers and try to understand other people's styles of interaction.
- Show appreciation for your advisor, committee members, coworkers and support staff.
- Remember people's names and address them accordingly.

Step 4: Apply your assertiveness skills to avoid the most common communication mistakes.

- Do not be afraid to express your opinions, even if you disagree with somebody.
- Listen to the other person first, to understand their point of view, rather than get involved in circular arguments.
- Clarify goals and expectations with your advisor before making assumptions.
- Communicate sensitive issues in person, rather than via e-mail.
- Be proactive about completing your dissertation and communicating the results to your advisor and committee members.

Step 5: Learn the necessary coping skills to deal with difficult people.

- Begin your discussion by assuming that the other person is reasonable and apply basic assertive communication skills to convey your ideas.
- If your interactions are repeatedly frustrating, listen to the other person and identify what type of difficult person they are.
- Use the appropriate coping skills depending on the type of difficult person you are dealing with.
- During your interaction with a difficult person remain polite and focus on the goals of your project.
- Seek help from other professors and coworkers, if it becomes too difficult to resolve a problem on your own.

Setting boundaries with a hostile-aggressive micromanager: *Sharon's story*

For Sharon, a chemist, the most difficult part of the Ph.D. process was learning how to get along with her advisor, a hostile-aggressive micromanager. He expected 12-hour workdays and humiliated her on a regular basis. No matter how much she worked, he accused her of being unproductive and not fit to earn a Ph.D. Sharon decided to set limits by negotiating with him. She made it clear that in order for her to be productive, he also had to give her more independence and not ask her about her progress on a daily basis. After these discussions, her advisor respected her hours more, but he still humiliated her occasionally. To make matters worse, Sharon did not receive constructive advice for her dissertation from him or her thesis committee. In order to get help, Sharon consulted with a senior professor in the department, who guided her during the dissertation process. In retrospect, Sharon believes she should have switched advisors, but she also feels that staying in this group taught her persistence and effective communication skills.

Dealing with issues of authorship: *Ed's story*

Ed, a physicist, worked with a supportive advisor, but he was frustrated by a graduate student who took credit for other people's work. The other graduate student came with high recommendations from a reputable university, and the professor gave him an exciting project to work on. In spite of his good reputation, this student had little expertise and somehow convinced other people to complete experiments for him. He was also unethical and put himself as the first author on publications. To make matters worse, he did not acknowledge his coworkers in the papers. Ed brought this to his advisor's attention, but the professor did not address the problem immediately. Ed had to be very persistent with his advisor, because in the meantime, the other student published more papers with only his name on them. "Eventually, my advisor caught up with this unethical behavior. It took some time for my advisor to realize the student's dishonesty, because he had been very manipulative. In the end, he was not allowed to publish any more papers and was dismissed from our group." Persistence is key to working with difficult people. While Ed's advisor was not a difficult person, it took some effort on Ed's part to convince him to confront the dishonest student.

CHAPTER 6:
WRITE AND DEFEND YOUR THESIS

"The art of communication is the language of leadership."
James Humes,
Author of *Speak Like Churchill, Stand Like Lincoln:*
21 Powerful Secrets of History's Greatest Speakers

A few years ago, I had lunch with Desiree, a senior graduate student who had recently handed in her doctoral thesis. "How are you doing?" I asked. " I think it will take me a few weeks to get over my caffeine addiction. I have been pulling all-nighters for the last three weeks," she replied as she buried her head in her crossed arms on the table. Desiree described the thesis-writing process as a roller coaster. She had a slow start because it was difficult to motivate herself to write, but after having occasional bursts of energy, she would get side-tracked by the job-searching process. After each relapse, Desiree found it difficult to write again. As the graduation deadline neared, however, she became frantic and worked on her thesis day and night. She finished on time, but felt she could have done a better job with a more consistent writing schedule. Did all former graduate students have a similar thesis-writing experience?

Interestingly, writing seemed to be either the least or the most challenging part of graduate school, for most of my interviewees. It was the easiest for those who perceived writing as a straightforward process, compared to the uncertainty of research. Students who had already published papers found writing even easier, as they could cut and paste sections from previous manuscripts into their theses. Other students, however, found writing cumbersome. Writing is a solitary act, and it requires daily self-discipline. Most people (even writers) do not feel like writing every day. With all of the new responsibilities that come with graduation (e.g., job-searching, moving), it can be difficult to focus on writing every day. Yet, under the pressure of a graduation deadline, you will need to motivate yourself to keep writing, despite distractions. In this chapter, I will show you how to develop your own writing process and build up your thesis, one stage at a time.

Once the writing of your thesis is completed, you still have one more challenge ahead of you: to defend it in front of your committee, and possibly an open audience as well. Fear of public-speaking is common, but this fear frequently lessens in graduate school, as students have the opportunity to improve their speaking skills by presenting at seminars or teaching undergraduates. Nevertheless, everybody wants to improve their presentation skills and impress their audience on the day of their defense. Another reason to enhance presentation skills is that most Ph.D.s will need to present their dissertations at conferences and as part of their job interviews. In the second part of this chapter, I will summarize the key strategies for preparing and delivering effective presentations.

In summary, this chapter will show you how to:

- Develop your writing process
- Edit your thesis efficiently
- Conquer nervousness before public-speaking
- Enhance your presentation skills

Challenge #1: Writing your dissertation

While talking with Ph.D.s, I realized that there are fundamental differences in the writing process between the humanities/social sciences/arts and the sciences/engineering/ mathematics. Students in the humanities/social sciences/arts usually begin writing their dissertations right after their qualifying exams. Their research and writing are closely intertwined, and their ideas emerge as they write their theses. In other words, the writing of the dissertation begins early, and can take several years to complete. Some students were even asked to write a chapter of their thesis as part of their qualifiers, and these students generally received a critique for one chapter of their dissertations as early as their second or third year.

Students in the sciences/engineering/mathematics usually write their dissertations in their last semester. They spend most of their time collecting data, developing devices or solving problems. Sometimes they also publish papers that are eventually incorporated into their dissertations. Thus, in the sciences/engineering/mathematics, the writing phase of the dissertation usually lasts about two to six months.

While the time span of the writing phase can be different in the humanities/social sciences/arts versus the sciences/engineering/mathematics, the underlying processes have much in common. First, regardless of your field of study, writing the dissertation will require self-discipline, most likely on a daily basis. Second, writing goes through three major several phases: collecting ideas, constructing the first draft and revising the final draft. Third, regardless of the time that it takes to write the dissertation, the final phase of the revision—right before the deadline—is usually intense for everybody. It is a time when students must remain motivated, creative and productive for 10–12 hours a day, for the last few weeks or months before the deadline.

What do you need to do during each of the three stages of writing? In the first phase, you will collect ideas, and you might not even be sure of the outline of your thesis. What should the different chapter and subject headings be? Students with publications (primarily in the sciences and engineering) usually have an easier time at this stage. In their case, the first phase of writing—where they determine what their thesis is to be about—already occurred to some extent during the preparation of their publications. For students with no publications this stage can be the most time-consuming, because they still need to define the central questions for their theses.

However, even students with publications occasionally struggle with the next stage: constructing a legible first draft. The first draft has to address questions such as: What is the central question or hypothesis that I am trying to answer? Do I have all of the supporting information that I need? How will I know when I am finished collecting data/information? Most Ph.D.s described this stage as time-consuming, and they usually had to go through many drafts and revisions before they felt ready to have their dissertations revised by someone else.

The final revision stage is busy, but not as intellectually challenging as the previous two phases. In this stage, students feverishly try to complete their writing by the graduation deadline. They isolate themselves from the rest of the world and work 10–12 hours a day proofreading and editing. Motivation is no longer an issue here; finding the time to do all the last-minute changes is the main challenge. At the end of this stage, however, it is common to be disappointed with the final version of your thesis. Many students feel it is not as good as they would have expected it to be, after three to seven years of research. Edgar, a chemist, was able to get over his "post-graduation blues" quickly because his advisor told him to expect these feelings. "When I finished my dissertation I was not proud of myself, but I was happy to be done with it," he said. His "post-graduation blues" also passed quickly as he started his new job.

Whichever the most challenging stage is for you, I am sure you will benefit from the wisdom of former graduate students. In this section, I will show you how to 1) move through the different stages of writing, 2) overcome the challenges of each phase and 3) keep yourself motivated throughout the writing process.

Stage I: Collect your ideas and develop your writing process

Whether you are writing your thesis or your first research publication, you need to develop a sustainable writing process. As with many other tasks, the most difficult part about writing is the beginning. It can be particularly challenging to motivate yourself to write if you have other priorities. "It was difficult to find time for writing, because I was collecting data until just a few weeks before my defense." said Zoe, a psychology major. "I had to isolate myself from my experiments in order to be able to concentrate on writing. With all of the distractions of a nearing graduation deadline, it can take a few weeks to get into the habit of writing daily. Once you begin writing, however, it will become easier—and possibly even rewarding. In order to incorporate writing into your daily routine you will need to experiment with various styles of working. Which time of the day are you most efficient? What is the best space for writing? How can you motivate yourself to write? How can you increase your creativity? In what order should you write the different sections of your manuscript? How many hours or pages per day should your write?

Remember that writing a thesis has several phases, and it is unrealistic to expect yourself to have a polished manuscript within a few days. The purpose of the first phase is to collect ideas on paper, and so they need not be organized or grammatically correct. When you begin writing your dissertation, you might already be ahead of the game if you have published papers or have a detailed outline of your thesis. If you do not have an outline yet, begin by defining the different sections and collect your ideas under the appropriate section headings. If you have publications (or written progress reports), you can also speed up the writing process by inserting your previously written materials into the draft of your thesis.

 Create a table of contents or detailed outline, and insert your ideas in the corresponding sections, to facilitate the editing process.

Some students do not have any written materials when they begin writing, and they need to construct a doctoral dissertation from scratch. If you are in this situation, your first job is collect ideas. You might feel confused if your ideas occur in random order, but this is a normal phase of writing. As John Boalker, author of *Writing Your Dissertation in 15 Minutes a Day* says, ideas frequently rise out of a "chaotic soup." At the first stage, when you are collecting ideas, you are generating a "zero draft." It is not a first draft that you need to show to anyone; the purpose of your zero draft is to clarify to *yourself* what you are going to write about. Accept your ideas as they come along, record them and polish them later. If you already have an outline, categorize your ideas into the appropriate sections, to facilitate the editing process.

CHALLENGE #1: WHEN IS THE IDEAL TIME TO WRITE?
Ronald, an education major, woke up every morning at 3 a.m. and worked on his dissertation until 6 a.m. before having breakfast with his wife and children. For Ronald, the mornings were the most productive time of the day. Other students preferred to write in the evenings after they completed other tasks, particularly if they were still collecting data. Does your schedule revolve around your family? Do you need to work, in addition to completing your degree? The time of day you write is not important; getting in the habit of writing every day is.

CHALLENGE #2: WHERE IS THE BEST PLACE TO WRITE?
Choose the place that has the least number of distractions. Melinda, an English major, discovered that her university library provided little offices (just big enough to fit a desk and chair) for students working on their dissertations. She went to this office at the same time every day and forced herself to write at least two pages a day. This was the only

Challenge #1: Writing your dissertation

place where she could concentrate, because when she wrote at home, she found herself checking e-mail frequently or watching TV. If you do not have the luxury of a private office, write in your home or office when there are the least number of distractions, such as early in the morning or late at night.

 The key to completing your dissertation is to be persistent about writing every day, preferably at the same time and in the same place.

CHALLENGE #3: WHAT SHOULD YOU WRITE ABOUT?

Once you are in the flow of writing, it is easy to keep going, but how do you begin? What are the first words to put onto a blank page? Do not expect to write your introduction first, and then proceed in order through all of your chapters. It very, very rarely happens that way. The introduction, which usually involves an in-depth literature search, is frequently the most challenging part of the dissertation. When you begin writing, your goal should be to collect as many ideas on paper as you can. Your ideas will arise in a scattered, random fashion, and your job is to record them without judgment. If you know your chapter titles already, you will save yourself time at the editing stage by placing your ideas into the correct sections of your manuscript.

Begin writing by trying to define the core of your dissertation. What is the central message you are trying to convey? Summarize your thesis in a few sentences, even if you do not yet have all the supporting data. After you have written down your fundamental question or hypothesis, begin to embellish it with the information or data that you *have* already collected. What was the motivation for this study? What methods did you use to gather the data? What are the results of your research? How does it compare with the research of others in the field? What conclusions can you draw from your research? If you are still doing research, composing your dissertation in such a way might help to clarify what data or information you still need to collect.

 Begin writing by summarizing your dissertation in a few sentences. If your central message has not yet been defined, work on clarifying the "take-home" message of your thesis.

WRITE AND DEFEND YOUR THESIS

How do you know which part of your thesis you should be working on? One way to facilitate the writing process is to finish writing every day by making a to-do list of the top five dissertation-related tasks you would like to complete the next day. Break down the tasks into small, realistic and specific parts: Instead of writing "complete introduction," write "proofread second paragraph of introduction," or "summarize the findings from the paper by Smith et al." The next morning, when you begin writing, you will already have defined what needs to be completed. Choose the task that seems the least daunting and force yourself to spend at least a few minutes on it. The first few minutes of writing are the most difficult, and once you are past this stage, the rest of the process will go relatively smoothly. As you near the deadline for your dissertation, an organized to-do list will become essential for optimizing the use of your time. You might be working 12 hours a day on your thesis, but you will *never* run out of things to do. If you have a to-do list in front of you, you can choose the items that are the most urgent.

 At the end of your writing period, construct a to-do list with the most important tasks for the following day. Break down the tasks into small, realistic and specific parts, to help ease yourself into the writing process.

CHALLENGE #4: HOW MUCH SHOULD YOU WRITE EVERY DAY?
At the beginning, your goal is to gather ideas onto a page. Should you set a goal for a certain number of hours, or for a certain number of pages? In general, setting a goal for a number of pages leads to more progress. It is easy to sit in front of the computer for a certain number of hours without producing anything substantial, particularly with all of the distractions from the Internet. If you predetermine a goal for a certain number of pages, you will see cumulative (and very tangible) daily progress. A typical goal is about two pages a day, which is enough to make a dent in your thesis, yet short enough to seem realistic. Some days you will finish the two pages in 20 minutes; other days, it might take you 10 hours. If you finish your two pages quickly, should you keep writing? Continue to write if you are in the flow (or under a deadline), but remember to leave a few simple items on your to-do list, so that you will have some warm-up exercises for your writing the

following day. Also remember to take frequent breaks while writing (e.g. 10-15 minutes every hour) in order to give your mind a rest and to stretch your limbs.

If you need to motivate yourself to write, remember one of the basic principles of behavioral psychology: Positive reinforcement will motivate you to work, but negative reinforcement will impede progress. If you tell yourself that you will not go out for your afternoon snack until you have written two pages, you will probably resist writing even more. Instead, get a little snack now to reward yourself for taking the time to write. You will still have a bigger treat to look forward to, once you finish working.

Commit to writing a certain number of pages every day (two pages a day is a typical commitment), and focus on getting your ideas on paper, rather than perfecting your grammar and style.

CHALLENGE #5: WHAT TO WRITE, WHEN YOU ARE OUT OF IDEAS
On some days, you will be out of ideas; the proverbial cupboard will be bare. You might not even know what to put on your to-do list. These are the days when you can use writing to explore your ideas. Write two pages about anything, such as the "big picture" of your thesis and why it is important to your field of research. You can also write about how much this dissertation is frustrating you, or complain about your advisor, wishing he gave you more useful suggestions. Also write down any questions that are bothering you. Why do your results contradict each other? Where can you find out more about a particular topic? If you cannot think clearly, is there another place where you could write without distractions?

Joan Boalker pointed out that many people believe that they need to think in order to write. According to Boalker, it is the other way around: You need to write in order to think, and once you begin writing, thoughts will come rushing into your head. As you begin pouring out your ideas and frustrations on paper, you might begin to develop a new to-do list. Your list might not be about the writing, but it will tell you what you need to do. Perhaps it is time to talk with your advisor and tell him or her how disappointed you are with the results of your experiments. Maybe you could suggest omitting a particular experiment from the thesis or designing a different study. Could you seek help from somebody else in the department, to wrap up this project? Do you need to do more library research, because your introduction is not detailed enough? Do you need to find an alternative place to write, or do you need to rearrange your apartment to make room for a desk? At the end of this writing session, you have probably cleared out some distractions from your mind, and possibly constructed a new to-do list. Spend 30–60 minutes on free writing, anytime that you experience writer's block and need to collect your ideas on paper.

 Use writing to explore your ideas freely.

CHALLENGE #6: CLEARING YOUR HEAD OF DISTRACTIONS

Distraction is an unavoidable part of writing. You can minimize distraction by choosing an appropriate place and time for working on your thesis. While you can remove external distractions, how do you deal with distractions inside your head?

Obviously, sidestepping these distractions is not as easy as unplugging the phone. Some distractions will pass. Your subconscious mind might try to lure you into checking e-mail or watching television, just after you have encountered a particularly challenging part in your thesis. Other distractions need to be addressed appropriately, because they might be calling your attention to an important issue. Most students have other commitments besides writing their dissertations. Some of them get married, have children, have mortgages to pay or work part-time jobs. If any concerns arise during writing, make note of them in your to-do list, so that you can attend to them after you have finished your daily writing goal.

Expect distractions to arise spontaneously—and sometimes often—during writing, even if you are not dealing with any major problems. If you notice your mind wandering off, gently guide it back and continue writing. Free writing is a good way to clear your head of distractions. Sometimes you might not know what is truly bothering you. When you begin free writing, you might realize that you cannot concentrate because of a personal situation. If free writing clarifies any subconscious concerns, note them down in your to-do list.

Record the mental distractions that occur while you write, but attend to them only after you have finished your daily writing goal (they might not seem so urgent by then).

WHY IT IS IMPOSSIBLE TO BACK UP YOUR WORK TOO MUCH

You must have heard countless times to "back up your work." I would now like to rephrase this: It is *impossible* to back up your work too many times. I was working on the last chapter of my thesis, just three weeks before the deadline. I saved my file under a different name every day; I backed it up on an external drive, as well as on the computer itself. Just as I wanted to save the last chapter, the unthinkable happened: the computer could not save the file because it was corrupt. Recall that I had saved my file under a different name every day (using the date in the file name), so I did have access to the file that I had saved on the previous day. On this very day, however, I had made significant progress on my final chapter. I had saved it several times during the day, but the file was corrupt and I had no access to my work.

Fortunately, I was able to print this file before the computer crashed. Once I had a hard copy in my hand, I was able to scan it and use optical character recognition (OCR) software to render the file back into an electronic format. The scanned-in manuscript was mostly correct, except for small nuisances such as the page numbers being scanned into the text itself and the margins being slightly off. It took a bit of cleaning up, but it was nowhere as onerous as it would have been, to re-do—from scratch—all the work I had done that day.

What is the lesson here? *You cannot back up your work enough times.* Have it on several external devices and make sure that you have as many previous versions as you think are necessary. Also, always have a hard copy of the most recent version of your thesis. You do not need to print the entire document every day, but consider printing individual sections, especially if you have made significant progress. I was lucky to be able to print my document before the computer crashed, but had it failed, I still would have lost only one day of work.

WRITING YOUR THESIS, IF YOU HAVE RSI

Writing your doctoral dissertation is an opportunity to perfect your writing process. The habits that you learn now will be the ones that you build upon when you write grant applications or progress reports at your job. If you have ever struggled with RSI, you already know that every minute at the computer has to count. If you have never struggled with RSI, your time at the computer is still valuable, especially if you are nearing a thesis deadline. How can you make your time on the computer more efficient?

Whenever you sit down at the computer, ask yourself what you need to accomplish. I frequently fell into the trap of beginning my day by e-mailing, but I could no longer afford this luxury when I was writing my thesis. Every minute at the computer had to count for something: revising the introduction, constructing tables, analyzing data or making slides for my defense. It took me a few weeks to get used to postponing e-mailing, until after I had finished my daily writing quota; once I changed my work habits, however, I was more productive and focused than before.

 Postpone recreational computer use (e.g., e-mailing and web-surfing) until you have finished your writing requirements for the day.

Depending on the severity of your RSI, you will need to adopt a different strategy for completing your thesis. If you have a very severe case of RSI, you might need to stay away from typing completely. Voice-activated software is now accurate enough to record your thoughts, almost as fast as you say them out loud; you can also train it to learn scientific terminology (see the appendix for a list of voice-activated software packages). You can also use voice-activated software for dictating into Excel spreadsheets and using the Internet. There is a learning curve for using voice-activated software, but if you have a severe case of RSI, it might be the only way you can complete your dissertation.

 Explore the different functions of voice-activated software, so you can learn how to browse the Internet, write documents and create spreadsheets without typing.

If you become proficient with voice-activated software, you might be able to complete your dissertation as fast—or even faster—than if you were typing. During the learning phase, however, you will most likely be frustrated as you try to dictate the tasks that would be significantly faster to do by hand. I wrote a large part of my dissertation with voice-activated software. My RSI was healing, but I did not want to risk another injury. Therefore, my strategy was to write my thesis as fast as I could with the voice-activated software. My progress was slow at the beginning, because I struggled with learning the different features of the software and memorizing all of the commands for editing my text. As I got more proficient with the software, I was happy to realize that typing was faster with the software than by hand, particularly when there were large blocks of text to dictate. Editing was also efficient, as I could select multiple paragraphs with voice commands, rather highlighting them with a mouse.

While you are recovering from RSI, keep in touch regularly with your doctor or physical therapist. It might not be enough to reduce computer usage. As mentioned in chapter four, you might experience pain in your hands when you are stressed, even in the absence of typing. Furthermore, if you need to work on your thesis for 10–12 hours a day, you need to be aware of your posture at the computer, even when using voice-activated software. Many Ph.D.s who did not experience RSI complained of backaches and neck strain during the writing of their dissertations. Being in a tense position will also slow your recovery from RSI, and possibly make you more tired throughout the day. Make sure that you take frequent breaks to stretch your body, especially if you were assigned physical therapy exercises by your doctor.

 Take typing breaks before *you feel pain*.

EVALUATE YOUR WRITING PROCESS ALONG THE WAY

It will take some time to optimize your writing process, and it is important to evaluate your efficiency from time to time. It's a matter of discovering what works best for *you*. In fact, one student of literature recalled that the German writer Goethe could only write if he had a rotting apple in his desk drawer. Your requirements need not be as eccentric. Ask yourself some key questions: Have you chosen a productive time of day? Is your location suitable for writing? Can you satisfy your writing goal every day? Are you making satisfactory progress? Are you able to let go of distractions? You might need to tweak the writing process as your circumstances change. Writing in your room, for example, might be productive during the day, but you might

WRITE AND DEFEND YOUR THESIS

be distracted by excessive noise in the evenings. For this reason, you might need to consider multiple places for writing your dissertation. University libraries are usually open on the weekends and evenings, and frequently have extended hours at the end of the semester.

In order to develop an efficient writing process, keep the following points in mind:

- Make a commitment to write every day, preferably at the same time and in the same place.
- Commit to writing a certain number of pages a day. (Two pages appears to be a realistic goal.)
- Collect all your ideas on paper and categorize them into the appropriate sections, if you already have an outline.
- Keep clarifying the central message of your thesis.
- Put together a to-do list at the end of every day, so you will know where to start writing the following day.
- If you do not know what to write about, use free writing to explore your ideas.

Stage II: Construct your first draft

At the end of the first stage of writing, you will have a collection—or "soup,"—of ideas. The purpose of the next stage of writing is to define the central arguments of your thesis and organize all of the supporting data and information for them. To simplify the writing process, define the main arguments for each chapter and section. Once you have clarified the primary questions, the next step is to build your story. You know that you have finished your first draft when you have defined your main questions and have a logical order of arguments. Your manuscript might not be grammatically correct, and it could be verbose. Nevertheless, your first draft will give you something to work with. At this stage, your attitude changes from "What should I write about?" to "Do I have enough data to support this argument?" You know you are on the right track, when you have moved from the stage of collecting ideas to filling in the gaps in your line of reasoning.

 The purpose of your first draft is to define the central questions of your thesis and to gather all your supporting arguments in a logical order.

It might seem challenging to "fish out" arguments from the collection of ideas you generated in the first stage of writing. If your manuscript is disorganized, consider printing it, so you can oversee the whole document at once. Your writing might appear chaotic at first, but remember that even experienced writers need to go through many drafts to polish their work. Start by defining the chapters (and even opening new computer files for each of them) and insert your arguments in the right places. Do not worry about grammar or style at this stage; simply move the paragraphs around until you have your arguments in the right order.

Constructing your first draft will take patience. You might have many pages of ideas, but not know how to clean them up. My first scientific publication was a review article; the "zero draft" was so messy that I did not know where to start organizing it. I had 40 pages of ideas, but I was overwhelmed by the mere thought of rearranging them into proper paragraphs. Finally, after reading my zero draft several times, I opened up a new file and wrote an outline. Once I completed the outline, I scanned through my zero draft again, because every paragraph there had to end up somewhere within the outline. As I had expected, many of my ideas were repeated several times, and I had to paste them into another file called "cut-outs." Remember not to throw out *any* of your writing; instead, have a "cut-out" file with all of the paragraphs that you have removed from your first draft. Occasionally, I did find that I needed to go back to this file and retrieve a paragraph that I had previously removed.

 Have a "cut-out" file, where you save all the writing you removed from your thesis or manuscripts.

Once I had all the arguments under the right section headings, I refined my editing by moving the sentences around and clarifying my arguments. In the end, my 40-page zero draft was transformed into a 10-page first draft. I felt much more confident about having an organized 10-page manuscript than 40 pages of ideas. I gradually added more data and arguments to the various sections, and my final draft was a polished 40-page manuscript.

Expect your outline to change during the editing process, especially as you discover new information in the literature. In other words,

WRITE AND DEFEND YOUR THESIS

it might be necessary to move around different sections of your thesis as you edit your document. One of my warm-up exercises for writing was to proofread what I had written the previous day. Even at the final stages of editing, there will be a lot to revise. How do you know when you are done? Balance clarity with perfectionism: If you have defined your central questions, and answered them with reliable supporting arguments, you are probably close to finishing your first draft.

 Balance clarity with perfectionism: Organize your ideas in a logical order, but avoid spending too much time editing and re-editing the same parts of your thesis.

Joan Boalker reminds us to avoid a type of perfectionism she calls the "Penelope syndrome." Penelope, the faithful wife of Odysseus in Greek mythology, spent her days weaving a burial shroud for her father-in-law, which she unraveled every night to keep her suitors away. Like Penelope, some writers also have a habit of writing and rewriting the same paragraphs over and over again. After they have produced a few paragraphs, they throw them away and try to rewrite them. If you find yourself struggling with the "Penelope syndrome," ask yourself whether you are still trying to define your central questions or if you are being a perfectionist. Remember that eventually, your thesis needs to be handed in; most likely, it will not be perfect, but it will be good enough to show that you are an independent researcher. If you are dissatisfied with the order of your arguments or your style of writing, leave the final revisions for the next stage.

DEVELOP YOUR STORY, ONE STEP AT A TIME

Once you have all your main arguments in place, you can enhance your document by adding layers of detail to it. I have developed a method of writing called the "onion approach." This is a top-down method, where you define the "big picture" first to clarify the main arguments, and then collect information to support your line of reasoning. You can build up your thesis in this way by gradually adding layers to it, as if you were building an onion from the inside out. Ways of "filling out" your thesis include citing the previous researchers who have tried answering these questions, finding papers that support your methods and interpreting your own results. During the revision process, you can increase the legibility of your thesis by organizing your data into tables, putting together graphs and illustrating your methods with flowcharts. Your first draft need not include all of these embellishments, but at this point, it should be a well-organized manuscript that tells a coherent story.

Construct your thesis around the "big picture" or core arguments, and gradually embellish your manuscript by adding layers of detail every day.

Recent doctoral dissertations from your department are an excellent resource for constructing your thesis, particularly if their topics are similar to yours. You can use previous theses as models for your own thesis. What was the scope of their dissertation? In how much detail did they discuss their results? How did they interpret their data? Some students overestimate the scope of their theses, and bite off a larger piece than they can chew. It is better to have a narrower, focused topic than an ambiguously defined question that you cannot answer adequately. Look over previous dissertations to understand how other students elaborated on their central questions. Many doctoral theses are constructed as two or three master's theses that are extensions of one central idea.

Borrow recent doctoral dissertations from the library as models for building your own thesis.

Once you are motivated to write, it can be tempting to sit in front of the computer for 12 hours a day. The problem with this schedule is that it is difficult to maintain. You might be productive for 12 hours one day, but if you tried to reproduce this achievement the following day, you might feel instantly overwhelmed. If you devote an entire day to writing, you will be more productive if you divide your time into shorter segments. Becky, a humanities major, went to a workshop on how to write a dissertation, and walked away with the following advice: "I heard at the seminar that our attention span can be sustained for only 45 minutes at a time. Therefore, I divided my schedule into 45-minute 'units.' It was much easier to get organized, if I knew that I would only be working for 45 minutes at a time. After each unit of work, I relaxed for about 15 minutes. My friends and I actually went out to buy timers, so that we could follow this advice." Remember Jim, the electrical engineer, from chapter two? You might recall that Jim also followed the 45/15-minute schedule for reading and writing papers, suggesting that these time intervals worked well for sustaining one's attention over extended periods of time.

 Divide your writing schedule into several short segments (approximately 45 minutes of work and 15 minutes of rest) to help you stay focused and organized.

What should you do if you feel that you have fallen behind your schedule in completing your thesis? Should you pile up yesterday's uncompleted assignments, together with today's challenges, and try to do everything in one day? Lori, a psychology major, found that the most useful advice she received for writing her dissertation was to start every day fresh. "On most days, you will probably not finish everything on your to-do list. It is pointless to pile everything from yesterday onto today's list. Just start every day fresh, and try to complete as much as you can."

 Start every day fresh. Do not worry about how much you did not complete the day before; just focus on being as productive as you can each day.

In summary, remember the following suggestions when you construct your first draft:

- In your first draft, aim to clarify your central question and organize your supporting arguments in a logical order.
- Avoid editing and re-editing the same paragraphs. Focus on conveying a central message and leave the editing for later.
- Build your thesis from the inside out, by defining the core of your dissertation and adding a few layers of detail to it every day.
- Borrow recent doctoral dissertations from the library to understand the expectations of your department.
- If you will be writing for long periods of time, alternate 45 minutes of writing with 15-minute breaks.

- Start every day fresh, rather than feeling guilty about not having made sufficient progress the previous day.

Stage III: Complete your final manuscript

The final revision can be time-consuming, but also exciting. Until now, your job has been to collect and organize your ideas, but now you are almost ready to hand in your thesis to your committee. At this stage, your data and ideas are under the right headings, although you might still need to shift some paragraphs around. You no longer need to struggle with generating new ideas or building up your arguments, but you do need to refine each section until the whole manuscript is ready to be handed in. In order to avoid confusion among the different parts of your dissertation, it is most efficient to focus on perfecting one section of your thesis at a time.

It is possible to engage in different stages of writing simultaneously. For example, you might be close to finishing chapter one of your thesis, but still struggling with the introduction. Wherever you are in the editing phase, remember that the writing process is the same. For each section, you will need to define the questions and organize your ideas in a logical order. Once your ideas are in place, go through the grammar and style, to increase your manuscript's readability.

 Go through the revision process by focusing on perfecting your thesis, one section at a time.

At the revision stage, you might already be nearing your graduation deadline. In chapter three, I talked about the "reverse calendar" strategy for constructing small deadlines that are based on long-term goals. When is your thesis due? Research the answer to this question carefully; the final thesis might be due at the end of May, but you probably have to submit a draft to your committee or advisor a few weeks before. You will also need to leave enough time for administrative details, such as paperwork for the registrar's office, printing your thesis and binding your final manuscript. Write down all the deadlines, but do not panic if you realize how little time you have left. You will probably be more efficient during the last few weeks, and will have the necessary energy to meet your deadlines—especially if you have been maintaining a healthy diet!

If you become anxious under time pressure, use deadlines to empower yourself. Begin by setting very small and realistic deadlines that you can definitely meet (e.g., organize bibliography, proofread a certain section or format your document). Once you have satisfied small deadlines, you will feel an immediate sense of satisfaction. It is easy to set high goals for yourself, but it is much harder to meet them. Setting unrealistic goals might even backfire if you are unable to reach them, as they can leave you with a feeling of failure. Instead, visualize writing your thesis, one tiny step at a time. If you had to spend the next five minutes writing your thesis, what would you do? Would you revise the introduction? Would you add a graph or construct a flow-chart of your methods? Remember that any progress will motivate you to work, so set yourself realistic deadlines that you can definitely meet. Expect your goals and deadlines to change on a daily basis, and that you will probably need to rewrite your to-do list as your thesis evolves. For example, you might realize that you need an extra graph—or that the graphs that you were going to add are no longer necessary.

 Set up several short, manageable and well-defined deadlines that you can meet, to give yourself a sense of control over the editing of your thesis.

As hard as you may try to meet all your deadlines, you will probably miss a few. Perhaps one morning you wake up with a splitting head-ache, or life will bring you an unexpected emergency, and you will not be able to meet your writing goal for the day. What can you do? Be persistent and continue writing as soon as you have the chance. Also, see what you have learned from missing the deadline. Did you set goals that were too high? Were you unable to meet your deadlines because your notes or references were not properly organized? Did you pack your schedule too tightly? While deadlines are important for getting your work done, do not put too much pressure on yourself. Distinguish what you can plan for, from what is beyond your control; pick up where you left off, as soon as you have the chance.

In order to speed up your progress, think about experts who could help you. Does your advisor counsel her students during the the-sis-writing process? Will she read drafts of your thesis? It is important to get your advisor's approval on your dissertation (after all, she has to sign it), but her input could also help you focus and get organized. Paige, a chemist, asked her lab mates to review individual chapters of her thesis along the way. Not only did she get valuable feedback from her friends, but the "need" to show them something new every few weeks also motivated her to continue writing.

Also, find out whether your university or department has thesis-writing support groups. If they do not, consider starting your own. Look for friends and colleagues who are finishing up their theses around the same time, and offer to proofread their theses in exchange for them reading your dissertation. Carol, an English major, benefited from an informal support group within her department. "We met about once a month, and we discussed our struggles with the writing process. We also read each other's dissertations and critiqued them." Finally, find out whether your university has a writing center, where you can receive help in improving the grammar, style and content of your thesis. "It was challenging for me to write my thesis, because English is not my native language," said Peter, an electrical engineer. "I was very fortunate to get help from writing experts at the university, who helped proofread my thesis."

If you have a support group, a friend, or a writing coach, think about your goals. What type of criticism are you looking for? Are you concerned primarily about your grammar, the layout or the structure of your argument? It can be frustrating to give your thesis to someone, hoping for constructive criticism on the structure of your thesis, and get comments on your font size and margins. Also, be prepared for disagreement, and if there is some, do not take it personally. After all, it is *your* thesis, and *you* decide how to write it. Listen to the suggestions of others, but do what you feel is right. If you do join a thesis-writing support group, avoid competitiveness and rivalry, even if two of you are in the same year. Remember that each thesis is unique, and it is difficult to compare progress. Rather than focusing on "who will finish first," think about making the best thesis that you can. Several years from now, it will not matter which semester you graduated, but a well-written thesis can lay the foundation for your future career. No one will remember when you actually received your degree, but the quality of your work will be on display, on your library's shelves, for many years to come. If you are organizing your own thesis-writing support group, you can decide who will be in it. Choose the members carefully, and include students who will be supportive rather than competitive. If you have RSI, look for support groups for your condition. I was fortunate to get help from other RSI "veterans," who gave me advice regarding voice-activated software and ergonomic keyboards and mice.

 Seek the support of professors, friends and proofreaders during the preparation of your dissertation.

It is also important to keep yourself connected to your friends and family throughout the writing process. You might need to decline invitations to some social events, but do make time to relax every day. In the final stages of thesis-writing, you need to sustain your productivity and creativity. If you push yourself to your limits every day, you will probably burn out and not be able to concentrate. Relaxing for a short time at a social event can boost your productivity; in fact, surrounding yourself with supportive friends was one of the top two pieces of advice for releasing stress. The other advice for dealing with anxiety was regular exercise. Many students kept their fitness routines throughout the writing process, because they felt that exercise was an indispensable component of their well-being.

 The top two pieces of advice for letting go of stress during the writing process (as well as throughout graduate school): socialize with supportive friends and exercise on a regular basis.

When is your thesis finished? To answer this question, clarify the expectations with your advisor and thesis committee. Take charge of your dissertation by deciding how it should be constructed, but do get approval from your mentors. Communicating with other professors will help you focus on the most important issues and obtain the resources needed to fill in the gaps. Even so, it will be hard to judge when your thesis is finished. Many students have great expectations from their doctoral dissertations, and they experience a sense of disappointment when they realize that their thesis is not as good as they had expected. Some thesis writers even " hit the wall"—or experience a writer's block—close to the end. They have come a long way, but it is hard to push themselves to go until the very end. They might be asking themselves questions such as: Is my thesis good enough? What if my committee rejects what I have written?

One way to fight off the inevitable feelings of self-doubt is to recognize how much you have already done. When I was nearing the completion of my thesis, I complained to a senior scientist about my struggles with writing my dissertation. As she listened to my complaints, she just shook her head and said, "Dora, you finished your experiments, your committee agreed to let you graduate, and you have put together most of your thesis already! I think you're 95% there!" When I realized that I only had about 5% of my thesis ahead of me (which consisted primarily of editing, rather than crossing my fingers for experiments to go well), I felt incredibly relieved. Anytime I have doubts about my ability to finish a project, I remind myself of this comment. Many students struggle until the very end, even when they see the light at the end of the tunnel. Just remember to push yourself a little bit every day, until all the pieces of your thesis are in place. With persistence, your thesis will come together.

 It can be hard to push yourself to finish writing at the very end; boost your self-confidence by realizing how much you have already done, and how little there is left to do.

Completing your doctoral dissertation can be scary, because it signifies the closing of an important chapter in your life. When you finish your dissertation, you will move on to a new life—a life full of new opportunities, but possibly more responsibilities, too. If you have to move out of your graduate student dorm, are you concerned about what it will be like to live in an isolated apartment or house? What will life be like once you are a Ph.D.? Changes can be scary, even when they are positive. If you have no plans after your defense, it is even harder to motivate yourself to complete your writing. You might ask yourself questions such as: "What now? What *will* I do after graduation?"

However, whether or not you have concrete plans, you will feel relieved once your thesis is complete. In the words of Joan Boalker, "The best dissertation is a done dissertation."

WRITE AND DEFEND YOUR THESIS

Having your committee accept your thesis on the day of your defense is a big step towards earning your Ph.D. Most likely, however, your committee will expect you to make revisions. In some cases, these revisions can be completed within a few weeks. Other times, especially if you have already started your job, it can take months or even a whole year to incorporate all the corrections. Changes to your dissertation can be time-consuming if you are asked to reanalyze your data, collect new information, or possibly perform additional experiments. Some graduates recalled having to work for a few hours every evening after their daytime job, just to finish their revisions. Burdensome as these revisions might be, you now have a clear path ahead of you. You have completed an original doctoral dissertation, and you successfully defended it in front of your committee.

In summary, the following strategies have helped former students complete their dissertations while maintaining a reasonable schedule:

- In order to avoid feeling overwhelmed, focus on revising only one section of your thesis at a time.
- Break down your to-do list into well-defined and realistic deadlines that you will be able to meet.
- Ask your advisor, committee members, writing coaches or friends to help you proofread your dissertation.
- Do not isolate yourself from your friends and family. Make time to relax every day.
- Watch out for "hitting the wall" at the very end. Push yourself a little bit every day, until your thesis meets all the requirements.

Challenge #2: Enhancing your presentation skills

Delivering effective public presentations is a skill that improves through repeated practice. In this section, I have compiled advice from my interviews as well as several resource books (see the appendix), to cover the most common concerns regarding public-speaking. What is the best way to begin your presentation? How do you capture your audience's attention? How do you make your presentation persuasive? What can you do, if you feel nervous before a presentation? How do you answer difficult questions? How can you use PowerPoint to your advantage? During my interviews, I found that the most common challenges for graduate students were:

- ◆ Overcoming nervousness before giving a talk
- ◆ Keeping the audience interested in your presentation
- ◆ Condensing all your material into a 20–30-minute presentation
- ◆ Dealing with people who ask difficult or annoying questions

In this section, I will show you how to address these concerns and to avoid many of the common mistakes that people make before and during their presentations.

Preparing properly for presentations

WHY DO PEOPLE EXPERIENCE A FEAR OF PUBLIC-SPEAKING?
Most people experience fear before speaking in public, because their goal is to impress their audience with their expertise, rather than to tell an interesting story. During practice sessions (possibly in front of a mirror), they try to emulate effective speakers by controlling their gestures, the tone of their voice and their exact choice of words.

Sound familiar? Do you worry about giving presentations, because they might not go as planned? Are you concerned that you will make mistakes and that people will discover that you are not really an expert? What if somebody told you that even professional speakers experience nervousness before each talk? Did you realize that almost all speakers make mistakes during their talks? What distinguishes experienced speakers from novices is that experts can use their nervousness to their advantage, by giving themselves a boost of energy before their presentations. Furthermore, professional speakers expect their talk *not* to go 100% according to plan, but they are able to recover from their mistakes and even make light of them.

Inexperienced speakers, however, increase their anxiety by trying to deliver the perfect presentation. They over-practice their body language and their jokes, and might put excessive effort into their attire and slides. They want to get every detail right, and so they mentally run-through all the "what if's," in case something does not go according to plan. By the time they need to give their presentations, they feel exhausted, and cannot wait to get their talk over with.

WRITE AND DEFEND YOUR THESIS

Most people experience anxiety before public-speaking because they try to deliver the perfect talk. You can overcome this nervousness by allowing yourself to be yourself, and to focus on the material rather than how you look in front of the audience.

What if you could be comfortable or even *look forward to* public-speaking? While preparing for presentations takes time and energy, most Ph.D.s acknowledged that giving talks was essential to career development. First, presentations force you to think critically about your work; you need to explain to an audience the motivation for your study, your methods, your results and your conclusions. Through the process of preparing your presentation, you will probably discover new ways to improve your research.

The second reason that it is important to practice public-speaking is that once you get a job, you will probably need to present your work on a regular basis. If you work at a teaching college, you will need to give lectures multiple times a week. In a research institution or at a company, you will be asked to give presentations, and you might also need to speak at conferences. Furthermore, the higher up you go at a company, research institution or university, the more presentations you will need to give.

Knowing that almost everybody is nervous before speaking in public, what can you do feel more comfortable?

How to prepare properly for your talk

Begin preparing for your presentation by forgetting that you will talk to a crowd. Imagine for a moment that you are sitting in a café, explaining your research to a friend who also has expertise in your field. If you knew in advance that you would need to explain your work to your friend, you would probably bring your materials so that you could illustrate your points. You would probably not practice your gestures or the tone of your voice, because you would trust that these would come to you naturally. It is also unlikely that you would worry about making mistakes; if you did, you would admit them quickly and honestly by saying something like, "Did I just say the mice were 25 years old? Oops, I meant that they were 25 *days* old. This sure would have been an interesting experiment, with 25 year old mice! Well, getting back to my previous point, our data analysis showed that...." Can you see how in a casual conversation, you focus on your material, rather than on how you look or sound? You do not worry about mistakes, because you know that you have all your materials for reference.

Of course, the stakes are higher in front of a crowd, especially when the audience includes your thesis committee or professionals in your field (if you speak at a conference). Nevertheless, the above example illustrates that if you were to give this presentation to a friend, you would not be nervous about presenting your material. While preparing for this conversation, you would focus only on organizing your materials, so that you could present them to your friend coherently. The most important part of a professional presentation is also to organize your information so that your audience understands your story. Instead of standing in front of a mirror and wondering whether you merely *look* professional, begin by practicing in your head and make sure that you have all the information that you need.

 Practice in your head, to ensure that you have all the information that you need. Practice out loud to check whether you are within the time limit, and know how to explain your research. Do not try to perfect your body language or tone of voice.

If you are still concerned about how you look, you can improve your presentation skills by videotaping one of your practice sessions. Most likely, you will find that you look and sound professional, and that your gestures fit well with your message. You might realize, however, that you frequently use verbal mannerisms such as: "you know," "uhm," or "okay," and you might also notice some nervous gestures such as playing with your hair or fumbling with change in your pocket. You will probably not realize these filler words and gestures if you practiced in front of a mirror, but they will come across on a video recording. Try to keep a good posture and a professional tone of voice during your practice sessions, but do not put too much emphasis on trying to eliminate your old habits completely. It is normal to use mannerisms or nervous gestures when you temporarily lose your train of thought. The more prepared and relaxed you are before and during your talk, the fewer filler words you will use.

Videotape yourself during practice sessions to become aware of your nervous gestures or verbal mannerisms.

Some people set themselves up for anxiety by telling themselves in advance that they are not good public speakers. Your self-talk has significant influence over your self-confidence and your actual performance. Athletes often visualize themselves jumping to a certain height or crossing the finish line, for months before the actual event. These mental exercises serve to increase their motivation and help them review the skills they will need to accomplish their goals. You can also visualize yourself delivering an excellent presentation. If you are accustomed to the idea of being an ineffective public speaker, it might take some time to change your self-talk.

Most Ph.D.s attributed improvement in their public-speaking skills to practicing their talks with advisors and colleagues. During these practice sessions, they received feedback on the content and appearance of their slides, including difficult-to-read font sizes or excessive use of color in their illustrations. Furthermore, they also received constructive criticism on their presentation styles, such as how well they projected their voice or if they engaged in distracting activities such as playing with the pointer. Most importantly, however, these practice sessions served to increase their self-confidence, because they were able to get through their talk once (or a few times) in front of a real audience. If you are shy in front of a crowd, remember that graduate school will give you many opportunities to speak in public, and your presentation skills will improve with time.

Practice with your advisor or group members before your actual presentation to help you decrease nervousness and to enhance the quality of your talk.

WHAT CAN YOU DO RIGHT BEFORE A PRESENTATION, TO FEEL MORE COMFORTABLE?

There is no way to ensure that your talk will go exactly according to plan, but you can still run through a checklist beforehand to confirm that everything is set up properly. First, familiarize yourself with the room and the audiovisual set-up. Check the connections between the computer and the projector and make sure that your slides are projecting well onto the screen. Try out the pointer to see whether it is still working or if it needs new batteries (definitely not something you want to discover in the middle of your talk). If you will be speaking in a large room, you might also have a microphone. Is it wireless? Do you know how to turn it on? Is there an audiovisual person who can help you if there is a problem?

 Allow a few minutes before your presentation, to check the technical set-up for your presentation and to make sure that everything (e.g., computer, projector, pointer, microphone) is working properly.

Also do a quick check on your appearance before your talk. Are there any leftovers from lunch on your face or between your teeth? Are your hair and (possibly) make-up in order? If you have a tendency to get nervous during presentations, keep a bottle of water on the table in case your throat gets dry during your talk. (Avoid using a glass of water, because it could spill.) If you have any notes, arrange them properly, so that you can refer to them without having to sort through your pile during your talk.

Finally, accept that you will feel a little bit nervous before you get up on stage. The nervousness is there to give you a boost the energy, so that you can perform in front of your audience. Rather than try to fight this nervousness, harness this excitement into your presentation. Most likely, you will find that the nervousness dissipates as soon as you begin talking. Dalia, a psychology major, recalled that her advisor told her students that nervousness was a good sign. "She told us that if you did not feel any nervousness, it meant that you were too complacent, and not excited about your talk."

 Expect that you will be nervous right before your talk. Remember that the nervousness is there to give you energy during your talk, so use it to become excited about your presentation.

Mitchell, an English major, was an instructor for a public-speaking course during graduate school. "Some of my students were really afraid to speak in public. I advised them to overcome this fear gradually, by asking questions at seminars or speaking up at group meetings." If you feel excessively anxious before speaking in front of a group, become aware of your breathing. How many breaths are you taking per minute? Gradually try to slow your breathing down by inhaling more deeply, pausing between the inhales and the exhales and making your exhales longer. When you slow down your breathing, you will feel more relaxed; it will also give you a chance to take your mind off your anxiety temporarily.

 You can gradually overcome fear of public-speaking by asking questions at seminars or voicing your opinions at meetings. If the nervousness becomes excessive, consciously slow down your breathing for a few minutes before you speak.

In summary, here are some of the key points that will help you practice properly for your presentations:

- Visualize yourself having a casual conversation, rather than talking to a large audience.
- Practice in your head, to ensure that you have all of the relevant information.
- Practice out loud with colleagues, to receive constructive criticism.
- Videotape yourself, to become aware of verbal mannerisms and gestures.
- Check the technical set-up for your talk, before you begin your presentation.
- Accept that you will feel nervous; use that energy to become excited about your presentation.
- If you feel excessively nervous, consciously slow down your breathing by focusing on deep inhalation and long exhalations.

Structuring your presentation, in seven steps
STEP ONE: DECIDE WHAT YOUR THESIS STATEMENT OR TAKE-HOME MESSAGE WILL BE

When preparing for your talk, decide what the take-home message of your presentation will be. Summarize this message into one simple and succinct sentence that will be easy for your audience to remember. This sentence—sometimes referred to as the thesis statement, which is a fitting terminology for students working on their dissertations—is what your audience will walk away with after your talk is over. How do you decide what your thesis statement should be? Briefly, your thesis statement will summarize how your work addresses an important research question. You will be repeating this message several times during your presentation, so make your thesis statement concise and memorable.

STEP TWO: TAILOR YOUR PRESENTATION TO YOUR AUDIENCE
Think back to the example of explaining your research to a friend. How would the presentation differ if your friend were an expert in the field versus somebody who is only interested in the "big picture"? When you give a presentation to your thesis committee, your material will be primarily technical and detail-oriented. If you talk at a conference where the audience has a diverse background, you will probably spend the first few minutes explaining the motivation of your study before getting into the technical details.

As you analyze your audience, think about their shared backgrounds. What do these people have in common? What is their expertise? Your presentation will be more effective if you can address issues that many of your audience members are familiar with. Nonetheless, do not try to please everybody, because that is an unrealistic goal. Instead, focus on a persuasive story that the majority of your audience will be interested in.

Understanding your audience's expectations is critical when you are presenting to your thesis committee. You do not want to walk away being criticized for not presenting a certain part of your research (after all, they might have forgotten what you showed them last time), nor do you want to leave insufficient time for questions. If you can, approach your committee members, or at least your advisor, individually before the meeting. Give them a written report, so that they can understand your progress and clarify what is expected at the meeting.

STEP THREE: CAPTURE YOUR AUDIENCE'S ATTENTION
How should you begin your presentation? Do you need to tell a funny story? While it is not necessary to tell jokes, you can make your presentation more memorable by sharing an anecdote or an interesting

statistic at the beginning of your talk. For example, you could recount how you started this research or give a historical perspective on your work. You can also think about rhetorical questions such as: "How many people here have heard of…?" As you prepare your introduction, think about a common ground with your audience. What information is this audience looking for? What is the problem that your presentation will address? How will your audience (or your field of research) benefit from your work? Open your presentation with a few sentences that introduce your topic and capture your audience's attention.

Another way to think about a good introduction is to visualize once again a conversation with your friend at a café. How would you begin your talk? You would probably thank your friend for his or her time, and then give an opening statement highlighting the important points in your research. Assuming that you are talking at a conference or department seminar, you might begin with something like: "Good afternoon! I am really glad/honored to be here and have the opportunity to tell you about my research on (insert your topic). Our work on this project started a few years ago, when we realized that (insert the motivation for your research, and a background story)…." Avoid irrelevant introductions such as: "Thank you very much for coming to my presentation. I realize that everybody must be tired at this time of the day, and you all want to go home and watch the exciting game tonight. I am a sports fan myself, and I will try to get through this presentation fairly quickly." This introduction is from an actual presentation that I attended. While the presentation itself was interesting, it reminded people of the time of day and the audience members spent more time looking at their watches than paying attention to the talk.

Once you have given your audience a brief introduction, clarify your thesis statement. In other words, tell them what your take-home message will be. For example, your thesis statement might be: "Through this research, we have discovered that…." In order to get your audience's attention, it is important to clarify *why* they should care about your research, and what your take-home message will be. For a thesis committee meeting, you might begin this part of your presentation with a statement such as: "Last time, we decided that the most interesting way to follow up on my previous results was to examine the…"

Capture your audience's attention by beginning your talk with an anecdote, startling statistic, or a rhetorical question relevant to your research.

STEP FOUR: OUTLINE YOUR TALK

After your audience has understood your thesis statement, sort your presentation into an outline. Try to stay away from pedantic outlines such as: "I will first discuss my methods, then my data, then give you my conclusions and some directions for future research." You can make your outline more interesting by including a few details on your protocol, methods, data or interpretations of your findings. Illustrate your outline with a flowchart that you can refer back to when you cover the different sections in your presentation. As you go through your outline, connect each section to your thesis statement. How do the different parts of your talk support your take-home message? In his book *Power Points!*, Harry Mills suggests the following breakdown for presentations:

- ◆ Introduction: 10–15% of your time
  - Capture your audience's attention
  - Give thesis statement
  - Present an outline
- ◆ Body: 80–85% of your time
  - Illustrate and cite evidence for the three to five points you are making
- ◆ Summary: 5% of your time
  - Summarize key points
  - Repeat your conclusions and the thesis statement
  - Present opportunities for future research

STEP FIVE: PRESENT THE BODY OF YOUR WORK

Eighty to eighty-five percent of your time will be devoted to this part of your presentation. First, divide your work into three to five major categories. Avoid too many sections, otherwise your talk will be too rushed. A good rule of thumb is to prepare one slide for every two minutes. In other words, if you have a 20-minute presentation, use approximately 10 slides. If you expect questions during your presentation, it might be a good idea to prepare even fewer slides, such as one every three minutes. With fewer slides, you will be able to talk at a reasonable pace and present your information thoroughly. Sometimes it will be to your advantage to summarize your research with visual aids such as charts or graphs. During your practice sessions, make sure that your graphs or charts can be explained and understood in less than 30 seconds; otherwise, your figures might have too much information and could be confusing. To keep your presentation easy to follow, illustrate only one major point per diagram.

If you use bulleted lists, include at most six points at a time, otherwise your slides will look too busy. It is not necessary to have complete sentences; just highlight the key results. Put the most important point at the top of your list, and then follow it with your other points in order of decreasing importance. If you do not want your audience to read the bulleted list in advance, you can use animation and have the points appear right before you read them aloud.

After you have covered one of your categories, you can summarize the key points for that section with a transition statement such as, "As I have just shown, one of the most important results of our work was that.... Another important issue to address is...." Now you have made a transition to your next point. A good way to make transitions is to refer back to the flowchart that outlined your presentation during your introduction. During transitions, you can repeat the points that you have already covered, and then point to the section that you are about to present. You can also have the heading of your currently discussed section highlighted in your outline, so that your audience will have an easier time following you.

 Use transition statements to explain how each part of your talk addresses your thesis statement.

STEP SIX: SUMMARIZE YOUR TALK AND CONNECT IT WITH YOUR THESIS STATEMENT

At the end of your talk summarize your presentation by going over each one of the points that you covered during your presentation. What was the original problem that you were addressing? How has your research addressed this issue? What were some of the key points that you made during your talk? You can make your conclusions more memorable by paraphrasing your talk, rather than reciting each point word by word. As you wrap up your presentation refer back to your thesis statement and show how your presentation supports your central message.

STEP SEVEN: SHOW OPPORTUNITIES FOR FUTURE RESEARCH
What is a good way to end your presentation? You have just told an interesting story, and the end of your talk is a good opportunity to show how to continue your research. It is also your chance to cover gaps in your story that you might have discovered during the preparation phase. It happens frequently that students realize a few days before their presentations that they should have done more work in a particular area, but did not have the time to collect more data or information before their presentations. You can include these missing pieces in the section for "future research." The end of your talk is also your opportunity to announce that you welcome questions from your audience.

Common advice for constructing an easy to follow presentations is to:
1) Tell them what you are going to tell them (introduction)
2) Tell them (body of your presentation) and
3) Tell them what you told them (conclusion).

WHAT SHOULD YOU DO IF YOU GET NERVOUS DURING YOUR TALK?
Most of your anxiety will probably pass once you begin your presentation, but you might experience some nervousness if you make a mistake or suddenly forget what you were supposed to say. First, do not worry about having short periods of silence. Silence is an excellent way to get your audience's attention, especially if you have just made an important point. It will give you an opportunity to look around the room, to assess whether your audience has understood your point and to collect your thoughts. If you become nervous, slow down your breathing. Take a deep breath, get a drink of water and repeat in your head the point that you have just made. Feel a little bit more collected? Now you can move on to make your next point.

Another way to relax during a public presentation is to make eye contact with individual people in your audience. Talking directly to someone will make you feel like you are having a conversation with a friend, rather than delivering a public presentation. Furthermore, frequent eye contact will allow you to get feedback from individual audience members. Are they interested in your talk? Do they understand what you are trying to say? If you notice confused looks, it might be time to adjust your plan. Repeat your point again, and paraphrase it in a way that you think will clarify your message.

If you still experience nervousness during your talk, focus on your presentation and do not worry about how you look. Remember the previous advice about videotaping yourself? If you have done that exercise, you probably know that you look quite professional when you give a talk. Remind yourself of this image and shift your attention to your material. Is your thesis statement succinct and clear? Is your story convincing? Did you include all the important information? If you are able to build up your self-confidence through your practice sessions, you will be more relaxed during the actual talk. It can take time to build up self-confidence, if you are used to telling yourself that you are not a good public speaker. Accept that you will make mistakes—just as everybody else does—and that the best way to reduce the number of mistakes is to practice properly and often. You need not be the world's leading expert, to deliver an effective talk; simply focus on having a conversation with your audience about the interesting story you are going to tell.

How can you answer difficult or annoying questions?
What if there are no questions?

If you are presenting your work on a controversial topic, you might get some pessimistic or hostile questions. First, keep in mind that the hostility is not personal. The person asking the questions probably has nothing against you, but they might disagree with your conclusions. If you do encounter such questions, stay calm. Let them voice their opinions, but do not let them have control of the situation. Once they are finished, repeat the question to show that you were listening. Some people just want their voice heard. If you do not know the answer, admit it honestly, but give them some ideas for finding out. For example: "Yes, we know this method is still in the development phase, and it might not be applicable in all situations. Our results show that it is reliable in this particular set-up, and we are looking into expanding its applications by experimenting with…."

You might also encounter "question hogs." These people try to dominate the question-and-answer session. Answer one or two of their questions, then give somebody else an opportunity to ask a question by saying: "Let me answer some questions from the other people in the audience. If you still have questions, I will be happy to answer them after my talk. " If the "question hog" is a committee member, you might need to allow yourself to be grilled, but they will probably give you valuable information for your thesis.

What if you have reached the question-and-answer session and there are no questions? Does that mean that your audience did not understand your talk? Not necessarily. Sometimes there might not be any questions, because your audience is shy or because they are still thinking about how they want to pose their question. You can break the ice by asking a question yourself. For example, you can say something like: "Well, a question that I frequently get it is…." After you answer your own question, you might find that the audience will warm up to asking more questions themselves. If there are still no questions, wrap up your talk by thanking the audience for their time and attention.

 When preparing for your talk, try to anticipate what the most common questions will be, and prepare some extra slides with additional information to answer them.

Using PowerPoint to your advantage

Not all presentations require PowerPoint, but it is important to familiarize yourself with the features of this software. The most common mistakes that people make with PowerPoint are as follows:

- Font size too small:
  - Make titles 24–36 points. For text, use a smaller font size (18–24 points).
  - Make bullets one or two sizes smaller than the text.
- Typeface difficult to read:
  - Use the same typeface throughout, unless you want to make a special point.
  - According to Harry Mills, author of PowerPoints!, if you want your slides to look different, Tahoma and

WRITE AND DEFEND YOUR THESIS

Verdana are good alternatives to Arial; Georgia is a good alternative to Times New Roman.
- ◆ Slides crammed with information:
  - Convey only one major point per slide.
  - Use at most six bullets per slide.
- ◆ Improperly labeled diagrams:
  - Use each diagram to illustrate one point, which should be summarized in the title.
  - Use a legible font size to label the axes and scales on the graphs.
- ◆ Hard-to-distinguish colors:
  - Have contrast between your background and your text color.
  - Use either a light background with dark text or a dark background with light text. Avoid bright background colors, which are difficult to look at for long periods.
  - The most common background colors are white and dark blue.
  - The most common text colors are black (for white background) and white or yellow (for blue background).
  - If you use multiple colors on graphs, check whether they can be distinguished from each other from the back of the room.
- ◆ Putting more emphasis on the software features than the talk itself:
  - Use animation only when needed.
  - Keep your diagrams simple; it is not necessary to use three-dimensional pictures unless they convey additional information.
- ◆ Using distracting clipart:
  - Limit the use of clip art on the margins of your slides.
  - Use clipart only if it is part of your story.

In summary, according to professors and other Ph.D.s that I interviewed, the following are the features of effective presentations:

- ◆ Speaker was relaxed and knowledgeable

- Background and motivation were explained clearly in the introduction
- Outline of presentation was clarified at the beginning
- Speaker addressed interests of audience
- Information was summarized succinctly in graphs and charts
- Logical order to the arguments
- Included stories to illustrate points

In contrast, these are the most common mistakes:

- Expecting yourself to deliver a perfect presentation
- Practicing your gestures, the tone of your voice and your body language, particularly in front of a mirror
- Recycling slides from a previous presentation, without analyzing your audience
- Not communicating a clear take-home message
- Not explaining the background or motivation for your study
- Trying to present too much information, too quickly
- Pretending that you know the answer to a question when you do not
- Reading slides, rather than talking to the audience

Drawing out your thesis before writing it: *Russell's story*

Russell, an education major, had an interesting strategy for writing his thesis. As a visual person, he wanted to see all of the connections in his research before writing about them. Instead of free writing, he drew maps to see how his studies and data supported his arguments and conclusions. "My office wall and floor were decorated with maps. I used maps throughout my dissertation to help me plan my studies and write about them. It was easier to write, once I saw how everything was connected." Drawing maps and flowcharts can help you collect your ideas and construct your line of reasoning.

Whether you draw maps or use free writing, the important part is to get your ideas out of your head before attempting to organize them. Your ideas will come to you randomly and you will be able to put them in order once you see the "big picture" on paper.

Being afraid to present dissertation work: *Diane's story*

Diane, an English major, became a professor after graduation. She gives lectures multiple times per week and also needs to speak at conferences frequently. Interestingly, she did not experience fear of public-speaking until she went to graduate school. "I did not worry about giving talks until I was asked to present my dissertation. I think that I was afraid of not having done good enough research." In retrospect, she realized that she was probably trying to give the perfect presentation in front of an intimidating audience of professors. She still gets nervous when she needs to talk about her thesis, but she reminds herself that her committee accepted it, and therefore she must have done a good job. She does not get nervous before her lectures, although she does acknowledge that they take a significant amount of energy. "While I am giving a lecture, I have to stay focused on my material and also process the feedback from my students. I need to keep paying attention to how they receive the material and whether they are following me. I am not afraid of speaking in public now, but I will say that giving lectures is tiring."

CHAPTER SUMMARY AND ACTION PLAN

Write and defend your thesis

Part I: Write Your Thesis

Step 1: Construct your zero draft.
- Make a commitment to write every day.
- Decide when and where to write.
- Begin writing by collecting the ideas and data that you want to include in your thesis.
- Define the questions your thesis will address.
- If you have a preliminary outline, categorize your ideas into the appropriate sections, to facilitate the editing process.
- Aim to write at least two pages a day.
- If you do not know what to write about, write freely for 30 to 60 minutes about anything that comes to mind.

◆ Keep an active to-do list, to help you make progress on your thesis.

Step 2: Write your first draft.
   ◆ The purpose of writing your first draft is to define the central question of your thesis, and to organize your data and ideas in a logical order.
   ◆ Focus on constructing a persuasive story; leave the grammar and style editing for later.
   ◆ Avoid spending too much time on editing and re-editing the same part of your thesis.
   ◆ Use a top-down approach by writing about the "big picture," and embellish your story by adding layers of detail to it every day.
   ◆ Model the structure of your thesis after previous doctoral dissertations from your department.
   ◆ If you need help, join a thesis-writing group, or ask friends and writing coaches to proofread your thesis.

Step 3: Complete your final manuscript.
   ◆ Correct your thesis, one section at a time.
   ◆ If you have many hours to write, divide your time into 45 minutes of working and 15 minutes of rest.
   ◆ Double-check deadlines for handing in your dissertation.
   ◆ Set up many small and realistic goals, rather than complicated or ambiguously defined tasks.
   ◆ Keep your advisor informed about progress on your thesis, so he or she can revise it before it goes to your committee.

Step 4: Maximize your progress and avoid common mistakes during the writing process.
   ◆ Back up your work up every day, on multiple devices, and create hard copies periodically.
   ◆ Persistently strive to achieve your daily writing goal.
   ◆ Maintain a comfortable posture and take frequent breaks, to avoid developing RSI.
   ◆ Schedule time for social activities and exercise, to avoid isolation and relieve stress.

Part II: Enhance your presentation skills

Step 1: Reduce anxiety before your presentation.
- Visualize having a conversation with a friend, rather than talking to a large audience.
- Aim to convey the central message of your research, rather than trying to deliver the perfect presentation.
- Resist practicing in front of a mirror.
- Do not try to perfect your gestures or tone of voice.

Step 2: Prepare properly for your talk.
- Practice your slides in your head, to determine whether you have all of the relevant information.
- Practice out loud, to make sure that you are within the time limit and you know how to explain your research.
- Videotape yourself to see whether you use frequent verbal mannerisms or nervous gestures.
- Ask your advisor, colleagues or friends to give you feedback on your slides and presentation style.

Step 3: Go through your checklist on the day of your presentation.
- Test the technical and audiovisual set-up for your presentation.
- Check your attire, to make sure that it is in order.
- If you feel nervous, practice deep breathing for a few minutes.
- Get a bottle of water, in case your throat gets dry during your presentation.
- Arrange your notes on the table, if you have any.

Step 4: Deliver a persuasive presentation.
- Capture the audience's attention with an interesting and relevant story.
- Summarize your thesis statement in your introduction.
- Tailor your presentation to the interests and background of your audience.
- Divide the body of your presentation into three to five categories.
- Connect each part of your presentation to your central message.
- At the end of your presentation, reinforce your key points and your thesis statement.

Step 5: Stay focused during your talk.

- Make frequent eye contact with individual audience members.
- Slow down and take deep breaths, if you experience nervousness.
- If you make a mistake, admit to it quickly and move on.
- Stay calm and professional if somebody asks a hostile question.
- If there are no questions, you can break the ice by asking a question yourself.

Step 6: Optimize the use of PowerPoint.

- Use PowerPoint to support you, rather than try to build your talk around the special features of the software.
- Check the legibility of your fonts from the back of the room.
- Use contrasting colors between your background and text.
- Convey only one major point per slide or diagram.
- Aim to have one slide for every two or three minutes of your presentation.
- Construct diagrams so that they can be understood in less than 30 seconds.

*"If one advances confidently in the direction of his dreams, and endeavors to
live the life which he has imagined, he will meet with a success unexpected
in common hours."*
Henry David Thoreau, American author (1817–1862)

How a job search can help you graduate sooner

After eight years in graduate school, Nicole thought that she would
never finish. She worked with a biology professor who was infamous
for never having any of her doctoral students graduate. All of her previous students left with a master's degree after they realized how high
her expectations were. In spite of this reputation, Nicole decided to
join her group, and had a productive research project with several
publications. In her ninth year, Nicole heard about a job opening at
a biotechnology company that was a perfect match for her skills. She
interviewed promptly, and they offered her the position. Her thesis
was not completed when she accepted the offer, but her advisor agreed
to schedule her defense a few months after she started her job. "I don't
think that she was trying to hold me back on purpose, but she always
found something for me to do. Once I received a job offer, she agreed
to let me go. I also had many publications and my committee was supportive as well."

Fortunately, most students do not need a job offer to graduate, but
a little bit of career planning can speed up progress on your dissertation in several ways. First, it will prepare you mentally for the "outside world." It is difficult to motivate yourself to finish, if you do not
know what you will do afterwards. Should you pursue an academic or
non-academic career? Which job will allow you to balance work and
family best? How should you look for a job, if you want to work in the
same geographical area as your spouse? The best way to answer these
questions is to research the job market early—at least two years before

your planned graduation date. Talk to professionals at conferences and recent alumni from your department, and ask questions about their careers and their job-searching experiences.

 Evaluate your career goals throughout graduate school, but particularly during the last two years. Attend networking and information resources to learn about the different types of jobs available to you.

Second, a job search will motivate you to acquire marketable skills, and enable you to articulate your transferable skills. If you are a biologist, for example, you might find that companies value expertise with mass spectrometers and liquid chromatographers. In order to assess how marketable you are, write your résumé and curriculum vitae (CV) a few years before graduation and keep it updated. Visualize the CV or résumé that you want to send out a few years from now, and aim to make that CV a reality.

 During the development of your dissertation, think about your career path and what skills you will need when you graduate.

The third and most important reason to begin your job search early is to open up communication with your advisor. Your advisor's support will significantly facilitate your job search. First, he or she will write your recommendation letters. Second, your advisor can help you network by introducing you to alumni or other contacts, who could advise you on the job-search process. Third, your advisor might be aware of job openings in academia or industry, and can arrange an interview for you.

 Involve your advisor in the job-search process. He or she will need to write a recommendation letter for you, and might also be able to connect you with academic and industry contacts.

Another reason to inform your advisor about your career plans is to clarify the expectations for your dissertation and agree upon a graduation date. Some students avoid the "talk" with their advisors (i.e. when they will graduate), because they are afraid of what they might hear:

"What if he thinks everything I did so far is useless? What if he puts me on another project that will take forever?" No matter how much such a response might scare you, you need to hear what your advisor expects from you. Regardless of how your advisor responds to your request for graduation (even if his or her response changes from day to day), remain assertive about your career plans. Your advisor might need time to get used to the thought of losing you, especially if you have been a valuable member of the group. If you think that your advisor is holding your graduation back, seek the support of your committee members, and possibly a dean.

In this chapter, you will learn how to:

- Decide between multiple career paths
- Know what steps to take (and in what order) to pursue either path
- Learn about career resources on the Internet
- Answer challenging interview questions
- Negotiate your hiring package

Deciding between academic and alternative career paths

Jordan, an electrical engineer, loved research, but was not sure what type of career to pursue after graduation. He knew that he wanted to be his own boss and find work that would allow him to be creative. "I heard stereotypes about the different kinds of career paths, but I wanted to find out for myself about the different jobs. I interviewed at several types of organizations, such as big companies, small companies, start-ups and academia before I decided to become a faculty member. It is very important to see for yourself what is out there, rather than rely on information from others."

If you are thinking about an academic career, but do not like the atmosphere at your university, remember that the working environment varies by school. Amy, a nutritionist, considered many types of careers before she applied to academia. "I was not sure I wanted to become a faculty member, because I did not like the atmosphere at my graduate school. I decided to give academia a chance after I saw a job opening that seemed like a good fit for me. When I interviewed there, I loved the people, the area and the working environment. I really think I found the perfect job for myself," she said.

Interview at different types of organizations and universities to help you choose the optimal career path for you.

An alternative to interviewing is talking to young alumni from your school. Tina, a biomedical engineer, contacted two recent graduates from her department. "I e-mailed two people from my department, one working at a teaching college and one at a research university. I asked them whether they could talk to me about their experiences as assistant professors. I knew both of them only superficially, and I was surprised by how quickly they responded. They spent almost an hour with me on the phone, and told me about their job responsibilities and lifestyles. After these conversations, I realized that academia was not the right path for me."

Some Ph.D.s felt that their advisors encouraged academic career paths more than non-academic jobs. Danny, a biology major, encountered significant resistance when he discussed careers outside academia with his advisors. "I felt that they looked down on me because I wanted to teach rather than do research. They almost made me feel like it had been a waste of time to earn my Ph.D. It is true that a Ph.D. is not required for my job as a high school teacher, but it taught me valuable leadership skills for my current position as department head. I think students should stand up for themselves and follow a career they are passionate about."

 Even if your department is not supportive of alternative careers, remain informed about your options. Do not feel like you failed, if you decide not to go to academia.

Can you return to academia after working in industry? Ryan, a biochemist, became a faculty member in a research university after a year in industry, because he did not like the corporate environment. "I was not happy, because most of my time was spent at meetings or managing other people. I would rather be a scientist in academia, where I can do hands-on research every day." On the other hand, some Ph.D.s love the corporate environment. Lydia, a biologist, considered an academic career but accepted a permanent position at a biotechnology firm. She loves her new job and does not want to return to academia. "I feel much more comfortable in the corporate environment, because

I interact with many people on a daily basis. We all collaborate to get a product to market, whereas in graduate school we all had our own projects and it was very isolating."

The table below lists twelve common criteria that Ph.D.s use to decide which career path to follow. Some of these criteria might not be relevant for all jobs. For example, if you work for a government research lab, you might still need to write grant proposals for funding. Or, if you decide to become a high school teacher, your salary will probably be less than if you became a faculty member. Nevertheless, the following list shows the typical advantages and disadvantages of academic and non-academic career paths.

Table 7-1: Reasons why Ph.D.s chose certain career paths.

Criteria	Academic route	Non-academic route
Teaching	Requires teaching	Little or no teaching
Applying for grants	Will need to write proposals for grants	Only a few non-academic jobs require writing proposals for grants
Research	Need to design and commit to a long-term research proposal	Do not have to commit to a long-term research plan
Interaction with students	Will need to supervise student research	Little or no supervision of student research
Job stability	Job guaranteed after tenure is granted	No job guarantee, but not required to go through tenure process
Being your own boss	No boss to report to on a regular basis	Will probably have a boss or manager to report to on a daily/weekly basis

Table 7-1: Reasons why Ph.D.s chose certain career paths. *(concluded)*

Criteria	Academic route	Non-academic route
Freedom to pursue creative projects	Can pursue creative projects if funding is available	Little or no freedom to pursue creative projects
Opportunities for consulting	Some or many opportunities for independent consulting	Fewer opportunities for independent consulting
Salary	Standard salary, depending upon university	Depends upon position, but frequently higher than in academia
Postdoctoral fellowships	Required in some fields	Rarely required in non-academic positions
Geography	Have to be flexible with geographical location	Usually more likely to find job in desired area
Work/life balance	Usually need to work during evenings and weekends, especially before tenure is granted	Can frequently "leave work at work," and enjoy hobbies and family time at home

What is the purpose of a postdoctoral fellowship?

Why should you do a postdoctoral fellowship? First, if you are not sure about your career path, a postdoctoral fellowship will give you more time to explore your options. Second, a postdoctoral fellowship allows you to expand your marketable skill set, broaden your publication record and possibly enhance your teaching experience. Finally, if you do need to obtain your own postdoctoral funding, you will learn how to write grant applications—a necessary skill for all faculty members.

 If you do a postdoctoral fellowship, choose a project that will allow you to learn new marketable job skills.

LAND YOUR DREAM JOB

A postdoctoral fellowship could boost your CV and résumé, particularly if you want to gain more experience. Dean, an English major, became interested in library science during graduate school. After he completed his Ph.D., he decided to pursue a postdoctoral fellowship in library and information sciences. With the additional experience and personal contacts, he felt more confident about his future career as a specialist in information sciences. Rhea, a biochemist, knew she wanted to work in industry, but the job market was very competitive the year that she graduated. Although she was not offered a Ph.D.-level job, she did have a choice between a postdoctoral fellowship and a master's-level scientist position at a company. "A friend of mine, who was a senior scientist, advised me to take the postdoctoral fellowship, because the master's-level position would hinder my career advancement. I am glad that I chose the fellowship, because I now have the opportunity to learn new skills. Just a year into my fellowship, I received phone calls for job interviews. I think that there are more career options available to me, now that I have additional experience and publications."

In some cases, a postdoctoral fellowship will not advance your career. Clark, a physics major, claimed that his postdoctoral fellowship was a waste of his time. "I did not learn anything new during those years, and I was looking forward to starting a real job with a real salary." While Clark did not benefit from the extra training, a postdoctoral fellowship might be worthwhile if you want to acquire more skills or need time to define your career path.

In summary, there are three major considerations in deciding your future career path:

- Professional interests and skills
  - What type of work or research are you interested in?
  - What are your marketable job skills?
- Family considerations and personal priorities
  - Do you have a preference for geographical location?
  - Do you have a preference for large cities, small towns or suburbia?
  - Is it important to have flexible hours?
- Personality fit
  - Do you want to be your own boss?

- Do you like supervising students?
- Do you like teaching?

Regardless of the career path you choose, the following strategies will significantly enhance your job search.

The top 14 job-hunting strategies

1. Have both your CV and a résumé ready before you officially begin your job search

If you see the light at the end of the tunnel (i.e., you will most likely graduate in the next year), it is time to put both your CV and résumé together. Most academic job applications require a CV, which is a comprehensive list of your professional experience, and is usually more than two pages long. Other types of job announcements, for example those published by companies, usually request résumés, which are typically only one page. (See the appendix for resources on writing your résumé and CV.)

Sean, a physics major, found out after three and a half years of graduate school that his advisor's funding would run out in six months. Fortunately, his CV was ready to be sent out when an attractive job listing was forwarded to him from the department headquarters. "I was surprised that they asked for a CV rather than a résumé, because it was a non-academic position. My CV was already completed, and I sent it in right away. I think multiple people applied, but mine was one of the first CVs they received. They interviewed me quickly, and I got the job. I think it is essential to have both your CV and résumé ready, so that you can leap for opportunities when they appear."

2. Write a detailed and specific cover letter for each position

Your cover letter is your chance to explain to a potential employer where you would fit into the company or university. A thoughtfully written cover letter will draw attention to your résumé; a cut-and-paste cover letter from a template will probably end up in the recycling bin, along with your résumé. Hannah, a biology major, interviewed at a pharmaceutical company and was surprised that one of the scientists asked very detailed questions about her cover letter. "She spent the entire interview asking questions about my cover letter. Later, I found out that employers do this to make sure that you are truthful in your application." (See the appendix for resources on writing outstanding cover letters.)

3. Research the university or company before your interview, to find out where you would fit in

Why should this employer hire you? What expertise would you bring? What would be your contribution to this university or company? Nora, an art history major, received three academic job offers. She attributes her success to thorough preparation before each interview. "Before my job interviews, I researched each university so I could explain how my background fit in with their program. I knew what courses I wanted to teach, and what methodology I would use to cover the material." The interview process for Ph.D.s is usually one day for non-academic positions, and two days for academic jobs. During this time, your potential colleagues will have many opportunities to ask you challenging questions. It is impossible to predict all the questions, but the more you know about each university or company, the more prepared you will be.

4. Avoid being arrogant or subservient during your interviews

The interviewers could be future colleagues. You will not impress them with arrogance (e.g., drown them with information during your job talk), nor is it to your advantage to be subservient (e.g., thank them profoundly for every small favor). In a tight job market, candidates want to make an outstanding impression during their interviews, but what is the right strategy? Ph.D.s who received multiple attractive job offers believe that employers consider two major factors: 1) academic excellence and 2) effective communication skills. If you were in the shoes of the interviewers, what characteristics would you look for? First, you would want somebody who has the expertise to do the job, but also somebody who is easy to work with. During your interviews, do not think about how much you need this job. Instead, give an enthusiastic job talk, answer the interview questions honestly and remain collegial throughout the day.

5. Check your department headquarters/career office for job listings

Companies will advertise positions through multiple channels, including department headquarters. Do not assume, however, that your department will automatically forward you job listings. If you are at a research-oriented university, your department might assume that everyone will follow an academic path, and therefore will not inform you about non-academic job openings. If you are thinking about an alternative career, you need to be proactive and ask your department, career office and advisor about job opportunities. Lloyd found a job listing in an e-mail from his department administrator: "I had never heard of that company before, but I applied and got an interview. After I received that e-mail, I asked my department administrators to forward me job listings because they usually did not do that. I found out that departments get a lot of job listings that they do not forward to students."

6. Join professional organizations and network at conferences (and have your business card ready!)

In a tight job market, you will need every opportunity to find job listings and professional contacts. Brad, an electrical engineer, traveled to many conferences during his last two years to find a job. "It was a great opportunity to meet professionals from all across the country. I also learned about the different jobs, and I came to realize that the non-academic path was right for me." If you attend conferences, do not be shy about starting up conversations with other professionals. Carry around a small stack of business cards (you can impress people just by having a business card as a graduate student), because there will be several opportunities for you to exchange contact information. The backs of business cards are also useful for writing down the e-mail address and phone number of professionals who might be able to recommend openings or job leads, but do not have their own card. Underneath their contact information, write down where you met them, so you can refer to it when you send them e-mail. Be sure to follow up with these contacts after your conference, and inquire whether they would like to see your CV or résumé. (If they do, also include a cover letter.)

7. Tailor your job talk to your audience

"After I gave my presentation, people told me that this was the first job talk that they actually understood," said Reba, a biochemist, who interviewed at a pharmaceutical company. According to her audience, the other candidates gave very technical talks about their dissertations, and they were not relevant to the company's work. Reba's presentation focused only on research that would be interesting to pharmaceutical companies.

During your job talk, you need to convince your audience that you have the expertise that they are looking for. If you research each company or university before you interview, you can customize your job talks by emphasizing the portions of your work which fit best with the interests of your potential employer.

8. Research the market so you can negotiate your hiring package accordingly

"I knew that my friend, who was also an assistant professor, received $5,000 more in salary than what my university offered me. I asked the chairman whether he would consider a salary increase or a more substantial research fund for me. He referred me to the dean, who agreed to a salary increase, but could not change my startup package," said Martin, a biologist. "I found out later that I received the standard startup package for my university, so I think I was treated fairly." If you want to negotiate your hiring package (in academia or industry), be sure you have a written offer. A verbal offer is not official until it is in writing. Universities will often publish information about salaries and startup packages, which you can use as reference in your negotiation. Remain friendly during the negotiation process (after all, they could be your future colleagues); ask whether your employer "would consider" a larger salary. Give your reasons—such as better salary at another university, or your need for additional benefits—but be prepared to have your request denied, even if the university is very interested in you.

9. Treat each interview as if it were your first choice

"I went to my first interview just as practice, because I was not interested in the position. I am glad that I was prepared, because once I had the interview, I fell in love with the place and they offered me the position," said Belle, a nutritionist. Employers are looking for candidates who are both qualified and enthusiastic about their positions. If an interviewer senses that they are just a "backup," they will probably not give you an offer. It is difficult to predict whether a job is a good fit before you visit, so prepare thoroughly for all interviews.

10. Put together a list of questions to ask from your potential employer

The best way to show enthusiasm for a potential job is to prepare questions in advance. Defer questions about salary and benefits until after you have received a job offer. Appropriate questions would include details about your first assignment, how many more faculty members/scientists they expect to hire, what types of expertise they are looking for, teaching requirements and library or research facilities.

11. Send postdoctoral applications by mail rather than e-mail

"When I was looking for a postdoctoral position, my advisor told me to send my applications via priority mail rather than e-mail, because most professors are too busy to respond to all of their e-mail messages. Now that I am a professor myself, I respond only to postdoctoral requests that come by priority mail, because I literally receive hundreds of applications by e-mail," said Sheila, a chemist. If you send your application with regular mail, include a cover letter as well.

12. Look for research opportunities outside of your group, such as industrial internships or collaborations at another university

"I think that the reason that many students are confused during their job search is that they have been isolated throughout their Ph.D. process, and are not familiar with the different types of career opportunities. It is especially important to look for industrial internships, if you are thinking about a non-academic route. Your advisor may or may not be happy about you leaving for a few months, but the additional experience could really enhance your résumé," said Aerin, a mechanical engineer. Industrial internships are frequently advertised through university career offices or department headquarters. If a job recruiter visits your school, you can also ask them about summer internships for graduate students. "I got my current job through a campus recruiter who was looking for summer interns," said Cara, a geologist. "I spent a few summers there, and I really liked the job. They offered me the position, so I did not have to worry about job-hunting while I finished my Ph.D." Collaborations at another university can also help you find a job, by giving you the chance to network with more professionals in your field. "I spent a few weeks collecting data at another university, and it was through that group that I found out about my current job," said Andrew, an electrical engineer.

13. Begin the job search early and apply to all attractive job listings, if you are part of a dual-career couple

As tough as it is to find a job, it is even tougher to find two jobs in the same town. For this reason, it is especially important to research the job market early if you need to look for a job at the same time as your spouse. Shirley and her husband, both mathematicians, wanted to find tenure-track positions in the same geographical area, and they applied to every job listing in the country. After nearly 200 applications, Shirley's job search was successful. "I was really stressed, because I felt that it was out of my control. In the end, it worked out really well, and my husband and I got professorships at the same university." Crystal, an engineering major, looked for tenure-track positions only in areas where there were also job opportunities for her husband, who worked in the semiconductor industry. "I researched the geographical locations where we could both find jobs, and I applied only to schools in those areas. I knew it was a competitive market, so I also considered non-academic jobs. I actually received an offer from one of my top-choice schools, and now my husband has an offer from a nearby company."

14. Consider alternative careers, if you want a part-time job

Alanna, a history major, looked for a part-time job that would allow her to spend more time with her baby. "Most of my classmates pursued an academic path, but it did not seem like the right fit for me. I searched around for a while, and I even volunteered at the Center for Women's Studies at my university. I loved the position, and they eventually offered me a permanent job. Now I work part-time, just the way I imagined it." Gail, a biologist, quit her job as a research scientist after her baby was born, because she no longer had the energy to work 12-hour days. A few months later, she found out that the director of her research center had decided to work part-time. "They called me up to see if I was interested in the position. Now we share the director's job, and we both work part-time."

The top 14 job-hunting strategies

Note: The suggestions in the following sections (for both academic and alternative career paths) were amalgamated from interviews with former graduate students and the job-search reference books listed in the appendix.

Working step-by-step towards an academic career

Ready to apply for an academic job? If you are in your last year, it is time to put together your package and even apply to a few schools. "It is never too early to start practicing interview skills," said Jessica, an art history major. "If you don't get a job, at least you will have your CV and application materials ready by the next season. You will also be less nervous the following year, if you have already gone through the process. And who knows? You might get a job the first time around."

 If you are less than a year away from graduating, put together your application package and ask your advisor and other mentors to help you revise it.

Do you need a Ph.D. degree before you apply for academic jobs? Some schools require their candidates to have defended their theses already, so you might not get any interviews if you have not yet finished. "I got my Ph.D. in the winter, so I was only called for interviews in the spring," said Eli, a history major. Other graduate students received job offers while they were still students. "I received a job offer before I defended my thesis, and they even asked me to do a postdoctoral fellowship for a year before starting the position," said Kenny, an electrical engineer. Before you apply, inquire about the school's policy and whether they require their candidates to have already defended their theses.

If you are not sure when you will finish, or you do not have time to apply for jobs, have a financial plan for the period when you will be between jobs. Dee, a biochemist, worked 12–14 hours a day on her thesis during her last year, and decided to postpone her job search. "My dissertation was a full-time job, and I was not able to focus on anything else until I finished my thesis. I saved money to pay for the bills after graduation, and I also negotiated a six-month postdoctoral fellowship with my advisor."

If you are too busy to look for a job during your last year, find a part-time position or a postdoctoral fellowship to cover you financially until you get an offer.

The academic job-search calendar

Academic job openings are usually advertised in journals, professional websites, professional conferences and university/department homepages. Your advisor, department administrator or career office will know where to look for academic job openings, because there are usually just a few sites for each field. You can expand your job search by looking at multiple departments related to your field. Cory specialized in marine biology, but did not realize that he could have applied to several types of departments: "I applied only to biology departments, but later on I realized that some of the geology departments were looking for candidates with my qualifications. I think it is a good idea to search through all the departments where you might fit in."

Apply to job listings in fields related to your major, if you have the qualifications for the position.

The calendar below is a general guideline for the timeframe for applying to academic positions. Most of the job openings are published in late summer or early fall, but some openings become available in the spring. If you do not get job offers by early spring, continue to look for more positions. While these timeframes are approximate and vary by school, the general calendar appears to be similar between mathematics/science/ engineering fields and the humanities/social sciences/arts. (See the appendix for more resources on academic careers.)

Phase I: (July/August–September)
Preparation and information gathering:
- Write your CV
- Ask for letters of recommendation
- Research the schools you want to apply to
- Obtain application packages from schools

Phase II: (September–December)
Job application and networking:

- Apply for positions
- Attend conferences
- Practice answering interview questions

Phase 3: (December–March)
Interviewing and applying for more positions:
- Practice job talk
- Travel to campus interviews
- Follow up on interviews
- Apply for positions

Phase 4: (March–August)
Negotiation and more job applications:
- Negotiate salary, benefits and start-up package
- If you have no offers, apply to other positions that might have opened late
- Continue to network

Preparing your application
COVER LETTER
Your cover letter might be the first document that the search committee will read from your application package. The cover letter gives you the opportunity to highlight your talents and to distinguish yourself from the other candidates. What should you include in the cover letter?

In the first paragraph:
- Write how you heard of this position. Was it an online job announcement (specify source) or a referral from someone?
- Explain your background: where you are finishing (or have finished) your Ph.D., and where you are working right now.
- Clarify why you are interested in the position and how your background would be an asset for the department.

In the middle paragraph(s):
- Provide an overview of your achievements that are relevant to the job posting.
- Emphasize the type of expertise that the job posting is looking for, such as a particular field of research or teaching experience.

LAND YOUR DREAM JOB

- You can also mention your published work or grant awards, to give you more credibility.
- In subsequent paragraph(s), insert your secondary interests. If you are applying to a teaching college, insert your research interests. If you are applying to a research-oriented university, mention your teaching experience.

In your final paragraph:
- Summarize the contents of your application package, such as your CV, teaching philosophy and research proposal.
- In your closing, thank the committee for their time and consideration.

(See the appendix for resources on how to write outstanding cover letters.)

THE CURRICULUM VITAE

Your curriculum vitae (CV) should summarize all of your credentials that are relevant to the job:

- Your name and contact information
- Education, from bachelor degree to Ph.D.
- Awards and honors
- Research experience since college
- Research interests
- Teaching experience
- University services
- Publications and presentations
- References

Place the teaching or the research experience first, depending upon which one you are putting emphasis on. (See the appendix for resources on writing résumés and CVs.)

LETTERS OF RECOMMENDATION

Recommendations letters should strengthen your application package and distinguish you from other candidates. Letters of recommendation are not the place for mentors to write about your shortcomings, but to be enthusiastic about your talents and achievements. Many jobs will require three to five letters. Whom should you ask for a recommendation?

- Dissertation and postdoctoral advisors
- Committee members
- A faculty member who supervised you as a teaching assistant
- A collaborating faculty member (at your university or somewhere else)
- Supervisor during an industry internship, particularly if it was during graduate school

When you ask for a recommendation letter, keep the following in mind:

- Give your referees a few months' worth of notice to write your letters of recommendation, and remind them occasionally as the deadline nears.
- Ask for letters in person (or over the phone), rather than via e-mail.
- Discuss the job description, so your mentors will know whether to emphasize your teaching experience or your research.
- Write a note to explain what information you hope your mentor will include in the letter. (You do not need to write the letter, but provide a bullet-point list of your major accomplishments.) Most professors will appreciate the summary as a starting point to write the recommendation.

Getting ready to interview

There are three different types of interviews:

- Conference interviews
- Telephone interviews
- Campus interviews

Conference and telephone interviews are used to screen a large number of candidates, and to narrow down the applicant pool to three to six people who will be invited for a campus interview. Conference and telephone interviews are usually a few minutes to an hour, and their purpose is to determine whether you would be a good fit for the school. Campus interviews are one to two days, and include one or two seminars and possibly a teaching demonstration. Regardless of the type of interview, you need to be able to answer questions on the following topics:

- Your dissertation
- Your research interests
- Teaching experience
- Grant proposal writing plans
- How you fit into the school and department

If you visit a school for a campus interview, remember to do the following:

- Do not pack anything indispensable in your checked baggage. (We all know that baggage gets lost from time to time.)
- Bring extra copies of your CV and other application materials, such as your teaching portfolio and research proposal.
- Research the school, to familiarize yourself with the curriculum. Be ready to point out specific courses that you would be interested in teaching.
- During your interview, treat members of the search committee like colleagues. Do not be subservient or arrogant; remember that your interviewers might be your future colleagues.
- If you are invited at the same time as the other candidates, do not be intimidated by them. They are probably just as nervous as you, and are also interviewing at other schools.
- Rehearse a five-minute overview of your dissertation for which you do not need any slides or overheads. This overview should be comprehensible for people in your field, even if they are not experts in your area of specialty. You will be asked to present this five-minute overview several times during your interview.
- Practice your job talk with your advisor and other colleagues before your interview.
- Always send a hand-written thank-you note you to the chairman of the search committee after your interview. Thank them for their time and offer to send additional materials.

Typical interview questions

DISSERTATION QUESTIONS

- Why did you choose this topic for your dissertation?
- How does your dissertation contribute to your field?
- What would you change if you could start your dissertation over?
- Why did you choose this particular method? Be prepared to answer very detail-oriented questions about your protocols.
- How did you arrive at your conclusions?
- What is your opinion regarding... (a research question or controversial issue related to your field)? The committee might ask open-ended questions to see how you think and whether you are on top of the literature.
- If you are in the humanities or social sciences, the committee will probably ask whether you have considered revising your thesis into a book.

RESEARCH PROPOSAL

- Why are you interested in this field of research?
- Where do you see your research in the next two, five and 10 years?
- How do you plan to apply for funding? Do you have sufficient data for a grant application?
- What facilities do you need for your research? What kind of startup package do you need?
- How does your research fit into the department?
- Whom would you collaborate with?
- Do you need your mentor's permission to bring some of your work with you?

TEACHING

- What courses are you interested in teaching?
- What courses are you prepared to teach?
- What is your approach to teaching this course?
- Which textbook would you use?
- Do you plan any demonstrations?

CONTRIBUTION TO DEPARTMENT AND SCHOOL

- Are you interested in developing new courses or seminars?

• What committees would you like to serve on?

• How do you and your family feel about living in this town?
• How do you spend your free time?

ILLEGAL QUESTIONS
• Are you married?
• How old are you?
• Do you have children, or do you plan to have any?
• What is your sexual orientation?
• What is your religion?

Employers are not supposed to ask you about your marital status, sexual orientation or your family. If they do ask an illegal questions, you can counter with another question, such as: "It seems to me that you are concerned about how my personal life will affect the department. Could you be more specific about that?"

Negotiating job offers
QUESTIONS TO ASK AFTER YOU HAVE RECEIVED AN OFFER
"Once I got an offer, the tables were turned. The school invited me back for a second campus interview, and the department really tried to impress me," said Keri, a chemistry major. Here are some questions that will help you prepare for your new job or decide between multiple job offers:

• Who decides the teaching assignments? Which courses will I be asked to teach?
• How many students are in each class?
• How many teaching assistants will I have?
• What is your tenure process?
• Do you have regular department seminars?
• What is the expected growth at your department?
• On which committees should I expect to serve?
• Also ask questions about specific facilities—such as special instruments or library collections—that are necessary for your research.

Questions for human resources:

- What is your vacation policy?
- What types of retirement accounts do you offer?
- What type of health insurance will I have?
- What is your family leave policy?

Some parts of your job offer are negotiable. For example:

- Startup/hiring package
- Teaching assignment
- Salary
- Vacation

See the end of the chapter for Donna's story on how she negotiated the terms of her dream job. The key is to construct an "ultimate wish list" and to separate needs from desires. Be firm when you ask for what you *really* need (e.g., financial support for graduate students) and more flexible when you negotiate non-essential desires (e.g., a slightly higher salary.)

 Before your negotiation process, construct an "ultimate wish list," but separate needs from desires.

What to do, if you do not get any offers or interviews

Search committees usually look for very specific types of candidates. Julianne, an art history major, has several friends who have been on the market for two or three years. "It is hard to predict what the search committees look for. They turn away many qualified candidates, because they want the perfect fit for the job. The best policy is to be yourself, because you do not want to get hired for a job that you are not prepared for."

What should you do if you keep getting rejection letters? First, have a job to cover you financially and to help you acquire more marketable skills. Second, contact the search committee and inquire why you were not selected for an interview, or why you were rejected after your interview. Your application package might have a serious problem such as missing recommendation letters or a poorly written research proposal. If your thesis was based on an obsolete field of research, you might have been rejected because you did not emphasize your marketable job skills. For example, you might get feedback such as: "We are not looking for somebody who specializes in...." Some search committees might not respond to your inquiries, but even a few responses will help you redraft your application package. If you believe that you have been rejected too many times, ask your mentors to help you improve your application package for the following season.

 Ask search committees for feedback, if you have been rejected repeatedly.

Navigating alternative career paths

Your friends pursuing academic careers are looking at a competitive market, but they have an easier time when it comes to finding job postings. Most academic jobs are listed in journals and professional websites, and there is usually a standard calendar for applications, interviews and negotiations. If you choose a non-academic career path, how do you start? How long before graduation should you start looking for a job? Where is the best place to find job listings? How do you prepare for interviews?

Since there is no standard application procedure for non-academic positions, you will need to pursue multiple job-search routes. It is possible that you will get lucky and find a job quickly through a friend or the Internet. Most likely, however, most job openings will not be appropriate for you. Companies might look for somebody with only a bachelor degree, or a Ph.D. with five years of industry experience. With so many qualified applicants entering the market every year, it is likely that you will need to apply to several jobs before you get an interview. In this section, I will discuss how to 1) find job listings, 2) prepare for your interviews and 3) negotiate your job offer(s).

Finding job openings

There is no universal rule regarding how long before graduation you should start looking for a job. Six months seems to be a common rule of thumb, but you need to ask alumni from your department about their experiences. Will employers interview you before you defend? When is the hiring season? Do most employers require a postdoctoral fellowship? Will employers wait for you, if you need to finish your Ph.D. or postdoctoral fellowship before starting a position?

Dawn was exhausted after six months of job-searching. She had had a few interviews, but no offers. "Finding a job is a full-time job," she remarked. According to Dawn, the most time-consuming aspect of the search was locating job listings. In order to discover the greatest number of job opportunities, you will need to balance your time among the following strategies and resources:

- Networking
- Internet job sites
- Company websites
- Recruiters
- Job fairs
- Campus recruitment at your department and career office

Keep a database of all the resources and contacts you make during your job search. Many people switch jobs every few years, and these contacts will be useful in case you need to find a new position. In order to organize your job search and contacts, set up separate folders within your e-mail account to file away job-search correspondence. Save all of your contacts before your university e-mail is deactivated, or set up a separate e-mail account (e.g., Yahoo!) that you can use after graduation. Also make sure that you choose an email address that sounds professional (i.e. avoid usernames like partygirl789@xyz.com).

 Maintain a database of job-search contacts for future reference.

Networking effectively

When you hear the term "networking," your first reaction might be: "I know I should network, but how do I do it effectively?" Where can you meet potential employers? Begin with work-related communities such as:

- Alumni associations from all the universities you have attended
- Alumni associations or contacts from previous jobs you have held
- Conferences
- Professional workshops/seminars
- Networking evenings of professional associations
- Contacts from your advisor
- Department events at your university
- Recent graduates from your department
- Company presentations

Networking will help you learn about open positions and increase your visibility within professional circles. Meetings of professional associations usually have a job bulletin board, either at the meeting or on their websites. One way to make your networking more efficient is to "work the room" with a friend. My friend Ava and I were looking for jobs simultaneously, but our skill sets were different, and we did not feel like we were competing with each other. We networked together at seminars ("Hey, you should talk to that guy in the blue shirt, I think he is hiring a Ph.D. with your background."), and we also informed each other of interesting job leads from the Internet. Ava actually e-mailed me the posting that led to my first job offer. It is impossible to find all job postings on your own, but with a little bit of collaborative effort, you can substantially increase the number of potential job leads.

In order to have fruitful networking sessions, remember to do the following:

- Carry around your business cards
- Have a notepad and pen ready to collect information about job leads
- Wear your name tag on your right-hand side so it is seen when you shake hands
- Do not be shy about starting up conversations
- Ask other people to talk about themselves
- Incorporate relevant job skills into the conversation
- Ask about job openings in their company. If they cannot offer you any, ask for leads: "Do you know anybody who might know about job openings in my field?"

- Do not talk about your dream job—most people will not be able to offer you that, and it will be a turnoff for the conversation
- Collect everybody's business card/contact information, and jot down any notes from your conversation on the back of the card
- Send follow-up e-mail to thank contacts for job leads, and as a way of keeping in touch

Non-professional communities also give you many opportunities to network with other people. At these events, job-searching is not the main focus, so do not rush into work-related conversations. You can steer the conversation toward jobs with a phrase such as: "I am also doing well. In fact, I just finished my Ph.D. and I am looking for a job in...." Always be ready to give your job-search synopsis should the opportunity a rise. Consider networking at non-professional gatherings such as:

- Sports and hobby groups
- Family events
- Friends' parties and barbecues
- Special-interest groups (e.g., minorities, disabilities, ethnic groups, new mothers)

Tia, a biochemist in her eighth year of graduate school, went grocery shopping after a frustrating day at work. Her results were not reproducible, and she had lost the motivation to finish her thesis. At the grocery store, she met an old friend who worked for a start-up company. Tia found out that his company was hiring, and she told him about her experience that was relevant to the position. They arranged for an interview a few weeks later, and she was hired for the position. Needless to say, her motivation perked up and she was able to finish her thesis within a few months.

 Always carry business cards with you, in case you learn about a job opening during a non-professional gathering.

During your search, you might hear about jobs that are suitable for your skills, but not for your level of education. For example, you might hear about a job that requires a bachelor degree with multiple years of industry experience. You have a Ph.D., and possibly no industry experience. Should you pursue this lead, if you have the required skills? Absolutely. Millie, a biologist, applied for a position that was advertised for a bachelor-level scientist with five years of experience. Millie had all the required job skills, and she got an interview and the job offer. The company also adjusted her salary to that of a Ph.D.-level scientist, which was slightly higher than the original salary for which they had budgeted.

 Apply for jobs if you have the qualifications, even if your level of education or years of experience do not match the job description.

In order to pursue all possible job leads, you will need to prepare your résumé in several formats:

- Formatted hardcopy, with bullets and italicized text, that looks professional; you can hand it out to campus recruiters or companies at job fairs
- Plain-text résumé that you can paste into
  - online job banks
  - the body of e-mail messages

Always include your cover letter as part of the body of the e-mail message, to catch the eye of the hiring manager. If you want to copy a plain-text résumé into an e-mail, save it as a "text only" file, to make the pasting easier.

Using Internet resources

The Internet has vast resources for job-searching, but you should not rely on it exclusively. I was fortunate to get an interview (and a job offer) after applying to 50 jobs on the Internet, but some Ph.D.s applied to over 100 positions without any success. In the appendix, I have listed the major job-searching sites, as well as some field-specific job sites.

Protect yourself by submitting your résumé only to those job banks that have an appropriate privacy policy. Read their policy and determine what they will do with your résumé and whom they will send to. Does the job site transmit information securely? If you are unsure about the security of a job bank, talk to career counselors at your university, or read more about job banks on the websites listed in the appendix.

Also, check how easy it is to retrieve résumés. If you can log on as an employer and retrieve other people's résumés, then the job site is not secure. Read over the services and do not fill out a profile unless the website has the right jobs for you. Find out which companies post to the sites. Does the site allow you to update your résumé periodically? Can you delete your résumé after you have found a job? (This can be very important, especially if your new employer finds your résumé on the Internet *after* you have already started working there). If they charge you for submitting your résumé, shop around for other services, to make sure you are getting your money's worth.

 Register only with job banks that have a secure site and which allow you to update or delete your résumé as necessary.

Before you post your résumé online, remember that you cannot guarantee the privacy of your résumé, no matter what precautions you take. Read articles on www.job-hunt.com about privacy; you will need to make the decision as to whether you are comfortable with putting your résumé electronically on the Internet.

Diversify your Internet job search through the following routes:

- ◆ Large job banks
- ◆ Field-specific sites, such as those of professional organizations
- ◆ City or region-specific job sites (such as the career section of your local newspaper)
- ◆ Recruitment firms
- ◆ Company websites (if you apply through a company website customize your résumé to their job description)

If you apply to jobs electronically, keep the following suggestions in mind:

- ◆ Include a subject in your e-mail (e.g., "Application for protein biochemist"), so that your e-mail does not get auto-deleted as spam.

- Virus-proof your computer, so that it does not transmit viruses through e-mail.
- Update your résumé as necessary.
- Make a professional looking personal website as your own "marketing collateral," which the employer can access for additional reference.

Employers search job banks for keywords, so include relevant keywords in your résumé as well in other sections of your job application. If you find an interesting posting on a job bank, also apply to it through the company, because they are more likely to hire from their own website. If you have a personal website, update it frequently, and include its address on your résumé.

 Do not rely exclusively on the Internet to find job listings. Most Ph.D.s get their jobs through networking or personal contacts.

Attending job fairs

Job fairs are a good opportunity to research multiple companies simultaneously. It is not common anymore for candidates to be interviewed at job fairs, but it still occurs occasionally. Dress appropriately and carry around a small briefcase with your résumé and business cards. Collect contact information from representatives, and e-mail them a few days later as a follow-up. If the company sounds interesting, ask whether you can arrange for a phone interview to ask about potential job leads.

To prepare for job fairs:
- Get a guest list, to find out which companies will attend.
- Look at the floor plan, to identify the locations of relevant companies in advance, and to organize your time so that you will have a chance to visit all of the interesting booths.
- Approach company representatives confidently by introducing yourself, telling them that you are finishing your Ph.D., and asking about job opportunities.
- If your résumé needs to be modified for a specific position, do not hand over a generic one. Ask for the representative's contact

information, and send an updated version of your résumé within a few days.

- ♦ Collect company brochures and business cards; write notes on them as needed.
- ♦ Follow up with company representatives after the fair:
  - • Thank them for their time
  - • Send your résumé or ask if they need more reference materials

Preparing for interviews

What is the best way to prepare for interviews? Sign up for a mock interview with your campus career services office, if they offer them. Apply for many positions, to get practice interviews; that way, you will be well prepared when you interview at your favorite company. Research companies to familiarize yourself with their work, and to find out where you would fit into the organization. In addition to reviewing the company's website, check on the company's performance and background on the Internet. Read newspaper articles, annual reports and Internet postings about their recent productivity. A friend of mine—who worked for a large consumer products company—was informed on her first day that she would be laid off in six months. Had she read the news about this company, she would have realized that experts had already been predicting a downsizing in this company for a few months. If you have doubts about the company, do not bring them up during your interview. Remember that your goal at the interview is to get an offer, because the more offers you have, the more marketable you are. After you have received an offer, you can make a decision regarding whether or not to accept it.

 Generate multiple interviews simultaneously, to increase your marketability; it will show companies that you are a desirable employee. This can be particularly critical if you are currently unemployed.

Typical interview questions

First and foremost, your interviewer wants to check whether you have the necessary skills for the job, and will probably ask you questions about your dissertation. In addition, you should be prepared to answer behavior-based questions that are meant to assess how organized you are and how well you work in teams.

Technical questions
(more common in the sciences/engineering than in the humanities/ social sciences)
- Why did you choose this topic for your dissertation?
- How does your dissertation contribute to your field?
- What would you change, if you could start your dissertation over?
- Why did you choose this particular method? (Be prepared to answer very detail-oriented questions.)
- Do you also have any experience with...? (They might ask if you have ever used a certain type of instrument or software. If the answer is "no," say so, and then give an example of a similar instrument/software that you do have experience with.)

Job-related questions
- Why do you want to work here?
- What kind of experience do you have?
- Where do you see yourself in five years?
- What are your biggest accomplishments?
- Do you work well under pressure?
- What are your greatest strengths/weaknesses?
- Describe a difficult problem you had to deal with.
- Do you have any questions?

Behavior-based questions
- Tell me about yourself.
- How do you get along with other people?
- Do you have experience working in teams?
- Do you consider yourself a leader or a follower?
- Did you have trouble getting along with your previous supervisor?
- Do you prefer to work with others or alone?
- Describe a situation where your work or an idea was criticized.
- What have you done that shows initiative?

It is impossible to prepare for all the questions that an employer might ask, but most employers will look for the following qualifications:

- Technical skills
- Willingness to cooperate and work in teams
- Good fit with the working environment
- Efficient time management
- Enthusiasm
- Motivation: Are you willing to go the extra mile?

Interviewers will probably also inquire about:

- Career vision: Where do you see yourself in five years?
  - Mention the technical areas in which you would like to grow and explain how employment with this company will help you to reach your goals.
- Good employment history:
  - Do not badmouth anybody from your previous jobs.
  - If they ask about previous employment/graduate school experience, mention what you learned and where you would like to grow.
- Healthy self-esteem:
  - If asked about your weaknesses, mention a technical skill that is not essential for your current job description, but one that you are working on. Give examples of workshops or seminars that you have attended to overcome this weakness.
  - If asked about your strengths, give concrete examples of your technical skills, particularly ones that are essential for the job opening. Also mention non-technical, transferable strengths, such as time management, ability to motivate others or good writing skills.
  - If they ask you to rate yourself on a scale of 1 to 10, emphasize your strengths, but do not give yourself a rating of 10, because that suggests that you consider yourself as having no more room to grow. A safe bet is a number between 5 and 10, such as 7 or 8.

If you are asked a general questions such as "Tell me about yourself," focus on your professional development. For example, tell the interviewer how you became interested in your field of research, what relevant job experience you have, what research experience you have, and what led you to pursue this particular career path. In your reply, give examples of leadership roles that show you are a motivated and dedicated person. (Prepare the answer to this question thoroughly, because it is a very common interview question.) Also think about specific answers to questions such as such as: "Are you a team player?," or "Are you an efficient time manager?" so you can reply with more than a "yes" or "no." Consider answers such as: "Yes, I have experience working in teams. In graduate school, I worked with two other students to develop...."

How to stay calm during interviews

Most interviewers just want to find a qualified candidate, and they will not try to make you uncomfortable. Some experienced interviewers, however, will probe you with many challenging questions, to see how you perform under pressure and to catch you if you are not telling the truth. If you encounter such a "stress" interview, do not get intimidated, because they probably have nothing against you personally. Remain friendly and polite throughout the interview, and answer all questions with specific examples that you have prepared in advance.

You might also encounter a disorganized or inexperienced interviewer, who might:

- Have a cluttered desk and need to look for your résumé
- Be constantly interrupted by phone calls or other people knocking on the door
- Engage in small talk and not discuss the job
- Describe drawbacks of the job or disappointments in previous candidates
- Ask a series of close-ended "yes" or "no" questions

Sit quietly and patiently, and wait for them to find your résumé or to answer any other interruptions. If the conversation derails to yesterday's sporting events, play along for a minute, and then guide the conversation back to the job with a transition such as: "Mr. Smith,

I actually had a question about the types of assignments I would have...."

If the interviewer is negative about the job, ask what he expects from his hires. Paraphrase what you hear from the interviewer, so that he or she knows that you are listening. If you are asked many "yes" or "no" questions (e.g., Did you like your last job? Did you get along with other people? Do you have any expertise with...?), elaborate on your response by giving an example: "Yes, I got along with my coworkers very well. In fact, we collaborated on a project that...."

You can also show enthusiasm by asking specific questions such as:

- What would be my first assignment?
- What are the challenges of the job?
- What projects will I work on, during the first six months?
- What skills are required for the job?
- How did the job open up?
- To whom would I report?
- What are the opportunities for growth within the company?

Following up after interviews

After an exhausting but exciting interview, you might walk away thinking that you nailed the job. Your interviewers might also think that they found the perfect candidate, until another qualified person walks through their door. To make sure that your interviewers do not forget about you, send a follow-up e-mail to the hiring manager. Keep your e-mail short (two or three paragraphs), but specific. First, thank him or her for their time and for giving you the opportunity to interview with their organization. Second, show your enthusiasm with examples such as:

"I was very impressed with the new technology that you have developed to analyze X. I hope that with my expertise with Y, I will be able to contribute to this project. I believe that this project will give me the opportunity to develop the technical skills I need to advance my career. If you would like for me to come in for a follow-up interview, or you require more reference materials, please let me know. I appreciate your consideration and look forward to hearing from you." (Expand where you think it is appropriate, but still keep the entire e-mail to no more than three paragraphs.)

 Always send a hand-written thank-you note to the hiring manager(s) after your interviews.

Waiting for the phone call

Regardless of how well you prepared, there is a chance that you will not get the job. Continue your search, even if you think your interview went well. The job is not yours until you get a written offer. It is difficult to predict when the company will call you back, especially if they are also interviewing other candidates. Until you have a formal offer, your aim should be to keep generating interviews. If you get an offer and are scheduled for another interview, ask the company how much time you have to accept the offer. At your other interview, let them know that you already have an offer, and that you have limited time to make a decision. If you do not hear back from the second company within a few days before your first offer expires, call human resources or the hiring manager and ask about their decision. Another option is to ask the first company if they can give you an extension on their offer. This option could be risky, because they might think that you are not truly interested, or that they are a mere "fall-back." If you have an offer and a few interviews pending, accept the offer only if you know it is the right place for you. There is always a chance that you will get an offer from a more desirable company later on, so only accept positions where you know that you will grow professionally.

 Keep generating interviews until you have a formal offer, even if you think that your interview went well.

If you are rejected (especially repeatedly), ask for feedback from the interviewer. First, thank them for their time, and let them know that you are still interested. If they give you feedback, show them that you understand their comments. Second, ask if there is a chance for another interview at their department—perhaps for a different position—or at another division. If the interviewers know you already, and you do not let them forget you, you will come to mind when they need to hire someone again.

Negotiating offers

Most employers expect their candidates to negotiate their hiring package. In order to determine your optimal salary, consider the following three questions:

- What are your financial needs? (This is your absolute minimum salary, but you should not share it with anyone.)
- How much are others with your job description and education paid typically? (This is the minimum that you should ask for.)
- What salary would make you happy? (This is the upper limit of your range.)

Since salaries are frequently negotiated, do not cite a specific amount on your application. Write "negotiable" or "competitive" if they ask you for a number. During the negotiation process, discuss job responsibilities before you talk about money, as a way to lead into the conversation (e.g., ask about first job assignment, whom you will report to, possible travel, etc.). When it comes time to discuss your salary, mention a range based on the market (your minimum) and the salary that would make you happy, but is still reasonable for your job description (your maximum). The negotiation process actually gives you the chance to show your employer that you have done your homework and know how much your skill set is valued in the market. (See the appendix for resources on finding salary ranges.)

 Do market research before you begin the negotiation process.

Other things that you can negotiate, besides salary:

- Sign-on bonus
- Moving expenses
- Vacation
- Stock options

Be careful about accepting stock options in lieu of salary increases. Stocks can go down, but if they offer you stock options in addition to a reasonable salary, accept them. Remember that settling for a lower salary will also decrease your raise in the future, because raises are

LAND YOUR DREAM JOB

calculated as a percentage of your base salary. Also ask about performance reviews that could increase your salary in the next few months.

If you need to relocate, ask about:

- Professional moving companies
- Moving your car(s)
- Cost of selling or buying a house
- Cost of a realtor
- Temporary housing costs
- Job assistance for spouse
- Assistance in finding a daycare facility or school for your children

In terms of relocation costs, do your research before you ask for a specific amount of money, so that you will know exactly how much it will cost. (The numbers might surprise you.) Many companies will offer you relocation assistance in their hiring package, but check whether they will cover all of your costs. The negotiation process can go back and forth for a few weeks—possibly even months. The company might not grant all of your wishes right away, but that does not mean that there is no room for negotiation. The hiring manager or human resources representative might need to check with their supervisor regarding your requests. If your deadline is nearing and you have not heard back from them yet, give them a call. They might be busy with a hiring boom, so it is best to be proactive about discussing your offer.

CHAPTER SUMMARY AND ACTION PLAN

How to land your dream job

Step 1: Begin thinking about different career paths two years before graduation:
- Attend networking sessions and career seminars, to learn about all the opportunities available to you.

- Write your résumé and CV and determine what marketable skills you still need to acquire.
- Talk to your advisor to finalize the expectations for your thesis and discuss career plans.

Step 2: If you decide to pursue the academic path:
- Find out where the job openings are listed for your field.
- Prepare your application package.
- Ask for input from your advisor(s) regarding your teaching philosophy/research proposal/grant proposal-writing plans.
- Tailor your CV and cover letter to each school to which you apply.
- Ask for recommendation letters and give your mentors at least a month of notice before the deadline.
- Practice your job talk and your answers to interview questions.
- Research the schools before the interviews, to determine how you would fit into their program.
- Prepare questions for the university about your teaching assignments, research facilities and support for graduate students.
- Find out what your startup costs would be.

Step 3: If you decide to pursue careers outside of academia:
- Always carry business cards with you and network actively at professional and non-professional meetings.
- Diversify your Internet job-searching by applying for positions through large job banks, region-specific professional sites, company websites and recruitment firms.
- Check the privacy policy of every website to which you plan to post your résumé, before doing so.
- Prepare a specific résumé and cover letter for each position and include important keywords, where appropriate.
- If you attend a job fair, determine in advance which companies you will visit, so that you can maximize the use of your time.
- Practice answering interview questions.
- Tailor your job talk to your audience.
- Prepare questions for your potential employer about your responsibilities, current projects and expected growth at the company.

Step 4: Follow up and negotiation for either path:
- ♦ Send a hand-written thank-you note to the head of the search committee/hiring manager, after your interview.
- ♦ If you get rejected repeatedly, ask for feedback, in case there is a serious problem with your application package.
- ♦ Before the negotiation process, research the market, to determine what would be a fair offer for your particular position.
- ♦ Separate your needs and desires during negotiation, and be firm when asking for things that you truly need.

A successfully negotiated academic position: Donna's story

Donna loved the academic job she was offered, but it was far away from her husband. Her husband had a private practice as a dentist, and moving near Donna's university would have meant losing all of his clients. Therefore, Donna and her husband agreed that he would move gradually, so he would have a chance to build up his practice in the new town. Donna knew that a long-distance relationship would be difficult for her marriage, and she decided to incorporate some requests into her negotiation process. Donna began her negotiation by constructing her "ultimate wish list," which included a higher salary, no teaching for one year (to have time to develop her research program) and only one class per semester after that. In addition, she requested to have a long weekend (Fridays and Mondays off) once a month, to have the time to visit her husband. The university agreed to her requests and they also arranged for career assistance for Donna's husband, to help him set up a new dental practice. Donna also received financial help for her move, and the university hired a realtor to help Donna find a new home. The negotiation process lasted for months, and Donna described it as a "gentle dance" between her and the department. She had had a long wish list, and the department did not grant her everything immediately. Donna negotiated firmly on issues that were essential for her, but was more flexible with the requests on which she was willing to compromise.

Throughout the negotiation process, it is important to distinguish between needs and desires. Needs are essential for you to perform your job, and it is important to be firm on these issues during negotiation. The department will understand if you are assertive about your needs, but they will probably not appreciate it if you push to get everything that you want, such as a slightly higher salary or a bigger office.

Keeping academic and alternative career paths open:
Anthony's and Ian's stories

Anthony, a chemist, had a very academic thesis topic with few "real world" applications. He had no exposure to industry and was not sure which path to follow. He decided to do a postdoctoral fellowship and chose a project that was relevant to industry. After his postdoctoral fellowship, he realized that he was more interested in applied research, and so he decided to take a job at a biotechnology company. "I like working on practical projects, but there are other reasons that I chose to work in industry. First, I really wanted to stay in California, and the academic job market is very competitive here. Second, I am not tied to a research group, and so I have the option of moving to a different department or company. Third, I do not have to write grant proposals, and I also have more free time. I am glad that I did the postdoctoral fellowship, because it left both career paths open, and it gave me time to think about what I really wanted to do."

Ian, an electrical engineer, interviewed at several companies and research laboratories during his job search. After his interviews, he realized that his real passion was research, but he was not ready to pursue an academic path. He saw his professors working long hours and struggling to get funding. How could he continue research, unless he became a faculty member? Ian found a "happy medium" between the two career paths by joining a government laboratory. "I still get to do hands-on research, which is what I really love. One of my colleagues went back to academia after working here for a few years, so I think the tenure-track faculty position is still an option for me."

Leaving academia after a professorship: *Ray's story*

After he completed his degree in sociology, Ray followed the same career path as his classmates: He became a professor at a university. His position was not permanent, however, and as he neared the end of his appointment, he realized that he no longer wanted to stay in academia. "I like the idea of not having a boss and having the freedom to pursue my own research project. On the other hand, I feel that being a professor is very isolating. There is no community I can interact with. I also find that our research is very removed from the problems of the real world." Finding a non-academic position with an academic résumé is a challenge, but Ray decided to combine the practical aspects from his thesis with additional training. "My thesis focused on collaborative politics and conflict resolution, and I'm looking to find a job in these areas. I am considering working as an independent mediator, an ombudsman or an executive coach. I am also taking some training courses in mediation and conflict resolution, to strengthen my résumé." Ray found job listings at career and company websites, but also took advantage of one of the most efficient job-searching strategies: networking. He had contacts at conflict-mediation organizations, and he followed their advice regarding appropriate training courses and networking sessions.

APPENDIX A
THE INTERVIEW PROCESS

Total number of Ph.D.'s interviewed: 100

Number of men: 51

Number of women: 49

Number of Ph.D.'s in the sciences, engineering, and mathematics: 70
Includes the following majors:
Aerospace Engineering, Astronomy, Biochemistry, Biology
(including Cell biology, Molecular Biology, and Microbiology),
Biomedical Engineering, Biophysics, Chemical Engineering,
Chemistry, Computer Science, Electrical Engineering, Geology,
Geophysics, Marine Biology, Mathematics, Mechanical Engineering,
Neuropsychology, Nutrition, Physics, Psychology, and Toxicology.

Number of Ph.D.'s in the humanities, social sciences, and arts: 30
Includes the following majors:
Architecture, Arts Administration, Art History, Comparative
Literature, Economics, Education, Egyptology, English, French, Fine
Arts, History, Library and Information Sciences, Linguistics, Media
Studies, Sociology, Theology, and others*.

Ph.D.-awarding institutions of interviewees:
(Number of schools: 46)

Baylor College of Medicine
Boston College
California Institute of
  Technology (Caltech)
Carnegie Mellon University
Columbia University

Duke University
Emory University
Florida State University
Fordham University
Georgia Tech University
Harvard University

*Some students majored in one-of-a-kind interdisciplinary fields, and the names of their
  departments have been kept confidential to protect the identities of their universities.

Indiana University
Iowa State University
Johns Hopkins University
Louisiana State University
Loyola University (Chicago)
Michigan State University
Massachusetts Institute of
  Technology (MIT)
Notheastern University
New York University (NYU)
Oregon State University
Polytechnic Institute of
  New York
Princeton University
Purdue University
Rutgers University
Stanford University
Stony Brook University
Syracuse University
Tufts University
University of California (UC)
  at Berkeley

UC Los Angeles
UC San Diego
UC Santa Barbara
UC Santa Cruz
UC Southern California
University of Massachusetts
  Amherst
University of Massachusetts
  Boston
University of Colorado
University of Delaware
University of Florida
University of Illinois at Urbana-
  Champagne
University of Miami
University of Pennsylvania
University of Utah
University of Virginia
University of Wisconsin

Interview questions:

- Why did you decide to earn a Ph.D.?
- What was your biggest challenge in graduate school, and how did you cope with it?
- Did you have previous work experience? If yes, did it help you in graduate school?
- Was graduate school what you expected? If not, what were the biggest surprises?
- How did you motivate yourself to work?
- What strategies did you use to become more efficient in your research?
- Did you set internal deadlines for yourself? If so, were they helful?
- How did you deal with stress?

- Did you develop repetitive strain injury? If so, how severe were your symptoms and what treatments did you seek?
- Did you maintain a healthy diet? Did caffeine or sugar affect your concentration, moods, or sleep quality?
- How did you deal with your advisor being unsupportive (in case they indicated they worked with a difficult professor)?
- What were the challenges associated with writing your thesis?
- Do you have any advice for students who want to become better public speakers?
- How did you choose your career path?
- How was the job-searching experience for you?
- What advice would you give to current and prospective graduate students?

APPENDIX B
RESOURCES TO HELP YOU PLAN AND APPLY FOR GRADUATE SCHOOL

Online graduate school resources

Overviews on graduate school and the application process

http://www.phds.org
http://www.phds.org/graduate-school/
http://gradschool.about.com/
http://www.princetonreview.com/grad/

Graduate school rankings by US News and World Report

http://www.usnews.com/sections/education

Sites to help you choose a graduate school

http://graduate-school.phds.org/

Statistics on US Doctorates in the 20th Century

http://www.nsf.gov/statistics/doctorates/

Resources for international students

http://educationusa.state.gov/

Resources for minority students

Equal Opportunity Publications
http://www.eop.com/

National GEM consortium
http://www.gemfellowship.org

Ron McNair fellowship
http://www.ed.gov/programs/triomcnair/index.html

Summer Research Programs
(For all undergraduates interested in pursuing a Ph.D.)

Amgen Scholars
http://www.amgenscholars.com

GREAT Group Summer Programs
http://www.aamc.org/members/great/summerlinks.htm

Online financial aid resources

Loans overview

http://www.gradloans.com
http://www.studentloannetwork.com/

Stafford loans

http://www.gradloans.com/stafford_loan/graduate-
    federal-loans.php
http://www.gradloans.com/stafford_loan/
http://www.studentloannetwork.com/graduate-students/
    graduate-stafford-loan.php

Graduate PLUS and private loans

http://www.gradloans.com/graduate-plus-loan/
http://www.gradloans.com/private/

Loan consolidation and repayment

http://www.gradloans.com/consolidation/
http://www.gradloans.com/repayment/

Filing your FAFSA application

http://www.fafsaonline.com/

Graduate fellowships, internships, and work-study programs

General resource center

http://www.nafadvisors.org/scholarships.htm

The Natl Science Foundation
http://www.nsf.gov/funding

Grantsnet (science, engineering)
http://sciencecareers.sciencemag.org/funding

Humanities Grant Information - National Endowment for the Humanities (NEH)
http://www.neh.gov/grants/index.html

Fulbright Program (US Dept of State)
http://fulbright.state.gov/

Student Programs (National Institutes of Health)
http://www.training.nih.gov/student

EPA Student Opportunities (US Environmental Protection Agency)
http://www.epa.gov/careers/stuopp.html

e-Scholar (US Office of Personnel Management)
http://www.studentjobs.gov/e-scholar.asp

Learn Without Borders (National Security Education Program)
http://www.worldstudy.gov

Jacob K. Javits Fellowship Program (US Deptartment of Education)
http://www.ed.gov/programs/javits/index.html

Public Health Training Opportunities (Centers for Disease Control)
http://www.cdc.gov/phtrain

Grants and Fellowships, AHRQ (US Dept of Health and Human Services)
http://www.ahrq.gov/fund/grantix.htm

White House Fellows Program (US Executive Branch)
http://www.whitehouse.gov/fellows

Internships and Student Programs (US Dept of Agriculture)
http://www.usda.gov/da/employ/intern.htm

Hubert H. Humphrey Fellowship Program (US Dept of State)
http://exchanges.state.gov/education/hhh

Books about applying to and surviving graduate school

Kaplan GRE Exam 2008 Premier Program. Kaplan Publishing, 2007.

Cracking the GRE with DVD, 2008 Edition by Princeton Review, 2007.

WEINER GREEN, Sharon Ph.D., Wolf, Ira K. *Barron's GRE 2008 with CD-ROM.* Barron's How to Prepare for the Gre Graduate Record Examination. Barron's Educational Series, 2007.

Graduate Schools in the U.S. 2008 (Peterson's Graduate Schools in the US)

ASHER, Donald. *Graduate Admissions Essays: Write Your Way Into the Graduate School of Your Choice.* Ten Speed Press, 2008.

BLOOM, Dale F. ; Karp, Jonathan D.; Cohen, Nicholas. *The Ph.D. Process: A Student's Guide to Graduate School in the Sciences.* Oxford University Press, 1999.

FEIBELMAN, Peter J. *A Ph.D. Is Not Enough: A Guide to Survival in Science.* Perseus Books Group, 1994.

MITCHELL, Leslie. *Ultimate Grad School Survival Guide.* Peterson's, 1996.

MUMBY, Dave. *Graduate School: Winning Strategies for Getting in With or Without Excellent Grades.* Proto Press Publications, 2004.

PETERS, Robert. *Getting What You Came For: The Smart Student's Guide to Earning an M.A. or a Ph.D.* Farrar, Straus and Giroux. 1997.

SELTZERM, Richard. *How to Write a Winning Personal Statement.* Peterson's. 1997.

APPENDIX C
ONLINE RESEARCH TOOLS

Field-specific free-access electronic databases

Architecture, Urban design

Architectural Publications Index
http://www.architecture.com/

Art, archeology

ArchNet
http://archnet.org/lobby/

Art and Archaeology Technical Abstracts (AATA)
http://aata.getty.edu/nps/

Artforum Index
http://www.mcgilvery.com/artforum/fm_afi.html

Sciences (General)

Science.gov
http://www.science.gov/

Astronomy, Space Exploration

ADS (NASA Astrophysics Data System)
http://adsabs.harvard.edu/ (astronomy)

NASA Extragalactic Database (NED)
http://nedwww.ipac.caltech.edu/

NASA History Office
http://www.hq.nasa.gov/office/pao/History/index.html

NTRS: NASA Technical Reports Server [NASA Database - Center for Aerospace Information (CASI) Technical Reports Server]
http://ntrs.nasa.gov/search.jsp

SIMBAD
http://simbad.u-strasbg.fr/simbad/

Biology, Chemistry, Medicine

ACS Directory of Graduate Research Web Edition
http://dgr.rints.com/ (chemical research)

Chemical Heritage Foundation
http://www.chemheritage.org/

MEDLINE / PubMed [Pub Med]
http://www.ncbi.nlm.nih.gov/sites/entrez?db=PubMed

National Medical Library Research Center
http://gateway.nlm.nih.gov/gw/Cmd

NCBI Bookshelf
http://www.ncbi.nlm.nih.gov/sites/entrez?db=Books

Organic Syntheses
http://www.orgsyn.org/

PubMed Central
http://www.pubmedcentral.nih.gov/

Physics

AIP Center for History of Physics
http://www.aip.org/history/about.html

SPIRES (high energy physics)
http://www.slac.stanford.edu/spires/

Economics, Business

Economic Indicators
http://www.gpoaccess.gov/indicators/index.html

Eurostat
http://ec.europa.eu/eurostat

IDEAS
http://ideas.repec.org/

Education

Education Resource Organizations Directory (EROD)
http://wdcrobcolpo1.ed.gov/Programs/EROD/

Engineering

American Society for Engineering Education Conferences
http://www.asee.org/conferences/v2Search.cfm

ASCE Civil Engineering Database
http://cedb.asce.org/

DOE Information Bridge (science and engineering)
http://www.osti.gov/bridge/

Electronic Engineers Master Catalog : EEM
http://www.eem.com/

IEEE History Center
http://www.ieee.org/web/aboutus/history_center/

PartMiner (electric engineering)
http://www.partminer.com/

SAE Store
http://store.sae.org/

ThomasNet (engineering equipment)
http://www.thomasnet.com/

Environmental and Geological Sciences

Conservation Directory (environmental)
http://www.nwf.org/conservationdirectory/

US Geological Survey Abstracts
http://infotrek.er.usgs.gov/pubs/

OSGeo (Open Source Geospatial Foundation)
https://www.osgeo.org/

Toxics Release Inventory (environmental)
http://www.epa.gov/tri/

Government Documents

Air University Library Index to Military Periodicals
http://www.dtic.mil/dtic/aulimp/index.html

Catalog of U.S. Government Publications
http://catalog.gpo.gov/F

CenStats
http://censtats.census.gov/usa/usa.shtml

GPO Access (government printing office)
http://www.gpoaccess.gov/

National Archives
http://www.archives.gov/

National Library Catalogues Worldwide
http://www.library.uq.edu.au/ssah/jeast/

National Union Catalog of Manuscript Collections (NUCMC)
http://www.loc.gov/coll/nucmc/

Statistical Abstract of the United States
http://www.census.gov/compendia/statab/

USA.gov (government information)
www.usa.gov

Weekly Compilation of Presidential Documents
http://www.access.gpo.gov/nara/nara003.html

Humanities, Social Sciences

History
AHA Directory of Affiliated Societies
http://www.historians.org/ (History)

In the First Person (Personal narratives)
http://www.inthefirstperson.com/firp/index.shtml

Social Science Research Network
http://www.ssrn.com/

Literature
AATA Online: Abstracts of International Conservation Literature
http://aata.getty.edu/nps/

Persee (Humanities and Social Sciences)
http://www.persee.fr/

TOCS - IN: Tables of Contents of Journals of Interest to Classicists
http://www.chass.utoronto.ca/amphoras/tocs.html

Media Studies
Film literature index
http://webapp1.dlib.indiana.edu/fli/index.jsp

Music
Doctoral Dissertations in Musicology Online
http://www.chmtl.indiana.edu/ddm/

Patent Information
Europe's Network of patent databases [espacenet]
http://gb.espacenet.com/search97cgi/s97_cgi.exe?Action=FormGen
&Template=gb/EN/home.hts

UK Intelectual Property Office
http://www.ipo.gov.uk/

International Patent Classification
http://www.wipo.int/classifications/ipc/ipc8/?lang=en

U.S. Patent Database
http://www.uspto.gov/main/patents.htm

Google patents
http://www.google.com/patents

Other

LibDex: the Library Index
http://www.libdex.com/

Webster's Dictionary
http://www.m-w.com/dictionary.htm

Smithsonian Institution Research Information System
http://www.siris.si.edu/

Google Scholar (search engine for most disciplines)
http://scholar.google.com/

Conference listings

www.allconferences.com

www.eventseye.com

www.conferenceguru.com.

Alerts and subscription services

*Current contents - table of content alerts for over 8,000 journals
(need subscriptions)*
http://scientific.thomson.com/products/ccc/

*Dialog: compilation of over 900 databases and real-time newsfeeds
(need subscriptions)*
http://www.dialog.com/

Factiva: business information (need subscription)
http://factiva.com/

Pubcrawler: free alerts for PubMed and Genbank
http://pubcrawler.gen.tcd.ie/

Google Alerts – news alerts (free)
http://www.google.com/alerts

Google government search engine
http://www.google.com/ig/usgov

RSS reader information

http://www.whatisrss.com/

http://www.google.com/reader (free)

http://my.yahoo.com/s/about/rss/index.html (free)

http://page2rss.com/: tracks non-xml pages (free, converts non-RSS pages into RSS feeds so you can browse the in your reader)

APPENDIX D
BOOKS TO HELP YOU GET ORGANIZED

ALLEN, David. *Getting Things Done: The Art of Stress-Free Productivity*, 2002.

EMMETT, Rita. *The Procrastinator's Handbook: Mastering the Art of Doing It Now.* Walker & Company, 2000.

FIORE, Neil. *The Now Habit: A Strategic Program for Overcoming Procrastination and Enjoying Guilt-Free Play*, Tarcher, 1989.

KOCH, Richard. *The 80/20 Principle: The Secret to Success by Achieving More with Less*, Currency, 1999.

MORGENSTERN, Julie. *Organizing from the Inside Out, second edition : The Foolproof System For Organizing Your Home, Your Office and Your Life*, Holtzbrinck Publishers,1998.

MORGENSTERN, Julie. *Time Management From The Inside Out:The Foolproof System for Taking Control of Your Schedule and Your Life*, Owl Books, 2004.

SECUNDA, Al. *The 15-Second Principle*, Career Press, 2004.

TEITELBAUM, Daniel. *Ultimate Guide to Mental Toughness: How to Raise Your Motivation, Focus and Confidence Like Pushing a Button*, Mental Toughness, 1998.

APPENDIX E
RESOURCES TO HELP RELIEVE
WORRY AND ANXIETY

BENSON, Herbert and Klipper, Miriam Z. *The Relaxation Response,* Harper Paperbacks, 2000.

BOURNE, Edmund J. *The Anxiety & Phobia Workbook*, New Harbinger Publications, 2005.

BRANTLEY, Jeffrey and Millstine, Wendy. *Five Good Minutes At Work,* New Harbinger Publications, 2007.

BURNS, David D. *The Feeling Good Handbook,* Plume, 1999.

CARNEGIE, Dale. *How To Stop Worrying And Start Living,* Pocket, 2004.

KASE, Larina; Vitale, Joe; Martin M. Antony. *Anxious 9 to 5: How to Beat Worry, Stop Second Guessing Yourself, and Work With Confidence,* New Harbinger Publications, 2006.

KHALSA, Gurucharan Singh, and Bhajan, Yogi. *Breathwalk: Breathing Your Way to a Revitalized Body, Mind and Spirit,* Broadway, 2000.

Relaxation CDs and audiobooks are available from:

The Body Mind Institute in Boston:
   http://www.mbmi.org/shop/default.asp

The Midwest Center for Stress and Anxiety:
   http://www.stresscenter.com

http://www.relaxation-cds.com/nature/

http://www.therelaxationcompany.com/

APPENDIX F
PREVENTING AND HEALING REPETITIVE STRAIN INJURY

Books

BUTLER, Sharon. *Conquering Carpal Tunnel Syndrome And Other Repetitive Strain Injuries,* New Harbinger Publications, 1996.

DAMANY, Suparna and Bellis, Jack. *It's Not Carpal Tunnel Syndrome! RSI Theory & Therapy for Computer Professionals,* Simex, 2001.

FELDENKRAIS, Moshe. *Awareness Through Movement: Easy-to-Do Health Exercises to Improve Your Posture, Vision, Imagination, and Personal Awareness,* HarperOne, 1991.

GELB, Michael J. Body *Learning: An Introduction to the Alexander Technique,* Holt Paperbacks, 1996.

MONTGOMERY, Kate. *End Your Carpal Tunnel Pain Without Surgery,* Rutledge Hill Press, 1998.

PASCARELLI, Emil. *Dr. Pascarelli's Complete Guide to Repetitive Strain Injury: What You Need to Know About RSI and Carpal Tunnel Syndrome,* Wiley, 2004.

PASCARELLI, Emil and Quilter, Deborah. *Repetitive Strain Injury,* John Wiley & Sons Inc. 1994.

VINEYARD, Missy. *How You Stand, How You Move, How You Live: Learning the Alexander Technique to Explore Your Mind-Body Connection and Achieve Self-Mastery,* Marlowe & Company, 2007.

WILDMAN, Frank. *The Busy Person's Guide To Use Your Movement,* The Intelligent Body Press, 2006.

Online Resources

Ergonomics

http://www.healthycomputing.com/

http://www.alimed.com/

http://www.tifaq.org/, includes links to ergonomic furniture, typing aides, typing break software, and voice recognition software

RSI resource pages

http://www.rsihelp.com/

http://www.repetitive-strain-injury.com/

http://www.rsi-relief.com/

http://www.tennis-elbow.net/

http://www.selfcare4rsi.com/

Ergonomic pipetts

Rainin: http://www.rainin.com/

Ovation: http://www.vistalab.com/epresentations.asp

Feldenkrais resources:
http://www.feldenkraisresources.com/

http://www.feldenkrais.com/

http://www.feldenkraisinstitute.org/order/

Alexander Technique resources

http://www.alexandertechnique.com/

http://www.alexandertech.org/

http://www.alexandercenter.com/

http://www.ati-net.com/

APPENDIX G
RESOURCES TO HELP YOU ENHANCE YOUR COMMUNICATION AND WRITING SKILLS

Communication skills

ALESSANDRA, Tony. *The Platinum Rule: Discover the Four Basic Business Personalities and How They Can Lead You to Success,* Grand Central Publishing, 1998.

BOLTON, Robert and Bolton, Dorothy Grover. *People Styles at Work: Making Bad Relationships Good and Good Relationships,* Better. AMACOM, 1996.

BRAMSON, Robert. *Coping with Difficult People,* Dell, 1988.

CARNEGIE, Dale. *How to Win Friends and Influence People,* Vermilion, 2007.

COVEY, Stephen. *The 7 Habits of Highly Effective People,* Free Press, 2004.

Thesis writing

BOLKER, Joan. *Writing Your Dissertation in Fifteen Minutes a Day: A Guide to Starting, Revising, and Finishing Your Doctoral Thesis,* Holt Paperbacks, 1998.

BOOTH, Wayne C., Colomb, Gregory G. Colomb, Williams, Joseph M. Williams. *The Craft of Research,* University Of Chicago Press, 2008.

RUDESTAM, Kjell E. (Author), Newton, Rae R. *Surviving Your Dissertation: A Comprehensive Guide to Content and Process,* Sage Publications, 2007.

STERNBERG, David. *How to Complete and Survive a Doctoral Dissertation,* St. Martin's Griffin, 1981.

STRUNK, William and White, E.B. *The Elements of Style,*. Longman, 2000.

TURABIAN, Kate L., Booth, Wayne C., Colomb, Gregory G. Colomb, Williams, Joseph M. Williams. *A Manual for Writers of Research Papers, Theses, and Dissertations*, (Chicago Guides to Writing, Editing, and Publishing). University Of Chicago Press, 2007.

Presentation skills

ALLEY, Michael. *The Craft of Scientific Presentations. Critical Steps to Succeed and Critical Errors to Avoid,*Springer, 2003.

ANHOLT, Robert. *Dazzle'em with Style: The Art of Oral Scientific Presentation*, Elsevier, 2006.

CARNEGIE, Dale. *How to Develop Self-Confidence And Influence People By Public Speaking*, Pocket, 1991.

MILLS, Harry. *Power Points!: How to Design and Deliver Presentations That Sizzle and Sell*, AMACOM, 2007.

Audiobook:

POOL, Steve. *Fearless Public Speaking,*Topics Entertainment, 2002.

JOB SEARCHING RESOURCES

Online job searching resources, job banks, and networking sites

These sites offer a listing of the most popular job searching tools and resources

http://www.google.com/Top/Business/Employment/Job_Search

http://dir.yahoo.com/business_and_economy/employment_and_work

Online job bank as well as general job searching guide

http://www.job-hunt.org

Official website for "What Color is Your Parachute?" by Richard Nelson Bolles

http://www.jobhuntersbible.com/

Hosted by Martin Yates, author of "Knock'em Dead", this site offers advice on how to write résumés and cover letters, prepare for interviews, and manage your career.

http://www.knockemdead.com/

Online resource for finding large as well as field-specific job banks, executive opportunities, find employment in certain geographical regions, and considerations for self-employment.

http://www.rileyguide.com/

Alumni networking site for companies, universities, and high schools

www.alumni.net

www.Monster.com

www.Monstertrack.com

Powered by monster.com, allows you to find local jobs in your area
www.flipdog.com

A job site specifically for executives and senior-level positions
www.6figurejobs.com

Allows you to send your résumé to companies, venture capital firms, and recruiters
www.resumemachine.com

Online matching service between employers and job seekers started by Rob McGovern, founder of careerbuilder.com
www.jobfox.com

America's Job Bank, allows you to find your local job bank
www.Ajb.org

On this site you can find your local job bank and also view company profiles
www.BestJobsUSA.com

One of the largest career web sites, includes job searching tools, local job fairs, salary calculator as well as advice on résumé writing
www.careerbuilder.com

The career section from the Wall Street Journal, allows you to search for jobs in your field, research companies, and read the recent news about the job market.
www.careerjournal.com

Includes interviewing tips, job searching tools and salary calculator
http://hotjobs.yahoo.com

www.Careeronestop.org

www.truecareers.com

www.usjobs.com

Job searching tools as well as résumé and CV writing advice
http://jobsearch.about.com

Job searching site from the Chronicles of Higher Education
http://chronicle.com/jobs

Career and graduate student advice for college graduates
http://www.gradview.com/careers/

Résumé and CV writing resources

http://www.resumesandcoverletters.com/sample_resumes.html

A critique of CV's in five different fields
http://chronicle.com/jobs/99/09/99091701c.htm

http://www.cv-resume.org/

Salary Information

www.Jobstar.org/tools/salary

www.Salary.com

Recruiting Firms

www.Findarecruiter.com

www.recruitersdirectory.com

www.recruitersonline.com

www.recruiterlink.com

Recruiter site for executive positions
www.searchfirm.com

Sites for Academic Positions

www.academickeys.com

www.academic360.com

http://chronicle.com/jobs

www.higheredjobs.com

Website of Women in Higher Education, a monthly news journal
www.wihe.com

Field specific job sites

Library science

The web site for the American Library Association
http://www.ala.org/

General Sciences

Job searching sites of the new scientist magazine
www.newscientistjobs.com

A free job searching site for postdoctoral positions
www.post-docs.com

Job searching site of Science magazine
http://sciencecareers.org

Serviced by nature magazine
www.naturejobs.com

Life sciences

www.biospace.com

www.medzilla.com

www.bio.com

Careers in the medical field advertised by the American Medical Association
www.Jamacareernet.com

Pharmaceutical industry

www.Inpharm.com

www.Pharmajobs.com

www.Pharmacyweek.com

Physical sciences

Homepage of the American Astonimical Society
www.aas.org

Job site of the American Chemical Society
www.CEN-Chemjobs.org

Resource for jobs in earth sciences

www.Earthworks-jobs.com

Career resource center for the environmental sciences
www.EnvironmentalCareer.com

Website for the American Meteorological Society
www.Ametsoc.org

www.Physicstoday.org

http://physicsweb.org

www.physlink.com

Public Health

Public health resources maintained by the University of California at Berkeley
http://Lib.berkeley.edu/PUBL/internet.html

Engineering

Job resource center for architects, engineers, and environmental consultants
www.Aejob.com

Homepage of the American Institute of Chemical Engineers
www.Aiche.org

Maintained by the American Society of Civil Engineers
www.Asce.org

Website for the American Society of Mechanical Engineers
www.Asme.org

Career site of the Institute of Electrical and Electronics Engineers (IEEE)
http://careers.ieee.org

www.Engineerjobs.com

www.Engineer.net

Maintained by the National Society of Professional Engineers
www.Nspe.org

Homepage of the Society of Women Engineers
www.Swe.org

Aerospace

Homepage of the American Institute of Aeronautics and Astronautics
www.Aiaa.org

Job resources for aerospace sciences and defense
www.Spacejobs.com

Biotech

Resource center for the medical device industry
www.Devicelink.com

Mathematics

Webpage of the American Mathematical Society
www.Ams.org

Optics

http://optics.org

www.photonicsjobs.com

Telecommunications

www.Rcrnews.com

www.Telecomcareers.com

www.Wirelessweek.com

Federal Jobs

www.Resume-place.com

www.Usajobs.opm.gov

Careers in Government

www.Careersingovernment.com

www.Govtjob.net

www.Govtjobs.com

International Opportunities

www.Internationaljobs.org

www.Ircjobs.org

www.Jobpilot.com

http://workabroad.monster.com

www.overseasjobs.com

Sites for minorities

www.Diversitycareers.com

Website of the Equal Opportunity Publications
www.Eop.com

www.Hirediversity.com

www.workplacediversity.com

http://www.black-collegian.com/

http://www.quintcareers.com/African-American_career_
resources.html

Homepage of the Society of Hispanic Professional engineers
www.shpe.org

www.Ihispano.com

www.Latpro.com

www.saludos.com

Career Resource Center for Native Americans
www.Nativejobs.com

Books about the academic job search

FORMO, Dawn M., and Reed, Cheryl. *Job Search In Academe,
Strategic Retorts For Faculty Job Candidates,* Stylus publishing,
1999.

HEIBERGER, Mary Morris, and Vick, Julia Miller. *The Academic Job
Search Book,* University of Pennsylvania Press, 2001.

HUME, Kathryn. *Surviving Your Academic Job Hunt, Advice For
Humanities PhDs,* Palgrave Macmillan, 2004.

REIS, Richard M. *Tomorrow's Professor,* Wiley-IEEE Press.1997.

Guides for applying to careers outside of academia:

BASALLA, Susan, and Debelius, Maggie. *So What Are You Going to
Do with That? Finding Careers Outside Academia,* University Of
Chicago Press, 2007.

BEATTY, Richard H. *175 High-Impact Cover Letters,* Wiley, 2002.

BOLLES, Richard Nelson. *What Color Is Your Parachute?* Ten Speed
Press, 2007.

DIKEL, Margaret Riley, and Roehm, Frances E. *Guide to Internet Job
Searching,* McGraw-Hill, 2006.

FISKE, Peter. *Put Your Science to Work: The Take-Charge Career
Guide for Scientists,* American Geophysical Union, 2000.

ROBBINS-ROTH, Cynthia. *Alternative Careers in Science: Leaving the Ivory Tower,* Academic Press, 2005.

WHITCOMB, Susan Britton. *Resume Magic: Trade Secrets of a Professional Resume Writer,* JIST Works, 2006.

YATE, Martin. *Knock'em Dead,* Adams Media, 2007.

INDEX